Illustrator:
Agnes Palinay

Editors:
Janet Cain
Dona Herweck Rice

Editor-in-Chief:
Sharon Coan, M.S. Ed.

Art Director:
Elayne Roberts

Cover Artist:
Karen Walstad

Product Manager:
Phil Garcia

Imaging:
Alfred Lau

Publishers:
Rachelle Cracchiolo, M.S. Ed.
Mary Dupuy Smith, M.S. Ed.

569

Interdisciplinary Unit

Heroes

CHALLENGING

NO LONGER THE PROPERTY OF THE UNIVERSITY OF R. I. LIBRARY

Authors:

Betty Burke and Janet Cain

Teacher Created Materials, Inc.
P.O. Box 1040
Huntington Beach, CA 92647
ISBN-1-55734-605-4

©1994 Teacher Created Materials, Inc.   Made in U.S.A.

Teacher Created Materials

The classroom teacher may reproduce copies of materials in this book for classroom use only. The reproduction of any part for an entire school or school system is strictly prohibited. No part of this publication may be transmitted, stored, or recorded in any form without written permission from the publisher.

Table of Contents

Table of Contents *(cont.)*

Introduction

Heroes contains a captivating, whole language, interdisciplinary unit about a variety of unique men and women. This unit has 176 exciting pages that are filled with a wide variety of lesson ideas and reproducible pages designed for use with intermediate and junior high school students. The theme is connected to the curriculum with activities in reading, language arts (including written expression), science, social studies, math, art, music, and life skills. Many of these activities encourage cooperative learning.

Heroes is divided into the following sections to allow for easy thematic planning: Superheroes, Ancient Greek Heroes, Medieval Heroes, Heroes of the Wild West, Wartime Heroes, Sports Heroes, Heroes of Science & Invention, Space Heroes, Medical Heroes, and Heroes of Social Causes. This unit focuses on some fictional superheroes and many real-life heroes. The fictional superheroes appear to be normal people but actually possess special powers that they use to fight world-wide problems, such as crime. The real-life heroes are the exceptional men and women found throughout history and in every culture. They have made unique contributions by struggling to overcome tremendous obstacles.

This interdisciplinary unit includes:

- **Bulletin Board Ideas**—time-saving suggestions and plans for bulletin boards that are related to the specific groups of heroes

- **Planning Guides**—background information and suggestions for sequencing lessons for each section

- **Overview of Activities**—a brief description of the activities included in each section

- **Articles and Discussion Questions**—one-page articles about specific heroes for students to read and discuss

- **Quiz Cards**—opportunities to assess students' understanding of the articles in each section

- **Map Studies**—activities that reinforce a variety of map skills

- **Curriculum Connections**—relating the theme to language arts, math, science, social studies, art, music, and life skills

- **Suggested Literature**—summaries, vocabulary, and activities that allow literature to be easily connected to the theme

- **Writing Ideas**—writing suggestions and activities that cross the curriculum

- **Group Projects**—to foster cooperative learning

- **Hands-On Activities**—providing opportunities for students to be active learners

- **Research Topics**—listing a variety of topics that can be used to extend and enrich learning

- **Bibliographies**—suggesting additional literature related to each section

- **Culminating Activities**—which require students to synthesize their learning and participate in activities that can be shared with others.

Why Whole Language?

A whole language approach involves children in using all modes of communication: reading, writing, listening, observing, illustrating, experiencing, and doing. Communication skills are interconnected and integrated into lessons that emphasize the whole of language rather than isolating its parts. The lessons revolve around a selected theme. Reading is not taught as a subject separate from writing and spelling, for example. A child reads, writes, speaks, listens, and thinks in response to a specific theme introduced by the teacher. In this way, language skills grow naturally, stimulated by involvement and interest in the topic at hand.

Why Interdisciplinary Planning?

One very useful tool for implementing an integrated whole language program is interdisciplinary planning. By choosing a theme for a unit of study, a teacher can plan activities throughout the day that lead to a cohesive, in-depth study of the topic. Students will be practicing and applying their skills in meaningful contexts. Consequently, they will tend to learn and retain more. Both teachers and students will be freed from a day that is broken into unrelated segments of isolated drill and practice.

Why Cooperative Learning?

Besides academic skills and content, students need to learn social skills. No longer can this area of development be taken for granted. Students must learn to work cooperatively in groups in order to function well in modern society. Group activities should be a regular part of school life and teachers should consciously include social objectives as well as academic objectives in their planning. The teacher should clarify and monitor the qualities of good group interaction, just as he/she would clarify and monitor the academic goals of the project.

To keep this valuable resource intact so it can be used year after year, you may wish to punch holes in the pages and store them in a three-ring binder.

Bulletin Board Idea

Use the following bulletin board idea to introduce the section on superheroes. The patterns shown below make the bulletin board quick and easy to create. Begin by covering the background with aluminum foil. Then use an opaque projector to enlarge and copy the patterns shown below. Finally, create the title "Superheroes." You may wish to display student work or the Quiz Cards (page 13) on the bulletin board. You may also wish to place a table in front of the bulletin board to create a learning/research center for students.

Introduction

The concept of a superhero was first introduced to the public in 1938 when *Superman* magazine was published. This magazine was in comic strip form. Since 1938, many different superheroes have emerged and become popular. These unique, fictional men and women have worked to fight against serious problems, such as crime and corruption, that seem insurmountable to the ordinary person. Superheroes always have special powers and talents that they use in their fight to make society a safer place. However, many superheroes have limitations placed on their powers. These limitations, or weaknesses, make these characters seem more real and give the illusion that anyone, even someone you know, could be a superhero in disguise. Today people can enjoy superhero adventures through a variety of media, such as newspapers, magazines, books, television, movies, and computer games.

The outline below is a suggested plan for using the various activities presented in this section of *Heroes*. Each lesson can take from one to several days to complete. You should adapt these ideas to fit your own classroom situation.

Sample Plan

Lesson 1
- Introduce section vocabulary (page 8).
- Introduce and discuss the concept of a superhero (page 8).
- Read and discuss the article about Spider-Man (page 9).
- Complete the Spider-Man Quiz Card (page 13).

Lesson 2
- Read and discuss the article about Spider-Woman (page 10).
- Complete the Spider-Woman Quiz Card (page 13).
- Learn about spiders (page 16).
- Begin reading a book related to the theme (page 17).

Lesson 3
- Read and discuss the article about Superman (page 11).
- Complete the Superman Quiz Card (page 13).
- Invent a superhero (page 19)
- Choose a Relating the Theme activity (page 15).
- Continue reading a book related to the theme (page 17).

Lesson 4
- Read and discuss the article about Storm (page 12).
- Complete the Storm Quiz Card (page 13).
- Choose a Relating the Theme activity (page 15).
- Begin research projects (page 20).
- Finish reading a book related to the theme (page 17).

Lesson 5
- Draw a map that shows a superhero how to get to your school (page 14).
- Make a Super Car (page 18).
- Choose a Relating the Theme activity (page 15).
- Do one or more literature-related activities (page 17).
- Continue working on research projects (page 20).

Lesson 6
- Complete and share research projects (page 20).
- Complete one or more Culminating Activities (pages 166-170).

Overview of Activities

Section Vocabulary: You may wish to introduce the following vocabulary words at the beginning of this section: arch-enemy, arch-rival, metropolis, bureaucrat, laser, technology, hazard, strategic, megaton, serum, transform, sonic, mutant, toxic, sensor, cosmic, avenge, urban, radiation, diabolical, nemesis, subterranean, combatant, teleport, civilization, humanoid, tyrant, mortal.

Background Information:
- A superhero usually has a transformed body.
- A superhero has extraordinary powers or talents.
- A superhero may have some kind of limitation on his or her powers or talents.
- A superhero often helps the police or the government and has a mission to preserve law, order, and justice.
- A superhero fights villains who are extremely dangerous.
- Ultra-technology is frequently used for weapons and protection.

Bulletin Board Idea: This bulletin board is extremely easy to construct and will help set the stage for introducing the section on Superheroes (page 6).

Articles and Discussion Questions: Four interesting articles about specific superheroes and related discussion questions are provided (pages 9-12).

Quiz Cards: These four cards provide questions about the articles to assess students' understanding of what they have read (page 13). Teachers may wish to make the Quiz Cards self-checking by duplicating the set of cards and placing the answers on the back.

Map Study: This activity helps develop map skills and provides an opportunity for students to make a route map (page 14).

Relating the Theme: These activities connect the theme to a variety of curriculum areas, such as language arts, math, science, social studies, art, music, and life skills (page 15).

Spotlight on Science: Students do an in-depth study of spiders (page 16). Then they are challenged to compare characteristics of real spiders to those of Spider-Man or Spider-Woman.

Literature Connection: A literature selection for this section is summarized, and related activities are suggested (page 17).

Make a Super Car: This hands-on activity gives students the opportunity to design a car that could be used by a superhero (page 18).

Invent a Superhero: Students work independently to create their own superhero (page 19).

Research Topics: These research ideas will help students better understand superheroes and the medium through which they are presented (page 20). It is suggested that students work in cooperative learning groups.

Bibliography: Additional literature and videos are suggested (page 21). They may be used in a variety of ways, such as in a learning center, for research projects, for book reports, to stimulate class discussions, or for creative dramatics.

Culminating Activities: Students will pick one or more culminating activities to help them synthesize and share what they have learned (pages 166-170).

Spider-Man

Spider-Man's real identity is Peter Parker, the freelance photographer. As a child, he lived with his Aunt May and Uncle Ben in New York City because his parents had been killed in a plane crash. Peter was not born with any special powers or talents. However, when he was a teenager, he was accidentally bitten by a spider while attending a presentation about how nuclear energy is used safely. This was no ordinary spider because it had been exposed to huge amounts of radiation. As a result, Peter became strong and agile like a spider and was able to cling to any surface, including walls and ceilings.

Peter thought that there should be a way to profit from his unique powers. He made a red and blue uniform for himself and created a mechanism for shooting a web. He decided to call himself the "Amazing Spider-Man," making sure to keep his real identity a secret so he would not be an embarrassment to his aunt and uncle. Spider-Man was hired as the star of a national television show. However, after Spider-Man's uncle was killed by a burglar, he quit his acting career and was determined to devote his life to fighting crime.

Spider-Man has two main powers that make him successful against criminals. The first is his spider-sense, or instinctive feeling of danger. This special sense is active at all times, and it is omnidirectional so Spider-Man can recognize danger coming from any direction. Spider-Man's other superpower is his ability to adhere to different types of surfaces. This allows him to climb up walls and across ceilings with ease as he pursues criminals.

Spider-Man has made several tools that he uses to find and apprehend the criminals. He wears a web-shooter around each wrist. These devices shoot out a super sticky web that hardens but dissolves after about an hour. This webbing can be used to trap criminals and to attach a swing-line to tall buildings so Spider-Man can get to high places. In addition to the web-shooters, Spider-Man has created several homing signals and a beacon. The homing signals are shaped like a small spider, and Spider-Man uses his spider-sense to detect the signals up to a mile away. Spider-Man wears a device hidden in his belt that projects a beacon with the symbol of a red spider. This beacon is used to startle criminals.

Spider-Man often photographs himself in action, using a camera that he wears in his belt. He does this so that his real identity, Peter Parker, can earn money by selling these photographs to a daily newspaper. Spider-Man gives this money to his Aunt May, who has no knowledge of his dual identity.

Over the years, other superheroes have come to recognize the important role Spider-Man plays in the fight against crime. As a result, Spider-Man has participated in a variety of cooperative adventures with many well-known superheroes.

Discussion Questions

1. What do you think Peter's life would have been like if he had never been bitten by the spider?
2. What do you think it would be like to be Spider-Man?
3. Why do you think Spider-Man stories have remained popular for so many years?

Now use the Spider-Man Quiz Card to check your understanding of this article.

Spider-Woman

No one knows the real identity of Spider-Woman. She has kept it a well-guarded secret. She refuses to reveal her identity because she wants to protect the people that she cares about from being harmed by her enemies. Unlike Spider-Man, it is unknown whether Spider-Woman was born with special powers or if she acquired them later in life.

Spider-Woman has extraordinary strength, endurance, and agility. This means she can outfight, outlast, and outmaneuver most criminals. Spider-Woman can move her body like a spider, climbing up walls and across ceilings. These special talents and powers make her a formidable superhero.

Spider-Woman's intuition is only average. She is not able to sense danger any better than the ordinary person. However, her psychic ability is exceptional. She can create a web by concentrating intensely and does not need any kind of device. Spider-Woman uses the web to trap criminals. The web is multidirectional and expands outward from Spider-Woman. One problem with the web is that it becomes increasingly weaker the farther away it is from Spider-Woman. Therefore, a criminal can easily break loose if caught in the outer boundaries of the web. The other problem with the web is that it can be torn. Consequently, sometimes criminals are able to tear the web and escape. If Spider-Woman loses consciousness, she cannot create or maintain a web.

Spider-Woman is a relatively new superhero. As a result many of the other superheroes do not know her. They are cautious about accepting her into their group. But Spider-Woman is trying to prove that she is a worthy ally so she can join forces with the other superheroes.

Discussion Questions

1. How do you think Spider-Woman got her special powers?

2. Where would you go if you could walk on any surface?

3. Why do you think the other superheroes are cautious about accepting Spider-Woman into their group?

Now use the Spider-Woman Quiz Card to check your understanding of this article.

Superman

Superman was born on the planet Krypton. His parents named him Kal-el. When he was just a baby, the gravitational forces on Krypton became unstable. Superman's parents realized that the planet was about to explode. They knew they could not abandon their people. However, they decided to save their son's life by placing him on a spacecraft and sending him to Earth. On Earth, young Kal-el was discovered by Jonathan and Martha Kent. They named him Clark and kept him as their own. As he grew up, it became apparent that he had extraordinary powers. However, the Kents taught Superman to use his powers wisely because they felt that there must be a special reason for them.

After Superman grew up, he moved to Metropolis. As Clark Kent, the ordinary person, he is a reporter for a newspaper called *The Daily Planet*. As Superman, the superhero, he fights crime and injustice. His transition from an ordinary person to superhero takes place in a phone booth when he changes into his Superman costume. Once in his costume, Superman's powers are almost unlimited. He can fly at incredible speeds, leap over even the tallest building, and pick up heavy objects such as a train. His breath is freezing cold like a blast of Arctic air. Superman can see through objects with his X-ray vision and can detect sound over long distances with his supersensitive hearing.

Superman has two weaknesses. First, he is not able to see through lead. Although it is a relatively minor weakness, it has caused him problems at times. Second, and much more serious, is his vulnerability to kryptonite. Kryptonite, especially if it is green, robs Superman of his powers. Someone must remove the kryptonite before Superman can regain his powers.

Superman is one of the most recognized and best-loved superheroes. He was first introduced to the public in 1938 in a comic strip published as a magazine entitled *Superman*. The magazine was written by Jerry Siegel and the illustrations were drawn by Joe Shuster. In the 1940's, a Superman radio series was developed. The first movie to feature Superman was released in 1950. This popular superhero was then seen in the television show "The Adventures of Superman" during the 1950's. In the next decade, Superman appeared in a cartoon series. Finally, in the 1970's and 1980's, four full-length feature films were made about Superman.

Discussion Questions

1. What would you have done if you had been Kal-el's parents?

2. Why did the Kents think Superman was given his powers for a special purpose?

3. Why do you think Superman is one of the best-loved superheroes?

Now use the Superman Quiz Card to check your understanding of this article.

Storm

Storm is an African-American superhero. In the Marvel Universe, she is considered to be a mutant. This means that she is human, but her DNA has been changed in some radical way that results in her having special powers. Mutants are considered to be higher on the evolutionary scale than ordinary humans. In general, people are afraid of mutants because of the tremendous power they wield.

Storm's real name is Ororo Monroe. She was born in the United States. When she was a child, her family moved to Cairo, Egypt. There was a terrible air raid, and Storm's parents were killed. She became an orphan and roamed the city streets. As she got older, she moved all around the continent of Africa. Storm fine-tuned her powers and became the leader of the X-Men.

Storm is an adventurer. She has special powers that allow her to control the weather. She can cause weather conditions, such as ferocious winds, torrential rains, and explosive lightning. Because Storm can manipulate the intensity of the wind, she is able to fly at amazing speeds. In fact, she is capable of creating so much wind that her enemies are sent flying in all directions. Storm is extremely agile and uses this ability to escape if she is captured. Although Storm only has average physical strength, she has remarkable endurance, making it possible for her to outlast her enemies in a battle.

Occasionally, Storm loses control of the weather she has created. When this happens, the effects are devastating. The area experiencing the storm will suffer massive destruction. Eventually, Storm regains control of the weather and is able to calm it down. Storm cannot control the weather if she is unconscious. Any weather disturbance she makes will disappear if she loses consciousness.

Discussion Questions

1. What would you do if you could control the weather?

2. How do you think Storm was able to obtain her superpowers?

3. What would be the benefits of being able to control the weather? What would be the dangers?

Now use the Storm Quiz Card to check your understanding of this article.

Quiz Cards

Use the following questions to assess your students' understanding of the articles on pages 9 through 12 of this unit. Have them write their answers on notebook paper.

Spider-Man Quiz Card

1. What is Spider-Man's real identity?
2. Who raised Spider-Man?
3. How did Spider-Man get his special powers?
4. What special powers does Spider-Man have?
5. Why did Spider-Man decide to devote his life to fighting crime?
6. What is a web-shooter used for?
7. How does Spider-Man use the beacon?
8. What two things does Spider-Man wear in his belt?
9. How does Spider-Man earn money to give to his aunt?
10. Which superhero would you like to see Spider-Man team up with? Explain your choice.

Superman Quiz Card

1. Where was Superman born?
2. Why did Superman have to leave the place of his birth?
3. Who adopted Kal-el when he came to Earth and what did they name him?
4. Where did Superman move to when he grew up?
5. What job does Superman do as a human being?
6. How does this person become Superman?
7. What special powers does Superman have?
8. Why is lead a problem for Superman?
9. Why is kryptonite a problem for Superman?
10. How and when was Superman first introduced to the public?

Spider-Woman Quiz Card

1. Why doesn't Spider-Woman reveal her true identity?
2. How did Spider-Woman get her special powers?
3. What are Spider-Woman's physical abilities like?
4. Why is Spider-Woman's intuition described as average?
5. How does Spider-Woman use her psychic ability?
6. What does Spider-Woman's web look like?
7. What happens if Spider-Woman uses her web to trap a criminal that is far away?
8. How could a criminal escape from Spider-Woman's web?
9. What happens if Spider-Woman is knocked unconscious?
10. Why don't other superheroes know Spider-Woman?

Storm Quiz Card

1. What is a mutant?
2. Why are most people afraid of mutants?
3. How did Storm become an orphan?
4. Where did Storm grow up?
5. Who does Storm lead?
6. Why does Storm control the intensity of the wind?
7. How does Storm use her agility?
8. Why is Storm's endurance important?
9. What happens when Storm loses control of the weather?
10. How could an enemy cause an end to the weather disturbance Storm has created?

Map Study

Pretend that you have invited your favorite superhero to be a guest speaker for your class. Your superhero has visited you at home before, but he or she has never been to your school. Use the box below to draw and label a map that shows how to get from your home to your school. Be sure to include the exact address of your home and school, important street names, and a compass rose. After you have completed your map, use the back of this page to write a paragraph that describes what the map shows. In your description, include some landmarks, such as a specific store or an unusual tree, that your superhero will pass along the way.

Relating the Theme

You may wish to use one or all of the following activities to supplement your own ideas about ways to integrate the *Heroes* theme into your curriculum.

Language Arts:

1. Show two or more video tapes about superheroes. A list is provided in the bibliography on page 21. Have students make a chart to compare and contrast the videos.

2. Have the students bring their favorite superhero comic book or comic strip to school and give an oral report about a superhero.

Science:

1. Have students research one of the following: bats for Batman, iron for Iron Man, shadows for the Shadow, or wasps for Wasp. Then have students write a paragraph explaining why they think that name is appropriate for that superhero.

2. Some superheroes have special powers because they have been irradiated. Have students research radioactivity and its effects.

Social Studies:

1. Explain that many superheroes fight against crime. Ask students to brainstorm a list of ways they think ordinary citizens can help fight crime in their community.

2. Have students label the places superheroes live or were born on a map of the United States. Display the maps on the superhero bulletin board (page 6).

Math:

1. Ask students to write their own word problems that relate to a superhero's speed or strength, the power of a weapon, or the speed of a special means of transportation, such as the Batmobile. Then have students trade papers and solve each other's problems.

2. Have students poll the class to determine the popularity of four or five superheroes. Then help students use the information from the poll to make a circle graph of the results.

Literature:

1. Explain that Spider-Man and Spider-Woman have been popular superheroes for years. Throughout time many cultures have admired spiders and created stories about them. Read aloud one or more spider stories from other cultures. Suggested stories: *Tales of an Ashanti Father* by Peggy Appiah (Beacon Press, 1989); *Naro, the Ancient Spider: The Creation of the Sun & Moon* by Susan Joyce (Peel, 1990); *The Story of Arachne* by Pamela Espiland (Carolrhoda Books, 1980). Ask students to discuss the stories.

Art:

Ask students to draw a sketch of a new supervillain that their favorite superhero will have to contend with in an upcoming story.

Spotlight on Science: Spiders

Use a variety of reference materials to learn more about spiders. Then use phrases to fill in the outline shown below. Remember to start each entry in the outline with a capital letter.

The Spider

I. Physical appearance
  A. Body
    1. _____
    2. _____
  B. Eyes
    1. _____
    2. _____
  C. Mouth
    1. _____
    2. _____
  D. Chelicerae
    1. _____
    2. _____
  E. Pedipalpi
    1. _____
    2. _____
  F. Legs
    1. _____
    2. _____
  G. Spinnerets
    1. _____
    2. _____

II. Food sources
  A. _____
  B. _____

III. Usefulness of spiders
  A. _____
  B. _____

IV. Spider silk
  A. _____
  B. _____

V. Types of spiders
  A. _____
  B. _____
  C. _____

VI. Enemies
  A. _____
  B. _____

Literature Connection

Title: *The Greatest Batman Stories Ever Told*
Author: DC Comics Staff
Publisher: Warner Books, Inc. (1988) *(212-522-7200)*

Summary: This is a compilation of 26 Batman comic books. In these comic book stories, Batman battles famous supervillains, such as the Joker, the Penguin, and Catwoman. He uses a variety of special tools and machines, such as the Baterang, the Batplane, and the Batmobile. Batman is sometimes helped by other superheroes, such as Robin, Superman, and Batwoman.

Vocabulary: mettle, uncanny, diabolical, quarry, plummet, transgression, pernicious, nemesis, domineeringly, transfixed, proverbial, invulnerable, enigmatic, masquerading, subterranean, silhouetted, implacable, antiquities, confrontation

Experiencing the Literature:

1. Have students create a Batman dictionary. Ask them to make a list of words from the book that they would like to include in their dictionary. Tell them to arrange the words in alphabetical order. Have students write the words and definitions in their Batman dictionary.

2. Have students pretend that they are Batman and keep a journal that tells about the adventures he has as described by each comic book story.

3. Have students use brown construction paper to cut out the shape of a bat. Then have them write an adventure story about Batman on the construction-paper bat. Display the stories on the superhero bulletin board (page 6) or hang them from the ceiling.

4. Have students make a Venn diagram and compare and contrast Batman, the superhero, to Bruce Wayne, the ordinary person.

5. Ask students to work in cooperative learning groups to make a model of Gotham City.

6. Provide long strips of paper for students. Have students create their own Batman comic strip. Tell them to be sure to include illustrations and written text in their comic strip.

7. Divide students into cooperative learning groups. Have students pick and role-play their favorite story. Students may wish to make simple props and costumes for this activity.

8. Provide students with posterboard. Have them work with a partner to create a Batman board game. Tell students to write a set of directions that tell how to play the game. Ask students to tell about their game. Then have student pairs trade and play each other's game, or place the games in a learning center so that students can play them while they are studying superheroes.

9. Have students write an advertisement for the book. Tell them to use illustrations and written text for the advertisement. Remind students that the purpose of the advertisement is to persuade people to buy the book.

10. Write the story titles on the chalkboard or on an overhead transparency. Have students take a poll to determine which five stories were liked the best. Have students work with a partner to make a bar graph that shows the results of the poll.

Make a Super Car

Pretend that you have been asked by your favorite superhero to design a SUPER CAR for him or her. Use your imagination to draw a diagram of a car that will help your superhero overcome any obstacles. Be sure to label the parts of your diagram. You may wish to include special features on your SUPER CAR, such as a way to become invisible, a flying and floating mode, a parachute, radar, weaponry, escape systems, high speed capabilities, and on-board computer systems.

18

©*1994 Teacher Created Materials, Inc.*

Invent a Superhero

In this activity you will invent your own superhero. Fill out the information about your superhero. Then draw a picture of him or her on the back of this page.

Superhero's Name:

Real Name (as a regular citizen):

Real Job:

Location:

Goals (What does your superhero hope to accomplish?):

Physical Description (What does your superhero look like?):

Physical Abilities (strength, endurance, agility, speed, etc.):

Physical Adaptations/Transformations (Is your superhero's body built especially well for a task, or is your superhero able to change his or her body in any way?):

Intelligence:

Special Talents or Powers:

Extraordinary Senses (vision, hearing, touch, smell, taste, or extrasensory perception):

Fighting Techniques:

Special Weaponry:

Protection Devices (How does your superhero protect himself or herself?):

Special Vehicles (What does your superhero use to travel by land, water, and air?):

Enemies:

Weaknesses:

Research Topics

Work in cooperative learning groups to research one or more of the areas mentioned below. Share your findings with the rest of the class in any appropriate form of oral presentation. Students may find it helpful to use comic books, computer game books, and children's almanacs to research specific topics.

Superheroes
Iron Man
The Fantastic Four
Dr. Strange
The Incredible Hulk
She Hulk
Wonder Woman
Supergirl
Batman
Captain America
Captain Marvel
The Green Hornet
Flash Gordon
Buck Rogers
The Avengers
The Phantom
The Shadow
X-Men
Wasp
Thor
Hawkeye
Professor X
Nightcrawler

Supervillains
Dr. Doom
Galactus
Molecule Man
Volcana
The Joker
The Penguin
The Riddler
Catwoman
The Turtle Man
Lex Luthor
Morbius
Black Cat
Lizard

Presentation of Superheroes
Comic Strips
Comic Books
Animation
Movies
Computer Games Software

Topics Related to Superheroes
Metamorphosis
Regeneration
Cybernetics
Cryogenics
Lasers
Robotics
Electromagnetic Energy
Telepathy
Extrasensory Perception
Hyperkinetic Energy
Astral Projection
Nuclear Energy
Thermonuclear Power
Gamma Rays
Radiation
Mutations
X-rays
Radio Waves
Force Fields
Biosphere
Criminology
Vigilantes
Mercenaries
Martial Arts
Espionage
Holograms
Titanium
Molecules

Bibliography

Books

Barrier, Michael & Williams, Martin, eds. *The Smithsonian Book of Comic Book Comics.* Smithsonian, 1982.

Blackbeard, Bill & Williams, Martin, eds. *The Smithsonian Collection of Newspaper Comics.* Abrams, 1978.

Blair, Preston. *Cartoon Animation.* W. Foster, 1989.

Dehnbostel, Nancy L. & Hartman, Mary E. *Superheroes.* DOK Publications, 1983.

Dooley, Dennis. *Superman at 50.* Octavia Press, 1987.

Dubowski, Cathy East. *Megazord to the Rescue.* Grosset and Dunlap, 1994.

Eastman, Kevin. *Teenage Mutant Ninja Turtles.* First Publications IL, 1988.

Fleisher, Michael L. *The Encyclopedia of Comic Book Heroes.* Macmillan, 1976.

Fleisher, Michael L. *The Great Superman Book.* Harmony Books, 1978.

Foster, Walter. *Comic Characters.* W. Foster, 1989.

Grant, Alan. *Batman: Knightfall and Beyond.* Bantam, 1994.

Hoff, Syd. *The Young Cartoonist.* Stravon, 1983.

Horn, M., ed. *The World Encyclopedia of Comics.* Chelsea House, 1976.

Kane, Bob. *Batman and Me.* Eclipse Books, 1989.

Kane, Bob. *Batman, the Dailies.* Kitchen Sink, 1990.

Laybourne, Kit. *The Animation Book.* Crown, 1988.

Lenburg, Jeff. *The Encyclopedia of Animated Cartoons.* Facts on File, 1991.

Maddocks, Peter. *How to Be a Cartoonist.* S&S Trade, 1982.

McCay, William. *It's Morphin Time!* Grosset and Dunlap, 1994.

Roncarelli, R. *Computer Animation Dictionary.* Springer-Verlag, 1989.

Rovin, Jeff. *Encyclopedia of Superheroes.* Facts on File, 1985.

Shade, Richard A. *Lights! Camera! Action! Film Animation in the Classroom.* Creative Learning, 1987.

Simon, Joe & Simon, Jim. *The Comic Book Makers.* Crestwood Two, 1990.

Waricha, Jean. *The Terror Toad.* Grosset & Dunlap, 1994.

White, Tony. *The Animator's Workbook.* Watson-Guptill, 1988.

Videos

Batman (1966)

Buck Rogers in the 25th Century (1979)

Captain America (1978)

Captain America II (1979)

Destination Saturn—from the Buck Rogers' serial (1939)

Flash Gordon Videos: *Flash Gordon's Space Soldiers* (1936)
> *The Deadly Ray from Mars* (1940)
> *Flash Gordon Conquers the Universe* (1940)
> *Purple Death from Outer Space* (1938)
> *Rocketship* (1936)

Hero at Large (1979)

The Incredible Hulk (1977)

The Incredible Hulk Returns (1988)

Spider-Man (1977)

Supergirl (1984)

Superman and the Mole Men (1951)

Teenage Mutant Ninja Turtles (1990)

Teenage Mutant Ninja Turtles II: The Secret of the Ooze (1991)

Teenage Mutant Ninja Turtles III (1993)

Bulletin Board Idea

Use the following bulletin board idea to introduce the section on ancient Greek heroes. The patterns shown below make the bulletin board quick and easy to create. Begin by covering the background with butcher paper. Then use an opaque projector to enlarge and copy the patterns shown below. Finally, create the title "Ancient Greek Heroes." You may wish to use the Greek alphabet to create the title. This bulletin board can be used to display student work or the Quiz Cards (page 29). You can create a learning/research center by placing a table with appropriate materials in front of the bulletin board.

Introduction

The earliest record of stories about Greek heroes was found on clay tablets that date back to about 1200 B.C. Some Greek heroes were entirely human. However, many of them were thought to be related to the gods so they were only partly human. These heroes provided a link between the Greek gods and the mortals. They could do amazing god-like feats, but they still had to deal with many of the same problems faced by ordinary people.

Ancient Greek heroes were able to overcome the odds regardless of the obstacles they encountered because they possessed great courage, tremendous strength, and a wily cleverness. They gave the Greek people a feeling of pride and a set of values upon which they could pattern their lives. Greek hero stories continue to be enjoyed by people of all ages.

The outline below is a suggested plan for using the various activities presented in this section of *Heroes*. Each lesson can take from one to several days to complete. You should adapt these ideas to fit your own classroom situation.

Sample Plan

Lesson 1
- Introduce section vocabulary (page 24).
- Introduce and discuss ancient Greece (pages 23-24).
- Explore a map of ancient Greece (page 30).
- Read and discuss the article about Hercules (page 25).
- Complete the Hercules Quiz Card (page 29).

Lesson 2
- Read and discuss the article about Atalanta (page 26).
- Complete the Atalanta Quiz Card (page 29).
- Choose a Relating the Theme activity (page 31).

Lesson 3
- Read and discuss the article about Alexander the Great (page 27).
- Complete the Alexander the Great Quiz Card (page 29).
- Begin reading a book related to the theme (page 33).
- Compare Athens to Sparta (page 32).

Lesson 4
- Read and discuss the article about Helen of Troy (page 28).
- Complete the Helen of Troy Quiz Card (page 29).
- Learn about The Greek Gods (page 35).
- Choose a Relating the Theme activity (page 31).
- Begin research projects (page 36).
- Continue reading a book related to the theme (page 33).

Lesson 5
- Make a Greek Tunic (page 34).
- Choose a Relating the Theme activity (page 31).
- Do one or more literature-related activities (page 33).
- Continue working on research projects (page 36).

Lesson 6
- Complete one or more Culminating Activities (pages 166-170).
- Share research projects (page 36).

Overview of Activities

Section Vocabulary: You may wish to introduce the following vocabulary words at the beginning of this section: shield, riddle, hideous, voyage, din, task, quest, oath, heralds, pyre, immortal, discord, acropolis, chariot, oracle, era, sorceress, odyssey, devour, plague, pierce, agora, classical, temple, bronze, marble, commerce, warrior, Cyclops, mortal, plight, exile.

Background Information:
- The heroes of ancient Greece were often of mixed parentage—part god and part mortal.
- The Greek heroes often had extraordinary tasks to do, such as fight strange and hideous monsters.
- The Greek heroes were brave, strong, and determined. They were role-models for the people.
- No mortal could escape the human frailty which is death, not even Greek heroes.
- The ancient Greeks placed great emphasis on human development—both mental and physical. Mastering the situation was important to the Greeks.

Bulletin Board Idea: This bulletin board is extremely easy to construct and will help set the stage for introducing the section on Ancient Greek Heroes (page 22).

Articles and Discussion Questions: Four interesting articles about specific Greek heroes and related discussion questions are provided (pages 25-28).

Quiz Cards: These four cards provide questions about the articles to assess students' understanding of what they have read (page 29). Teachers may wish to make the Quiz Cards self-checking by duplicating the set of cards and placing the answers on the back.

Map Study: This activity helps develop map skills while providing background information about the location of ancient Greece (page 30). Students should use the map for reference throughout their study of ancient Greek heroes.

Relating the Theme: These activities connect the theme to a variety of curriculum areas, such as language arts, math, science, social studies, art, music, and life skills (page 31).

Spotlight on Social Studies: Students use a Venn diagram to compare and contrast life in Athens and Sparta (page 32).

Literature Connection: Literature selections for this section are summarized, and related activities are suggested (page 33).

Make a Greek Tunic: This hands-on activity gives students the opportunity to dress like the ancient Greeks (page 34).

The Greek Gods: Students work in cooperative learning groups to find out about the Greek gods (page 35).

Research Topics: These research ideas will help students better understand ancient Greece and the heroes associated with this place and time period (page 36). It is suggested that students work in cooperative learning groups.

Bibliography: Additional literature is suggested (page 37). The books may be used in a variety of ways, such as in a learning center, for research projects, or for book reports.

Culminating Activities: Students will pick one or more culminating activities to help them synthesize and share what they have learned (pages 166-170).

Hercules

Hercules is a great hero in Greek mythology. He was the son of Zeus, king of the gods of Olympus, and a mortal woman named Alcmena. He was born in the ancient Greek city of Thebes.

When Hercules was just a baby, he began showing that he had great strength by killing two serpents who were about to attack him. As he grew up, he became famous for his strength and his kindness to those in need. He learned wrestling, archery, and fencing. Although Hercules was basically a good person, he had one serious problem. He had a terrible temper. His temper was so uncontrollable that he had been banished from Thebes. Hercules was told that the only way he could make up for his behavior was to serve King Eurystheus of Argolis for 12 years. During this time, Hercules was given many difficult tasks to accomplish, but he was determined to do them all.

Here are the tasks Hercules had to do:

First, Hercules had to go to Nemea and kill a fierce lion that lived there. Hercules wore the lion's skin to show that he was successful. Second, he had to kill a horrible serpent called the Hydra of Lerna. The hydra had several heads which could grow back if they were cut off. Hercules found a way to keep the heads from growing back and was able to defeat the hydra. His third feat was to capture the Arcadian stag with golden horns. Then the fourth thing Hercules had to do was to catch the huge boar of Erymanthus. The fifth task required Hercules to go to Lake Stymphalus and scare some vicious birds away from the woods there. Then Hercules used two rivers to clean the king's stables. Hercules had to go to Crete to complete the next task. There he had to capture the bull that belonged to King Minos. For his eighth task, Hercules had to take human-eating horses from King Diomedes of Thrace to his king. Hercules had to defeat the queen of the Amazons for his ninth task. The last three tasks made Hercules immortal. He had to take cattle away from the monster called Geryon, steal Golden Apples from the Tree of Life, and catch a three-headed watchdog named Cerberus.

Discussion Questions

1. How would you describe Hercules?
2. Why do you think Hercules was unable to control his temper when he was young?
3. Which task do you think would be the most difficult? Explain your answer.

Now use the Hercules Quiz Card to check your understanding of this article.

Atalanta

Atalanta's father was the king of Arcadia. He was very angry when she was born because he wanted a son. So he took Atalanta and left her on a mountain. Atalanta was rescued by a female bear who eventually raised her to be a strong, athletic young woman.

One day Atalanta met a prince named Meleager. Meleager had come to the mountain because he loved to hunt. He was very impressed by Atalanta's skill as a hunter and fell in love with her. He soon realized that he wanted to marry Atalanta. However, Meleager's family was very unhappy about this and tried to block the marriage. The hate that Meleager's mother felt for Atalanta was very strong. His mother decided that she would rather see Meleager dead than married to Atalanta. As a result, Meleager did die.

Atalanta loved Meleager very much and was overcome with grief. She decided that she could no longer live on the mountain where she had lost the love of her life. Atalanta journeyed to Arcadia, the place where she was born. She was soon reunited with her father. Atalanta's father was very proud that this strong and mighty hunter was his daughter. He was sorry that he had left her on the mountain when she was a baby. Atalanta started living in her father's castle, and her story was told throughout the kingdom. Soon many men wished to marry her for her beauty, courage, and strength. However, Atalanta could not bear the thought of marrying anyone other than Meleager. Not wanting to insult these powerful men, Atalanta announced that a special competition would be used to determine which one she would marry. She declared that she would marry the man who could beat her in a race. However, anyone who competed and lost would pay with his life.

One by one, the men came to compete against Atalanta, hoping to win her as the prize. Each competitor paid with his life after failing to beat Atalanta. Hippomenes loved Atalanta dearly and wanted to marry her, so he decided to enter the race. However, Hippomenes was determined to race and win Atalanta's heart. While Hippomenes was racing against Atalanta, he distracted her by throwing three golden apples in front of her feet. Hippomenes won the race and Atalanta. Atalanta found Hippomenes to be a kind, brave, and cunning champion.

Discussion Questions

1. What would you have done if you had been Atalanta and loved Meleager?

2. Why did you think Atalanta decided to return to Arcadia instead of going somewhere new?

3. How would you have decided which person to marry if you had been Atalanta?

Now use the Atalanta Quiz Card to check your understanding of this article.

Alexander the Great

Alexander was born in 356 B.C. in Pella, Macedonia, which was located in the northern part of ancient Greece. His father was King Philip II, and his mother was Olympias. As a boy, he learned about military tactics from his father and about Greek culture from his tutor, Aristotle. In 336 B.C., after his father was murdered, Alexander became the ruler of Macedonia. He was only twenty years old when he took over the throne. After successfully suppressing some revolts in his kingdom, he set about fulfilling his father's dream of conquering the Persian Empire. One year after becoming king, Alexander led an army of 35,000 soldiers on a journey of conquest that covered an incredible 20,000 miles. Despite his young age, Alexander was an excellent general with a keen understanding of military strategy. As a result, he was able to conquer an enemy's army even when his troops were greatly outnumbered.

As Alexander conquered the foreign lands, he had new cities built that were similar to those he had left behind in Greece. The cities were situated in good locations and had ample water supplies. Many Greeks liked the new cities and chose to settle there. The conquered peoples were introduced to and became immersed in the Greek culture and language. This worked to greatly extend the influence of Greek civilization.

However, Alexander was not content to live in one of the cities he had built. He left Greeks behind to govern his kingdom and continued his conquest east, past the Indus River in India. People admired Alexander for having spread Greek culture throughout his vast empire, and they began calling him Alexander the Great. In 323 B.C., Alexander died from an illness while in Babylon. In all the years he had spent creating his empire, he had never returned to his home in Greece.

Discussion Questions

1. In what ways do you think Alexander was a hero?

2. Why do you think Alexander was a successful leader?

3. How did Alexander help promote the spread of Greek culture to other areas of the ancient world?

Now use the Alexander the Great Quiz Card to check your understanding of this article.

Helen of Troy

It is uncertain as to whether Helen was a real person or part of a myth created to explain the Trojan War. It is said that Helen's father was the god Zeus and her mother was Leda of Sparta.

Stories about Helen's beauty were told throughout the land. Princes from all over Greece came to court her. Finally, she decided to marry Menelaus, who was the king of Sparta. Helen and Menelaus were happily married until they had a visit from Paris, who was a Trojan prince. Paris had come to see if Helen was as beautiful as he had heard. Helen's beauty was breathtaking, and he became obsessed by this. Paris kidnapped Helen and took her back to Troy with him. When Menelaus found out that Paris had taken his beautiful wife, he became enraged.

Menelaus asked the Greek warriors to help him go to war against Troy and retrieve his wife. Many warriors wanted to help the king so they boarded their ships and sailed to Troy, which was located in Asia Minor. The Greeks expected to celebrate a quick victory over the Trojans. But they were never able to penetrate the walls around Troy. The Greeks and Trojans fought for ten years before there was an end to the bloodshed. Some say that Helen spent all those years in the Trojan castle weaving a tapestry that would tell her sad story.

Finally, a man named Odysseus thought of a clever plan to defeat the Trojans and rescue Helen. He secretly built a large wooden horse. Fifty soldiers hid inside of it. The remaining Greeks moved the horse next to the city walls so it could be seen by the Trojans. Then they left and appeared to sail away. The Trojans were curious about this huge, wooden horse so they took it inside their city walls. When it was nightfall, the Greeks inside the horse came out and opened the city gates for the other Greek warriors. As a result, the Greeks defeated the Trojans, and the beautiful Helen of Troy was returned to her husband, Menelaus.

Discussion Questions

1. Why do you think people say that Helen's was "the face that launched a thousand ships"?

2. If Helen hadn't been kidnapped, do you think the Spartans and Trojans would have remained peaceful forever?

3. How would you try to find out if Helen was a real person or the creation of a myth?

Now use the Helen of Troy Quiz Card to check your understanding of this article.

Quiz Cards

Use the following questions to assess your students' understanding of the articles on pages 25 through 28 of this unit. Have them write their answers on notebook paper.

Hercules Quiz Card

1. How did Hercules show his strength as a baby?
2. What was the serious problem Hercules had?
3. What happened as a result of this problem?
4. How many tasks did Hercules have to complete?
5. What was dangerous about the Hydra of Lerna?
6. What was the sixth task Hercules had to do?
7. Why did Hercules go to Crete?
8. What was dangerous about the horses he stole from King Diomedes?
9. Which tasks made Hercules immortal?
10. Would you like to be immortal? Why or why not?

Alexander the Great Quiz Card

1. When and where was Alexander born?
2. What kinds of things did Alexander learn about as a boy?
3. Why did Alexander become king at such a young age?
4. Why did Alexander leave his home in Greece?
5. Why was Alexander considered a military genius?
6. How do you think Alexander chose the locations for his new cities?
7. How was Alexander able to spread Greek culture?
8. How far east did Alexander's empire extend?
9. Why did Alexander become known as Alexander the Great?
10. What do you think happened to Alexander's kingdom after his death?

Atalanta Quiz Card

1. Why was Atalanta abandoned on the mountain?
2. Who raised Atalanta?
3. Who was Meleager?
4. How do you think Meleager's family interfered in his life?
5. What happened to Meleager?
6. Where did Atalanta go when she left the mountain?
7. Why do you think Hippomenes was hesitant about entering the race?
8. How was Hippomenes able to win the race?
9. Do you think Atalanta made a wise choice about how to decide who to marry? Why or why not?
10. What character traits are important to you?

Helen of Troy Quiz Card

1. What stories did people tell about Helen?
2. What happened after Paris meet Helen and Menelaus?
3. What would you have done if you had been Helen?
4. What did Menelaus do when he found out what Paris had done?
5. What would you have done if you had been Menelaus?
6. Why couldn't the Greeks immediately defeat the Trojans?
7. How long did the Greeks and the Trojans fight?
8. What plan did Odysseus use to get inside the walls around Troy?
9. Why do you think the Trojans were fooled by what the Greeks had done?
10. How do you think Helen and Menelaus felt about being reunited after all those years?

Map Study

Western civilization was born in ancient Greece about 2,500 years ago. Examine the map of ancient Greece that is shown below. Use a reference book, such as an atlas or an encyclopedia, to locate and label the following places on the map.

Ionian Sea	Crete	Troy	Knossos
Aegean Sea	Rhodes	Corinth	Delphi
Mediterranean Sea	Ithaca	Thebes	Olympia
Mount Olympus	Sparta	Athens	Pella

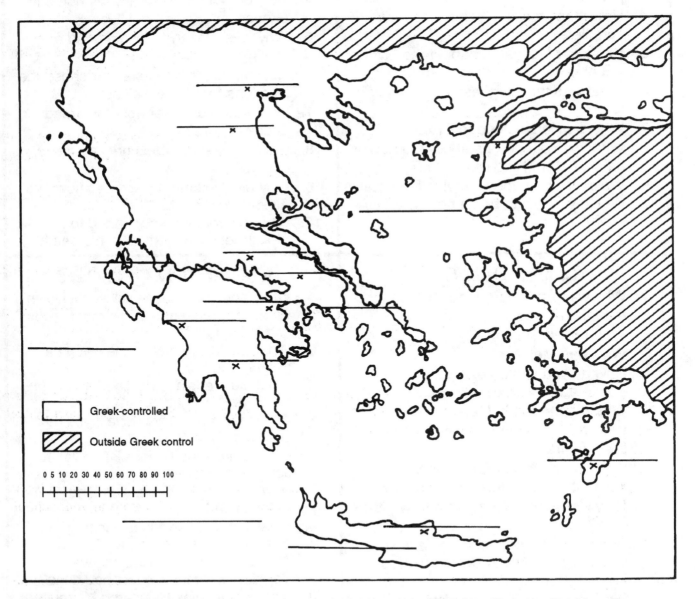

Greek-controlled

Outside Greek control

0 5 10 20 30 40 50 60 70 80 90 100

After you have finished labeling this map, compare it to a map of modern Greece. How has Greece changed from ancient times? How has it remained the same?

©1994 Teacher Created Materials, Inc.

Relating the Theme

You may wish to use one or all of the following activities to supplement your own ideas about ways to integrate the *Heroes* theme into your curriculum.

Language Arts:

1. Show a video tape of an ancient Greek hero and discuss the way that hero deals with problems. Suggested videos: *Jason and the Argonauts* (1963, British); *Ulysses* (1955, Italian); *Hercules* (1959, Italian); *Helen of Troy* (1955). After students view the video tape, have them read a book or an article about the same hero. Ask them to compare and contrast the characteristics of that hero as presented in writing and on the video.

Science:

Have students make a chart to compare the following information about ancient Greece and your community: climate, rainfall, and major crops. Ask them to draw conclusions about how the climate, rainfall, and terrain help determine what crops people grow.

Social Studies:

1. Have students draw a map showing Alexander's empire. Ask them to show the route Alexander took to conquer colonies in Egypt and the Middle East. Have students label the places and dates of important battles.

2. Ask students to write an essay explaining direct democracy and representative democracy.

Math:

1. Have students use the map on page 30 to determine the distances between cities and towns labeled on the map.

2. Archimedes was a great mathematician in ancient Greece. He discovered a scientific principle known as Archimedes' Principle. Ask students to research the principle and explain it in their own words.

Literature:

Read aloud a story about a Greek hero. Ask students to name the character traits of that hero. Ask them to make a chart that compares and contrasts the ancient Greek hero to a modern hero of their choice.

Physical Education:

Have students learn about the Olympics in ancient Greece. Then have them work in cooperative learning groups to organize some "Olympic" games at your school.

Life Skills:

Provide books with pictures of ancient Greek architecture for students to examine. Then have students look at buildings in your community. Ask students to sketch a building that has a design they think was influenced by ancient Greek architecture.

Spotlight on Social Studies: Athens and Sparta

By the 700's B.C., the people living in the small farming communities of ancient Greece began organizing themselves into larger political groups called city-states. A fortress, which was usually built on a hill, provided protection for the people in a city-state. Most of the citizens in a city-state shared the same heritage, customs, dialect, religion, and concerns.

Athens and Sparta were two city-states in ancient Greece. Use reference books to learn what life was like for the people who lived in Athens and Sparta. Compare and contrast these two city-states by completing the Venn diagram shown below.

Try to include information about the following:

- geographic location   • economy   • education
- citizenship   • culture   • allies and enemies
- government   • life-style   • beliefs/philosophies

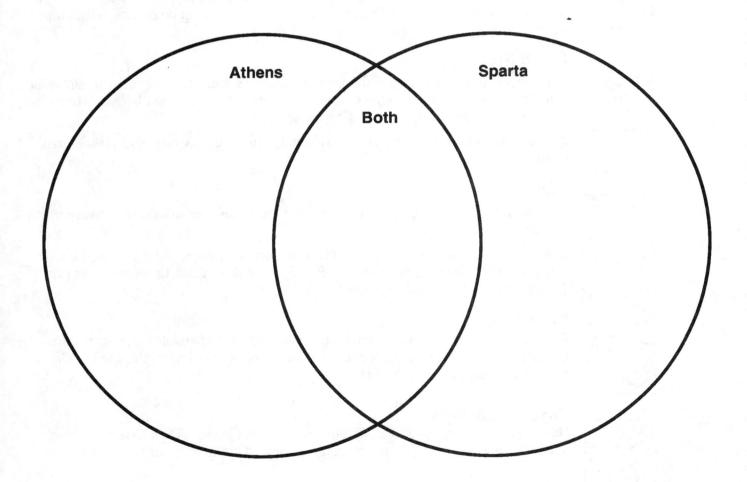

Literature Connection

Title: *Jason and the Argonauts*   **Author:** Bernard Evslin
Publisher: Morrow & Company, Inc. (1986) *(Canada: Gage Distributions; UK: International BK Dist. ; AUS: Kirby Book Co.)*

Summary: Jason and his Argonaut friends set out on a dangerous expedition to retrieve the Golden Fleece which would allow Jason to reclaim the throne of Iolcus. While on their journey, they encounter the bulls of Daedalus, huge boulders that exist to destroy ships, and a gigantic serpent.

Vocabulary: gargoyle, inviolate, regent, realm, decrees, mortals, tyrant, usurper, prophecies, relic, falconry, demons, antagonists, dignitary, treachery, noncombatants

Experiencing the Literature:

1. Have students trace Jason's journey on a map.
2. Ask students to pretend they are Jason and write journal entries about the journey.
3. Have students write a poem about Jason's journey to obtain the Golden Fleece.

Title: *Theseus and the Minotaur*   **Author:** Leonard Everett Fisher
Publisher: Holiday House (1988) *(Canada: Thomas Allen & Son; UK and AUS: Baker and Taylor Int.)*

Summary: This is the story of a prince named Theseus. When Theseus was born, his father, the king, buried his favorite sword and sandals under a rock. The king said that Theseus could not inherit the throne until he was strong enough to get the sword and sandals from under the rock. When Theseus grew up, he moved the rock and retrieved his father's sword and sandals. He journeyed to Athens to see his father. His father told him how Athens was defeated by King Minos of Crete years ago and that every year that defeat was paid for with the lives of 14 people. The 14 people were sent into the labyrinth to be killed by the Minotaur. Theseus successfully defeated the Minotaur, so no one else had to die in the labyrinth.

Vocabulary: successor, banquet, obliged, maidens, labyrinth, perish, mooring, hoist, dungeon, bellowing, hideous

Experiencing the Literature:

1. Have students fold a sheet of paper to make an eight page mini-book that shows some of the main events in the story.
2. Have students write a story that tells about another adventure Theseus has.
3. Ask students to work with a partner to make a model of the labyrinth.

Title: *The Great Deeds of the Superheroes*   **Retold by:** Maurice Saxby
Publisher: Peter Bedrick Books (1989) *(Canada: Publishers Group West; UK: Dragon's World; AUS: Lothian)*

Summary: This is a compilation of stories, five of which are about ancient Greek heroes.

Vocabulary: prophecy, immortals, sickle, chariot, catapult, peril, oracle, enchantress, suitors

Experiencing the Literature:

1. Have students make a Venn diagram to compare and contrast two ancient Greek heroes.
2. Have students study the family trees shown in the book. Ask them to create their own family tree.
3. Supply butcher paper and have students make a mural about the adventures of one ancient hero.

Make a Greek Tunic

In this activity you will work with a partner to make a tunic and sandals so you can dress like an ancient Greek.

Each of you will need the following materials:
- two old sheets
- needle and thread (a stapler can be used instead)
- tape measure
- rope or belt
- chalk
- safety pins

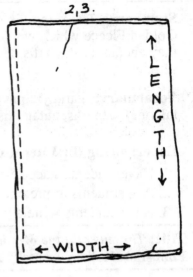

Directions:

Step 1: Have your partner use the tape measure to find out how long you are from the base of your neck to the tops of your knees. Add 12 inches (30 cm) to that length. For example, if your partner measures 36 inches (90 cm) and you add 12 inches (30 cm) to that, you will have a total of 48 inches (120 cm).

Step 2: Place the two sheets with the right sides together and cut two rectangles that are the length you got in Step 1 and 36 inches (90 cm) wide.

Step 3: Sew or staple the sides together along the length of the rectangles.

Step 4: Turn the sheets so that the right sides are showing. You may wish to sew or staple decorative trim onto the bottom of your tunic.

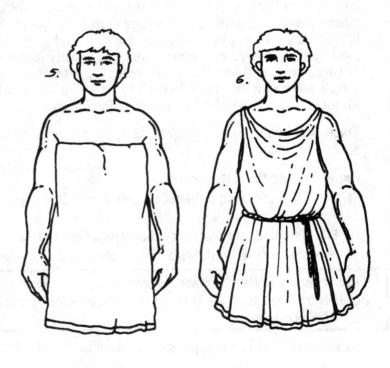

Step 5: Put the tunic on over your head, holding the top of it under your arms. Have your partner pull and pin the top edges together at your shoulders.

Step 6: Tie a rope or belt around your waist. Then pull the tunic over the rope or belt until the bottom of it is just above your knees.

Step 7: Now help your partner make a tunic following these same steps.

        ©1994 Teacher Created Materials, Inc.

The Greek Gods

The ancient Greeks enjoyed telling myths, or stories, about gods who had special powers. They often used their myths to explain things that they did not understand in the world around them. In addition, the behavior of the gods was intended to serve as a model of correct and moral behavior for the ordinary people, though certainly many gods did not exhibit such model behavior.

Work with a group of three or four other students to learn more about the Greek gods. Use books about Greek mythology or encyclopedias to complete the chart. The first one is done for you.

Name	Information
Aphrodite	*goddess of love*
Apollo	
Ares	
Artemis	
Asclepius	
Athena	
Atlas	
Cronus	
Demeter	
Dionysus	
Eros	
Gaea	
Helios	
Hephaestus	
Hera	
Hermes	
Hestia	
Hypnos	
Pan	
Pluto (or Hades)	
Poseidon	
Rhea	
Uranus	
Zeus	

Research Topics

Work in cooperative learning groups to research one or more of the areas mentioned below. Share your findings with the rest of the class in any appropriate form of oral presentation.

More Heroes
Odysseus (Ulysses)
King Minos
Homer
Phidippides
Socrates
Perseus
Plato
Herodotus
Aristotle
Aristarchus
Pythagoras
Hippocrates
Pericles
Myron
Theseus
Thales of Miletus
Democritos of Abdera
Aesop
Thucydides

Places
Mount Olympus
Peloponnesus
Mycenae
Attica
Thessaly
Corfu
Troy
Knossos
Ithaca
Crete
Athens
Sparta
Delphi
Delos
Eleusis

Architecture
Types: Doric, Ionic, Corinthian
Buildings: Acropolis, Parthenon, Amphitheater

Government
City-States
Monarchy
Oligarchy
Birth of Democracy
Tyrants

Life and Culture
Farming
Sea Trade
Barter System
Coins
Slave Labor
Citizen-Soldiers
Greek Alphabet
Olympic Games
Greek Gods
Theater: Comedies and Tragedies
Lyric Poetry
Sculpture
Mythology
Symposiums

Bibliography

Aesop. *Aesop's Fables.* Viking, 1981.

Artman, John. *Ancient Greece.* Good Apple, 1991.

Ash, Maureen. *Alexander the Great.* Childrens Press, 1991.

Asimov, Isaac. *Words from the Myths.* Houghton Mifflin, 1961.

Bloom, Harold, Introduction by. *Homer's Odyssey.* Chelsea House, 1987.

Bulfinch, Thomas. *Bulfinch's Mythology: The Age of Fable, the Age of Chivalry, Legends of Charlemagne.* Crowell, 1970.

Cohen, Daniel. *Ancient Greece.* Doubleday, 1990.

Colum, Padraic. *The Golden Fleece and Heroes Who Lived Before Achilles.* Macmillan, 1983.

Evans & Millard. *Greek Myths and Legends.* EDC, 1986.

Evslin, Bernard. *The Adventures of Ulysses.* Bantam, 1978.

Evslin, Bernard. *The Greek Gods.* Scholastic Inc., 1988.

Evslin, Bernard. *Hercules.* William Morrow and Company, 1984.

Fisher, Leonard Everett. *Jason and the Golden Fleece.* Macmillan, 1993.

Fisher, Leonard Everett. *Olympians: Great Gods and Goddesses of Ancient Greece.* Holiday, 1984.

Fisher, Leonard Everett. *Theseus and the Minotaur.* Holiday, 1985.

Gates, Doris. *A Fair Wind for Troy.* Viking Press, 1976.

Glubok, Sherley and Tamarin, Alfred. *Olympic Games in Ancient Greece.* Harper Collins, 1976.

Graves, Robert. *Greek Gods and Heroes.* Dell, 1973.

Green, Roger L., retold by. *Heroes of Greece and Troy, Retold from the Ancient Authors.* Walck, 1961.

Green, Roger L. *Tales of Greek Heroes.* Puffin Books, 1989.

Hutton, Warwick. *Perseus.* McElderry, 1993.

Hutton, Warwick. *Theseus and the Minotaur.* McElderry, 1989.

Hutton, Warwick. *Trojan Horse.* McElderry, 1992.

King, Perry. *Pericles.* Chelsea House, 1988.

Kingsley, Charles. *The Heroes.* Macmillan and G. Cave, 1980.

Low, Alice. *The Macmillan Book of Greek Gods and Heroes.* Macmillan, 1985.

McLean, Mollie. *Adventures of the Greek Heroes.* Houghton Mifflin, 1961.

Oldfield, Pamela, retold by. *Tales from Ancient Greece.* Doubleday, 1989.

Reeves, James. *Heroes and Monsters: Legends of Ancient Greece.* Blackie, 1977.

Richardson, I. M. *The Adventures of Hercules.* Troll Associates, 1983.

Saxby, Maurice. *The Great Deeds of the Superheroes.* Peter Bedrick Books, 1989.

Schwab, Gustav. *Gods and Heroes: Myths and Epics of Ancient Greece.* Random House, 1977.

Serraillier, Ian. *The Clashing Rocks: The Story of Jason and the Argonauts.* Heinemann, 1970.

Snow, Pegeen. *Atalanta.* Dillon, 1988.

Swaddling, Judith. *The Ancient Olympic Games.* University of Texas Press, 1984.

Warner, Francis. *Healing Nature: The Athens of Pericles.* Dufour, 1989.

Wise, William. *Monster Myths of Ancient Greece.* Putnam, 1981.

Teacher Created Materials

144   *How to Manage Your Whole Language Classroom*

145   *Portfolio Assessment for Your Whole Language Classroom*

163   *Writing a Country Report*

297   *Thematic Unit: Ancient Greece*

373   *Thematic Bibliography*

423   *Literature Unit: D'Aulaires' Book of Greek Myths*

906   *Newspaper and Reporting Set*

Bulletin Board Idea

Use the following bulletin board idea to introduce students to the section on Medieval Heroes. The pattern shown below makes the bulletin board quick and easy to create. Begin by covering the background with butcher paper. Then use an opaque projector to enlarge and copy the pattern. Glue aluminum foil over the knight's armour. Use a black permanent marker to redraw the lines on the suit of armour. You may wish to glue other types of materials, such as yarn for the mane and tail of each horse, onto the bulletin board. Finally, create the title "Medieval Heroes." This bulletin board can be used to display student work or the Quiz Cards (page 45). You can create a learning/research center by placing a table with appropriate materials in front of the bulletin board.

Introduction

Medieval times, or the Middle Ages, refers to the period of time in European history from about A.D. 450 through the 1400's. Most historians break down medieval times into three parts: the Early Middle Ages, the High Middle Ages, and the Later Middle Ages. During the Early Middle Ages, the Roman Empire fell, invasions by barbarians were common, Charlemagne became the Frankish king, and Christianity became popular. During the High Middle Ages, the rules of a feudal political system were enforced, the invaders were driven off, the Crusades took place, and the creation of art and literature were encouraged. During the Later Middle Ages, the people had to deal with tragedies resulting from famine, the Bubonic Plague, and the Hundred Years' War. However, those who lived through all of these usually found that their quality of life had improved.

The outline below is a suggested plan for using the various activities presented in this section of *Heroes*. Each lesson can take from one to several days to complete. You should adapt these ideas to fit your own classroom situation.

Sample Plan

Lesson 1

- Introduce section vocabulary (page 40).
- Introduce and discuss the medieval time period (pages 38-40).
- Explore a map of Europe during medieval times (page 46).
- Read and discuss the article about King Arthur (page 41).
- Complete the King Arthur Quiz Card (page 45).

Lesson 2

- Read and discuss the article about Robin Hood (page 42).
- Complete the Robin Hood Quiz Card (page 45).
- Choose a Relating the Theme activity (page 47).
- Make Robin Hood's Hat (page 50).

Lesson 3

- Read and discuss the article about Joan of Arc (page 43).
- Complete the Joan of Arc Quiz Card (page 45).

- Begin reading a book related to the theme (page 49).
- Learn about ballads (page 48).

Lesson 4

- Read and discuss the article about Vassilissa (page 44).
- Complete the Vassilissa Quiz Card (page 45).
- Make a medieval diorama (page 51).
- Choose a Relating the Theme activity (page 47).
- Begin research projects (page 52).
- Continue reading a book related to the theme (page 49).

Lesson 5

- Choose a Relating the Theme activity (page 47).
- Do one or more literature-related activities (page 49).
- Continue working on research projects (page 52).

Lesson 6

- Complete one or more Culminating Activities (pages 166-170).
- Share research projects (page 52).

Overview of Activities

Section Vocabulary: You may wish to introduce the following vocabulary words at the beginning of this section: chivalry, page, squire, Christendom, lance, realm, armor, steed, knight, joust, feint, succumb, pallet, summon, pilgrimage, the Crusades, damsel, pavilion, liege, chalice, visor, drawbridge, moat, esquire, cathedral, crypts.

Background Information:

- Medieval times span from about A.D. 450 until the late 1400's.
- Feudalism provided the political structure, while agriculture and trade were the basis for the economy.
- Boys were encouraged to study the arts, education, theology, law, or medicine. Girls were usually taught at home, although they occasionally went to school at a convent.
- Christianity grew during this period.
- Townspeople had increasing power as they gained wealth and military strength.

Bulletin Board Idea: This bulletin board is extremely easy to construct and will help set the stage for introducing the section on Medieval Heroes (page 38).

Articles and Discussion Questions: Four interesting articles about specific medieval heroes and related discussion questions are provided (pages 41-44).

Quiz Cards: These four cards provide questions about the articles to assess students' understanding of what they have read (page 45). Teachers may wish to make the Quiz Cards self-checking by duplicating the set of cards and placing the answers on the back.

Map Study: This activity helps develop map skills while providing background information about Europe during medieval times (page 46). Students should use the map for reference throughout their study of medieval heroes.

Relating the Theme: These activities connect the theme to a variety of curriculum areas, such as reading, language arts, math, science, social studies, art, music, and life skills (page 47).

Spotlight on Music: Students study what a ballad is and then write their own ballad (page 48).

Literature Connection: Literature selections for this section are summarized, and related activities are suggested (page 49).

Make Robin Hood's Hat: This hands-on activity gives students the opportunity to make a hat like the one Robin Hood wore (page 50).

A Medieval Diorama: Students work in cooperative learning groups to make a diorama that shows a scene from medieval times (page 51).

Research Topics: These research ideas will help students better understand medieval history and the heroes associated with this time period (page 52). It is suggested that students work in cooperative learning groups.

Bibliography: Additional literature is suggested (page 53). The books may be used in a variety of ways, such as in a learning center, for research projects, or for book reports.

Culminating Activities: Students will pick one or more culminating activities to help them synthesize and share what they have learned (pages 166-170).

King Arthur

King Arthur was and continues to be one of the greatest British heroes of medieval times. Although it is believed that there really was an Arthur, the adventure stories that have been told about him for nearly 1,000 years are generally thought to be legend. According to the Latin versions of the story, King Uther Pendragon was Arthur's father. However, the king was not allowed to raise Arthur himself because he had made a special pact with Merlin, a Celtic magician. As a result, Merlin raised Arthur as his own son and never told him that his father was a king.

According to the legend, there was a sword imbedded in a stone that was located in a churchyard. The sword, called Excalibur, was said to be magical and that anyone who could remove it from the stone would become the king of Britain. Many nobles and knights tried to remove it, but they could not. Then Arthur tried and easily pulled Excalibur from the stone. This amazing feat proved that he was royalty, so he became Britain's king. At some point after Arthur became king, he fell in love with Princess Guinevere and married her. Although they had several castles to choose from, Arthur preferred to stay at Camelot which was located somewhere in southern England.

Arthur tried to rule with fairness and wisdom. As a result, most knights greatly respected Arthur and wanted to serve him. They came from many countries in hopes of being chosen as a knight of the Round Table. This table was round in shape and could seat 1,600 knights without any one knight having a better seat than the others. Arthur felt that this was the best way to prevent his knights from arguing. Some of the stories say that Arthur had this enormous table built, while others say that it was given to him as a wedding gift.

The legend of King Arthur tells about his many heroic adventures. He is said to have conquered most of western Europe by defeating the Roman Empire. Unfortunately, while he was away, his nephew Mordred captured his kingdom. When Arthur returned home, he fought and killed Mordred. Although he was victorious, he received grievous wounds during this battle and later died. Some say that Arthur was taken to the mystical island of Avalon so that his wounds would heal. Many believe that he will return someday.

Discussion Questions

1. Why do you think the legend of King Arthur is so popular?

2. What would you have done if you had been able to pull Excalibur from the stone?

3. What would be the benefits of being a knight during medieval times? What would be the hardships?

Now use the King Arthur Quiz Card to check your understanding of this article.

Robin Hood

Robin Hood is a legendary English hero whose rebellious nature made him a popular character in stories and ballads beginning sometime during the 1300's. The ballads written about Robin Hood that were popular during medieval times were entitled, "Robin Hood and the Monk," "Robin Hood and Guy of Gisborne," "Robin Hood and the Potter," and *"Lytyll Geste of Robin Hode."* Some scholars believe that the adventures of Robin Hood are strictly fictional, while others believe that they are based on a real person. To this day, no one knows for sure.

The legend begins when Robin Hood is rescued by a group of outlaws who live in Sherwood Forest in Nottinghamshire. He finds that he has much more in common with these outlaws than anyone else so he becomes their leader. Robin Hood's followers include the beautiful Maid Marian, the love of his life; Friar Tuck, a rather portly and good-hearted priest; and Little John, a seven-foot giant of a man who is a marksman with a bow and arrow.

Robin Hood's popularity comes from the way he fights corruption and injustice. He treats corrupt officials, such as the sheriff of Nottingham, with contempt. However, he treats women and poor people with respect. He and his band of outlaws steal from the rich, such as wealthy landowners, and give to the poor. The commoners praise him as a hero, while authority figures proclaim him an outlaw.

Today, people of all ages continue to enjoy reading books and watching movies about Robin Hood's adventures.

Discussion Questions

1. Do you think Robin Hood was a real person? Explain your answer.

2. What do you think Robin Hood's life would have been like if he had never met the band of outlaws in Sherwood Forest?

3. If Robin Hood lived in today's society what type of corruption or injustice would he fight?

Now use the Robin Hood Quiz Card to check your understanding of this article.

Joan of Arc

Joan of Arc was a real person who lived between 1412-1431. She was the daughter of a farmer in Lorraine, France. Joan helped her family by herding sheep and cattle and working in the fields. Joan, like most of the people who lived at this time, had a strong religious upbringing. Joan believed that visions of the saints appeared and told her to take King Charles to the place where he would be crowned and to defeat the English army. She dressed up as a soldier and journeyed about 300 miles across enemy lines. The king was impressed by Joan's courage and tenacity, and he believed that she was sent to help France defeat the English. King Charles asked Joan to go to Orleans where the English were winning a battle against the French.

Once Joan arrived at Orleans, the soldiers thought she must be a saint because of how daring and brave she was. The soldiers fought valiantly and became more aggressive. As a result, the French were able to defeat the English and King Charles was crowned. Although the army had been defeated, many English continued to live on French soil. Joan told the king that they must return to England.

King Charles did not care about the English living on French soil, but he allowed Joan to continue fighting alongside any soldiers who would follow her into battle. In 1430, Joan was captured by the soldiers from Burgundy. Burgundy was an English ally, and they turned her over to the English. Joan was tried in a church court that was controlled by the English, who hated her. She was found guilty of heresy and sorcery. Her punishment for these crimes was to be burned to death at the stake. In 1456, she was given a new trial and was found to be innocent. In 1920, she was canonized as a saint.

Discussion Questions

1. What character traits do you think are unusual about Joan?

2. Why do you think Joan was so successful?

3. Why do you think the church decided to issue a new verdict after Joan's death?

Now use the Joan of Arc Quiz Card to check your understanding of this article.

Vassilissa

Vassilissa was a hero who lived in medieval Russia. She was very intelligent and courageous, and she had tremendous strength. Vassilissa was married to Staver, a young and sometimes foolish prince. Staver was invited to a feast in Kiev given by the Grand Duke Vladimir. Vladimir loved to brag about his wealth. Staver was tired of hearing Vladimir brag, so he decided to do some bragging of his own. He told his friend, Pavel, that his wife, Vassilissa was his most valued treasure. Staver said that she could compete against any man and win.

The Duke was outraged by this claim. He could not believe that it was true. He threw Staver into a dungeon and sent his soldiers to get Vassilissa. In the meantime, Staver's friend, Pavel, warned Vassilissa that the Duke's soldiers were coming to get her. Vassilissa promptly dressed like a man, took her bow and arrow, and rode off toward the Duke's castle with 12 men dressed up as Tartars riding behind her. When Vassilissa met the Duke's soldiers along the way, she told them that she was the messenger for the Great Tartar Kahn and that the Duke owed the Kahn a huge gold tribute. She also told them that Vassilissa had escaped and they did not need to go any farther. The Duke's soldiers were afraid of the Kahn and returned to the castle.

When Vassilissa arrived as the messenger of Kahn, a great feast was given on her behalf. The Duke's wife saw Vassilissa and knew at once that she was a woman. She told her husband that she was sure the Kahn's messenger was a woman. Duke Vladimir decided to put the messenger to the test. First, the Duke had the messenger wrestle three strong men. Each time, Vassilissa won. Then the Duke proposed an archery contest, and again Vassilissa won. Finally, the Duke asked the messenger to play a game of chess with him. The messenger offered to take a musician, which was Staver, to the Kahn in place of the gold if he won the chess game. The Duke was delighted by this since he did not have the large amount of gold. Of course, Vassilissa won the chess game and took her husband home. The Duke was never the wiser as to her identity.

Discussion Questions

1. What would you have done if you had been Vassilissa?

2. Why did the Duke challenge the messenger to so many types of contests?

3. How do you think Staver will act in the future? Explain your answer.

Now use the Vassilissa Quiz Card to check your understanding of this article.

Quiz Cards

Use the following questions to assess your students' understanding of the articles on pages 41 through 44 of this unit. Have them write their answers on notebook paper.

King Arthur Quiz Card

1. Who does the legend say is Arthur's father?
2. Who raised Arthur?
3. How did Arthur learn that he should be the king of Britain?
4. Who did Arthur marry?
5. Which castle was Arthur's favorite?
6. Why did so many knights from different countries come to Arthur's kingdom?
7. Why did Arthur feel that it was important for his knights to be seated at a round table?
8. What conquest was attributed to Arthur?
9. What happened while Arthur was away from his kingdom?
10. What do you think happened to Arthur after his battle with Mordred?

Joan of Arc Quiz Card

1. What did Joan do to help her family?
2. What kind of visions did Joan believe she was having?
3. When the visions took place, what was Joan told to do?
4. How was Joan able to pass through enemy lines on her way to the king?
5. Where did King Charles ask Joan to go?
6. Why did the king send Joan to this place?
7. What happened after the English were defeated?
8. What happened in 1430?
9. What happened at Joan's trial?
10. About how old was Joan at the time of her death?

Robin Hood Quiz Card

1. During the 1300's, how was the legend of Robin Hood usually told?
2. What is the name of one medieval ballad about Robin Hood?
3. Why did Robin Hood become the leader of the outlaws rather than just a member of the band?
4. How does Robin Hood meet the outlaws?
5. Where do the outlaws who rescued Robin Hood live?
6. Who was Maid Marian?
7. Who was Friar Tuck?
8. Who was Little John?
9. Who was one of the corrupt officials Robin Hood treated with contempt?
10. Why was Robin Hood popular with the common people?

Vassilissa Quiz Card

1. Why did Staver go to Kiev?
2. What did Staver brag to Pavel?
3. What did Vladimir do when he heard Staver's claim?
4. Who warned Vassilissa that the Duke's soldiers were coming to get her?
5. Why did Vassilissa dress up as a man before leaving for the Duke's castle?
6. Why didn't the Duke's soldiers go to Vassilissa's home?
7. What had the Duke done to prepare for the messenger's arrival?
8. What was the first challenge that the Duke proposed to the messenger?
9. What was the second challenge that the Duke proposed to the messenger?
10. How did Vassilissa obtain her husband's freedom from the dungeon?

Map Study

This map shows what Europe looked like during medieval times.

Use a current atlas to find a map of modern Europe. Compare the two maps to answer the following questions.

1. During medieval times, what was the land that is now Spain called?
2. During medieval times, what was the land that is now Portugal called?
3. During medieval times, what was the land that is now Great Britain called?
4. During medieval times, what was the land that is now the Netherlands called?
5. During medieval times, what was the land that is now Italy called?
6. During medieval times, what was the land that is now Sweden called?

Relating the Theme

You may wish to use one or all of the following activities to supplement your own ideas about ways to integrate the Heroes theme into your curriculum.

Language Arts:

1. Have students watch and discuss one or more of the following videos: *The Adventures of Robin Hood* (1938), *Joan of Arc* (1938), *Camelot* (1967), *Henry V* (1990), Ivanhoe (1952), and *Sword of Lancelot* (1963).

2. Have each student do research to learn about an important person who lived during medieval times, such as Robin Hood, Joan of Arc, Charlemagne, Otto the Great of Germany, William Duke of Normandy, Henry Tudor, Eleanor of Acquitaine, Pope Urban II, Richard the Lion-Hearted, and King Henry V. Ask students to use their research to write a speech that that historical figure might have given. Have students present their speech to the class.

Social Studies:

1. Have students research what a coat of arms is and the symbolism it represents. Then have them design a coat of arms for themselves.

2. Have students learn about the following types of medieval craftsmen: architects, master masons, master stone cutters, stone dressers, stone carvers, carpenters, sculptors, mortar makers, blacksmiths, plumbers, roofers, glass blowers, and stained glass craftsmen. Together, draw a mural showing these craftsmen at work.

Math:

1. Have students do research to find the average weight of a knight's armor. Have students weigh themselves and then determine how much they would weigh if they were wearing a suit of armor.

2. Ask students to determine the value of these medieval measurements: four and twenty, a score, a league, a rod, a township, a peck, and a pennyweight.

Literature:

Have students read one of the books from the Literature Connection (page 49). Then ask them to make a set of cards with illustrations and short summaries that show the sequence of story events.

Art:

Have students make stained glass windows, using black construction paper and tissue paper in a variety of colors. Have students cut out a design from the black construction paper. Then show them how to glue pieces of tissue paper to the back of the construction paper for a stained glass effect. Hang the stained glass windows in the classroom window.

Life Skills:

1. Have students write and/or make recipes that could be used at a medieval banquet. Some suggestions include: Welsh rabbit, Yorkshire pudding, wassail, bangers, and scones.

2. Have students do research to find out how medieval technology has influenced today's technology.

Spotlight on Music: Ballads

During medieval times, musical entertainment was often in the from of a ballad. A ballad is a song that tells a story in a rhyming verse. Most ballads use phrases or sentences that are organized into four-line stanzas. The rhyme scheme of a ballad is A-B-A-B. This means that the last word in every other line rhymes.

Read the following example of a stanza from a ballad.

A handsome knight rode through the wood.	A
He saw a fair maiden by a cool stream.	B
The knight rode by as quietly as he could.	A
But she disappeared as if part of a dream.	B

Now use the space below to write your own ballad. Be sure to give your ballad a title.

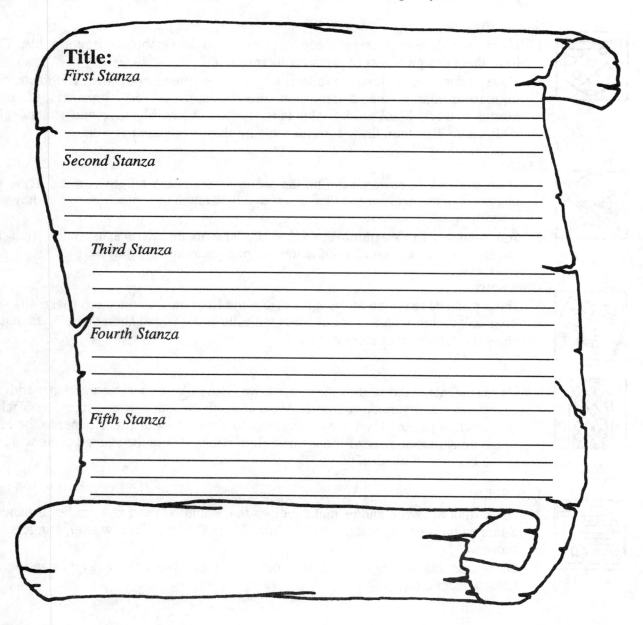

Title: _____

First Stanza

Second Stanza

Third Stanza

Fourth Stanza

Fifth Stanza

Literature Connection

Title: *Robin Hood*   **Retold by:** Sarah Hayes
Publisher: Henry Holt and Company (1989) *(Canada: Fitz, Henry & Whiteside; UK: Walker Bks.; AUS: CIS Publishers)*

Summary: This story tells about the legendary hero, Robin Hood. It begins in Sherwood Forest with Robert Locksley (Robin Hood) being falsely accused of killing a deer that belongs to the king. Sir Guy of Gisborne apprehends him, but Robin Hood is rescued by a group of outlaws who live in the forest. At first, Robin and the outlaws are wary of each other. But they soon learn to trust and respect each other. Robin Hood becomes the leader of the outlaws, and together they "rob from the rich and give to the poor."

Vocabulary: unmistakable, unkempt, procession, cavalcade, disheveled, treacherous, betrothed, brandished, minstrel, downtrodden, starveling, grievance, doublet, tarnished, quarry, tunic, garland, amiably, avenged

Experiencing the Literature:

1. Have students list the names of Robin Hood's men and briefly describe each of them. You may wish to have students draw a sketch of each outlaw.
2. Have students write a paragraph to describe Sherwood Forest.
3. Ask students to pick an event that is described in the story. Be sure that every student picks a different event. Have students draw a picture of the event. Arrange the pictures in the order that they occurred, and display them along the hallway.

Title: *King Arthur*   **Author:** Howard Pyle
Publisher: Troll Associates (1988) *(Canada: Vanwell Publishing; AUS: Capricorn Link)*

Summary: This legend tells about a young man named Arthur who pulls a sword from an iron anvil, which is a sign that he should become the king of England. King Arthur's castle is located at Camelot, and many knights gather there to serve him. Some years later, Arthur fights a battle against the Black Knight. He is seriously injured during this battle. Merlin and Lady Guinevere help to cure him. Arthur vows to fight the Black Knight again, but he needs a sword. He receives the sword, Excalibur, from a lady who lives in an enchanted lake. Arthur defeats the Black Knight, but rather than kill the knight, Arthur forgives him and they become allies. Some years later, Arthur's half-sister, Morgana, grows to hate him. She and her son plot against Arthur. Arthur and Morgana's son fight a battle, and both are mortally wounded.

Before Arthur dies, he asks his knight to throw Excalibur back into the lake. Then he boards a ship and floats away to die. Some people say that he will return some day.

Vocabulary: chivalry, turmoil, anvil, jousting, tournament, sheath, proclamation, covenant

Experiencing the Literature:

1. Have students draw an illustration of the knights at the Round Table. Then ask them to write an adventure story about the knights.
2. Have students write a paragraph describing Excalibur.
3. Provide poster board for students. Have students make a poster that advertises the book.

Make Robin Hood's Hat

In this activity you will make a hat like the one that Robin Hood wore.

Materials: butcher paper, ruler, scissors, stapler, chalk, a large feather (A paper feather may be substituted.)

Directions:

Step 1: Cut a piece of butcher paper that is 17 inches by 20 inches (43 cm by 51 cm). Place the paper on a table with the wrong side up and the 17 inch (43 cm) lengths at the top and bottom. Fold over 1.5 inches (3.8 cm) of the left side. If the hat is too large, make a wider strip along the left side.

Step 2: Fold the paper from top to bottom, making sure to match the corners. Staple the left side together.

Step 3: Use a ruler and chalk to make a mark that is 3 inches (7.6 cm) from the top right-hand corner. Then draw a line from that mark to the bottom right-hand corner. Cut along the line you have drawn and throw away the triangular piece of paper.

Step 4: Fold down the line you have just cut until it is even with the bottom of the butcher paper.

Step 5: Make a cuff on the hat by folding up 1.5–2 inches (3.8–5.1 cm) of the bottom edge. If necessary, use staples to hold the cuff in place.

Step 6: Glue or staple a feather in place on the hat.

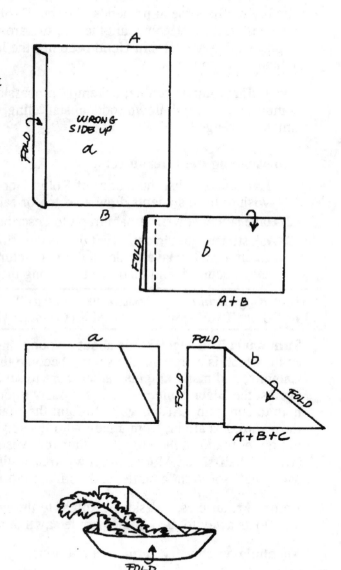

A Medieval Diorama

Think about the things that were popular during medieval times. Then work with three or four other students to create a diorama that shows a medieval scene. You may wish to include some of the following in your diorama: a king, knights in armor, banners, shields, a minstrel, peasants, a castle or cathedral, a dungeon, and a waterwheel or windmill.

Here is what you will need to make a medieval diorama:
- a rectangular box (preferably a shoe box) with a lid
- a pair of scissors
- cardboard, construction paper, fabric, cellophane, wood, clay, aluminum foil, etc.
- any objects, such as a toy horse
- glue

Here are the directions for how to make your medieval diorama:

Step 1: Use your scissors to cut a peephole, that is about ½ inch (1.3 cm) in diameter, in the center of one short side of the box.

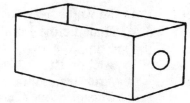

Step 2: Create your background scenery and glue it onto the end of the box that is opposite the peephole.

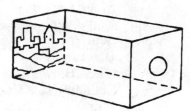

Step 3: Use a variety of materials to create the characters and objects for your diorama. You may want to draw a sketch to show where these will go in your diorama.

Step 4: Glue the characters and objects to the bottom and sides of the box. As you are gluing, be sure to look in the peephole occasionally to see how your diorama looks. Allow the glue to dry.

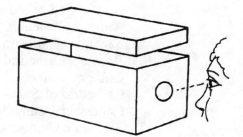

Step 5: Create a sky or ceiling by decorating the inside of the box lid. Allow the glue to dry. Then place the lid on the box. If you need additional light in your diorama, try cutting some slits in the top of the box. You can create some special effects with the lighting by covering the slits with wax paper or tissue paper.

Research Topics

Work in cooperative learning groups to research one or more of the areas mentioned below. Share your findings with the rest of the class in any appropriate form of oral presentation.

Occupations
Knight
Scribe
Noble
Lord
Overlord
Mercenary
Peasant
Serf
Tenant
Mason
Minstrel
Squire
Benedictine Monk
Friar
Alchemist
Architect-engineer
Master Stone Cutter
Stone Dresser
Stone Carver
Carpenter
Sculptor
Blacksmith
Glass Blower
Stained Glass Craftsman
Plumber

Technology
Waterwheel
Windmills
Mechanical Clocks

Cathedrals
St. Mark's Cathedral *(Italy)*
Lincoln Cathedral *(England)*
Ely Cathedral *(England)*
St. Peter's Cathedral *(England)*
Amiens Cathedral *(France)*
Salisbury Cathedral *(England)*
Brussels Cathedral *(Belgium)*
Cologne Cathedral *(Germany)*
Cathedral of Santa Maria del Fiore *(Italy)*
Canterbury Cathedral *(England)*
St. Paul's Cathedral *(England)*

Entertainment
Whittling
Jousting Tournament
Archery
Ballad

Weapons
Lance
Long Bow and Arrow
Mace
Dagger
Battle-axe
Crossbow and Arrow
Sword
Scabbard
Halberd
Bludgeon
Hawk's Beak

Related Topics
Lute
Castle
Dungeon
Stained Glass
Coat of Arms
Banners
Shields
Parchment
Scroll
Armor
Chivalry
Monarchy
Feudalism
Old English
The Crusades
Dragon
Plagues
Magna Charta
Guilds
Crypt
Vikings
Barbarians
Attila the Hun
War of the Roses
The Inquisition
The Holy Grail

Bibliography

Historical Background

Adams, Brian. *Medieval Castles.* Watts, 1989.
Aliki. *A Medieval Feast.* HarperCollins, 1986.
Cairns, Trevor. *Medieval Knights.* Cambridge University Press, 1991.
Caselli, Giovanni. *The Middle Ages.* P. Bedrick Books, 1988.
Conway, Lorraine. *The Middle Ages.* Good Apple, 1987.
Cooney, Ellen. *The Quest for the Holy Grail.* Duir Press, 1981.
Corbin, Carole L. *Knights.* Watts, 1989.
Gies, Joseph and Gies, Frances. *Life in a Medieval Castle.* HarperCollins, 1979.
Hindley. *Knights and Castles.* EDC, 1976.
Sabin, Louis. *Middle Ages.* Troll Associates, 1985.
Sauvain, Philip. *Castles & Crusaders.* Watts, 1986.
Saxby, Maurice. *The Great Deeds of the Superheroes.* Peter Bedrick Books, 1989.
Williams, Ann. *The Crusaders.* Longman, 1975.
Windrow, Martin. *The Medieval Knight.* Watts, 1986.

Biographies

Banfield, Susan. *Charlemagne.* Chelsea House, 1986.
Banfield, Susan. *Joan of Arc.* Chelsea House, 1985.
Brooks, Polly Schoyer. *Beyond the Myth (Joan of Arc).* Lippincott, 1990.
Brooks, Polly Schoyer. *Queen Eleanor.* Lippincott, 1983.
Creswick, Paul. *Robin Hood.* Macmillan, 1984.
Haynes, Sarah, Retold by. *Robin Hood.* Henry Holt & Company, 1989.
Pyle, Howard. *The Merry Adventures of Robin Hood.* Dover, 1968.
Smith, Dorothy. *Saint Joan: The Girl in Armour.* Paulist Press, 1990.

Legends

Artos, Allen. *Arthur: The King of Light.* Lorien House, 1986.
Barber, Richard, ed. *The Arthurian Legends: An Illustrated Anthology.* Littlefield, 1979.
Lang, Andrew, ed. *King Arthur: Tales of the Round Table.* Schocken, 1987.
Lawrence, Ann. *Merlin the Wizard.* Raintree Publications, 1986.
Pyle, Howard. *The Story of King Arthur & His Knights.* Macmillan, 1984.
Pyle, Howard. *The Story of Sir Lancelot & His Companions.* Macmillan, 1985.
San Souci, Robert D. *Young Guinevere.* Doubleday, 1993.

Teacher Resource Units

Birt, David. *The Medieval Town; The Murder of Becket; The Norman Conquest.* Longman, 1974.
Nichol, Jon. *The Castle; The First and Third Crusades; Ships and Voyages.* Longman, 1974.
Wright, Rachel. *Knights: Facts, Things to Make, Activities.* Watts, 1991.

Teacher Created Materials

144 *How to Manage Your Whole Language Classroom*
145 *Portfolio Assessment for Your Whole Language Classroom*
291 *Thematic Unit: Medieval Times*
373 *Thematic Bibliography*
481 *World History Simulations*
906 *Newspaper and Reporting Set*

Bulletin Board Idea

Use the following bulletin board idea to introduce students to the section on Heroes of the Wild West. The patterns shown below make the bulletin board quick and easy to create. Begin by covering the background with butcher paper. Then use an opaque projector to enlarge and copy the patterns. Have students take turns painting the bulletin board scene. After the paint has completely dried, glue some gold glitter in the man's pan. Finally, create the title "Heroes of the Wild West." This bulletin board can be used to display student work or the Quiz Cards (page 61). You can create a learning/research center by placing a table with appropriate materials in front of the bulletin board.

54   ©*1994 Teacher Created Materials, Inc.*

Introduction

In the early 1800's, a few adventurers made their way across the mountains to go to the western frontier. However, it was not until the mid-1800's that large numbers of settlers called the wild West their home. Although life in the West was exciting, it was also filled with a variety of dangers, including hostile Indians, wild animals, and vicious outlaws. Farmers came to the West and worked endlessly to transform the prairies into fields of crops. Cowboys came to the West and used the wide open prairie as grazing land for their cattle. Prospectors came to the West and hoped to strike it rich. By the turn of the century, the West was well populated and no longer considered wild.

The outline below is a suggested plan for using the various activities presented in this section of *Heroes.* Each lesson can take from one to several days to complete. You should adapt these ideas to fit your own classroom situation.

Sample Plan

Lesson 1
- Introduce section vocabulary (page 56).
- Introduce and discuss the wild West (pages 54–56).
- Explore a map showing famous cattle trails (page 62).
- Read and discuss the article about Sacajawea (page 57).
- Complete the Sacajawea Quiz Card (page 61).

Lesson 2
- Read and discuss the article about Wild Bill Hickok (page 58).
- Complete the Wild Bill Hickok Quiz Card (page 61).
- Choose a Relating the Theme activity (page 63).

Lesson 3
- Read and discuss the article about Bill Pickett (page 59).
- Complete the Bill Pickett Quiz Card (page 61).
- Begin reading a book related to the theme (page 65).
- Learn about the Gold Rush (page 64).

Lesson 4
- Read and discuss the article about Annie Oakley (page 60).
- Complete the Annie Oakley Quiz Card (page 61).
- Define terms that the cowboys used (page 67).
- Choose a Relating the Theme activity (page 63).
- Begin research projects (page 68).
- Continue reading a book related to the theme (page 65).

Lesson 5
- Make a model of a covered wagon (page 66).
- Choose a Relating the Theme activity (page 63).
- Do one or more literature-related activities (page 65).
- Continue working on research projects (page 68).

Lesson 6
- Complete one or more Culminating Activities (pages 166-170).
- Share research projects (page 68).

Overview of Activities

Section Vocabulary: You may wish to introduce the following vocabulary words at the beginning of this section: wagon train, trail boss, chuck wagon, hobbled, stampede, rustler, tumbleweed, sage brush, brand, mustang, roundup, bunkhouse, range, roam, longhorn cattle, head of cattle, livestock, frontier, Stetson, chaps, spurs.

Background Information:

- The westward movement took place throughout the 1800's.
- Many people moved west because there was plenty of land and natural resources.
- The first people to move west were usually farmers, ranchers, miners, and fur traders. Later, other people moved west and opened different types of businesses.
- Settling the West was an arduous and often dangerous job.

Bulletin Board Idea: This bulletin board is extremely easy to construct and will help set the stage for introducing the section on Heroes of the Wild West (page 54).

Articles and Discussion Questions: Four interesting articles about specific heroes of the wild West and related discussion questions are provided (pages 57-60).

Quiz Cards: These four cards provide questions about the articles to assess students' understanding of what they have read (page 61). Teachers may wish to make the Quiz Cards self-checking by duplicating the set of cards and placing the answers on the back.

Map Study: This activity helps develop map skills while providing background information about famous cattle trails (page 62). Students should use the map for reference throughout their study of heroes of the wild West.

Relating the Theme: These activities connect the theme to a variety of curriculum areas, such as reading, language arts, math, science, social studies, art, music, and life skills (page 63).

Spotlight on History: Students examine the events of the Gold Rush (page 64).

Literature Connection: Literature selections for this section are summarized and related activities are suggested (page 65).

Make a Covered Wagon: This hands-on activity gives students the opportunity to make a model of a covered wagon (page 66).

Cowboy Talk: Students work in cooperative learning groups to identify the meanings of terms used by cowboys (page 67).

Research Topics: These research ideas will help students better understand the Wild West and the heroes associated with this place and time period (page 68). It is suggested that students work in cooperative learning groups.

Bibliography: Additional literature and resource books are suggested (page 69). They may be used in a variety of ways, such as in a learning center, for research projects, or for book reports.

Culminating Activities: Students will pick one or more culminating activities to help them synthesize and share what they have learned (pages 166–170).

Sacajawea

Sacajawea, whose name means Bird Woman, was a Shoshone Indian who was born sometime around 1787. Sacajawea has been honored as one of the greatest women in American history. In 1800, Sacajawea was captured by another tribe and sold to Toussaint Charbonneau, a French-Canadian trapper. Charbonneau married Sacajawea. In 1804, two United States army officers, Meriwether Lewis and William Clark, hired Charbonneau as an interpreter and guide for an expedition to explore the Northwest. Sacajawea accompanied her husband when he joined the expedition.

Sacajawea proved to be indispensable as an interpreter and as a guide. She knew the secrets of living off the land. While crossing the Rocky Mountains, the expedition met a band of Shoshone Indians. She saved the expedition members from being harmed by the Indians. She was also able to convince the tribe to give horses and supplies for the expedition. She was an energetic member of the team and was looked after by all of the members of the group.

Sacajawea lived to be more than one hundred years old and spent her last years as an agent of good will between Native Americans and the settlers. Throughout the West, many monuments have been built to honor her. There is an especially famous statue of her in Washington Park, which is located in Portland, Oregon.

Discussion Questions

1. Why do you think Sacajawea was so helpful to the members of the expedition?

2. What was exciting about this expedition? What was dangerous about it?

3. Would you want to be a guide for an expedition like this one? Explain your answer.

Now use the Sacajawea Quiz Card to check your understanding of this article.

Wild Bill Hickok

Wild Bill Hickok represents the heroes who tamed the rough and rugged West. He was born with the name James Butler Hickok in Troy Grove, Illinois, in 1837. He was the son of a Presbyterian deacon. When he was 18 years old, he moved to Kansas. While there he worked as a farmer and was a soldier in the Free State Army, which was active in the antislavery movement. In 1858, he started working as a constable for the city of Monticello. One year later, he became a teamster for a Sante Fe freight caravan. Later, he took a job as a stagecoach driver on the Oregon and Sante Fe trails.

In 1861, Hickok was attacked by a bear. He moved to Rock Creek, Nebraska, in order to recover from his wounds. While living in Rock Creek, he got into a dispute with some settlers. He killed three of them and was tried for murder. The shooting was ruled self-defense and he was freed. Later that same year, Hickok helped the Union's Civil War effort by taking charge of a wagon train that took supplies from Fort Leavenworth, Kansas, to Sedalia, Missouri. After that, he worked as a Union scout and guerrilla fighter for the remainder of the war.

Hickok had a reputation for being a marksman. So, in 1869, he was hired as the marshal of Hays City, in Kansas. Three years later, he was the marshal of Abilene, a cattle town in Kansas. He brought law and order to these wild frontier towns. As a result, he became famous for his courage and sense of fairness.

In 1872, Hickok went East with Buffalo Bill's Wild West Show. Two years later he went to Cheyenne, Wyoming, to marry Agnes Lake. In 1876, Hickok met an untimely death when he was shot in the back by Jack McCall during a poker game. McCall was tried, convicted, and hanged for Wild Bill Hickok's murder.

Discussion Questions

1. Why do you think Hickok worked at so many jobs?

2. Would you like to have met Hickok? Explain your answer.

3. What do you think was hard about being a marshal of a lawless town?

Now use the Wild Bill Hickok Quiz Card to check your understanding of this article.

Bill Pickett

Bill Pickett was born near Liberty Hill, Texas, which is located on the South San Gabriel River. His exact date of birth is not known, but most historians believe it was sometime between 1860 and 1870. He was the son of Thomas and Virginia Jefferson. Pickett's mother was a Choctaw Indian. His father was reported as being part African American, Caucasian, and Native American.

After completing the fifth grade, Pickett took a variety of odd jobs in towns, such as Georgetown, Taylor, Florence, and Round Rock. Then he started working on the Garrett King Ranch. He was a range rider and helped tame wild horses and mules. One day, Pickett was trying to load a steer onto a stock car in Taylor. The steer tried to run away. Pickett grabbed the steer's horns, turned its head, bit it on the lip, and wrestled it down to the ground. This was so effective that Pickett used it as a stunt in the rodeo. Audiences were very impressed, and Pickett became a star.

Shortly after the turn of the century, Zack, Joe, and George Miller were organizing the Miller Brothers 101 Wild West Show. They invited Pickett to perform his "bulldogging" stunt as part of their show. Audiences enthusiastically watched Pickett as he seemed to fly off of his galloping horse, grab and position the steer, and throw it down to the ground with nothing but his teeth touching the steer.

Pickett worked with the Millers for almost thirty years. He performed his bulldogging stunt for audiences throughout North America and England. He performed with noted celebrities, such as Will Rogers and Tom Mix.

Pickett retired in the early part of the 1930's. He purchased land in Oklahoma near Chandler. One day he was stomped by a wild horse while trying to rope it. Pickett died as a result of those injuries on April 2, 1932. Bill Pickett was honored as the first African American cowboy by the Rodeo Hall of the National Cowboy Hall of Fame in 1972.

Discussion Questions

1. What do you think Pickett's life would have been like if that steer had not tried to get away?

2. Would you like to be a cowboy? Explain your answer.

3. Why do you think it took so long for Bill Pickett's contributions to be recognized?

Now use the Bill Pickett Quiz Card to check your understanding of this article.

Annie Oakley

Annie Oakley was born in 1860 in Darke County, Ohio. Her name at birth was Phoebe Ann Moses. By the age of eight, she had learned to shoot and helped her family by hunting animals for food. Annie became a professional marksman by the time she was 15. She participated in many shooting contests that took place in Cincinnati. She beat Frank Butler in a shooting match, which sparked a romance between them. Annie and Frank were married in 1876. Soon afterwards, Annie started calling herself Annie Oakley. In 1885, Annie joined Buffalo Bill's Wild West Show. She gave a fascinating performance with the assistance of her husband. She would shoot a dime that was in his hand or a cigarette that was in his mouth. Annie also did a trick during which her husband, who was standing 90 feet (27 m) away from her, threw a playing card into the air and she shot it. Annie's accuracy amazed audiences. She was often called "Little Sure Shot," a nickname that was given to her by Sitting Bull, a Sioux Indian chief.

Annie's performances were extremely popular. She went on tour in Europe and did shows for a variety of people, including the Queen of England and the German Crown Prince Wilhelm. Unfortunately, in 1901, Annie was seriously injured in a train accident. As a result of her injuries, she had to resign her position with Buffalo Bill's Wild West Show. However, after she recovered she started working with a theatrical group. In 1902, Annie starred in *The Western Girl*. In 1914, World War I broke out. For the duration of the war (1914-1918), Annie worked with American soldiers to show them how to shoot. Annie died on November 3, 1926.

Discussion Questions

1. Do you think Annie's ability to shoot was skill or talent? Explain your answer.

2. Why do you think Annie's performance was so popular?

3. How do you think Annie felt when she had to leave Buffalo Bill's Wild West Show?

Now use the Annie Oakley Quiz Card to check your understanding of this article.

Quiz Cards

Use the following questions to assess your students' understanding of the articles on pages 57 through 60 of this unit. Have them write their answers on notebook paper.

Sacajawea Quiz Card

1. Why don't historians know Sacajawea's exact date of birth?
2. What does the name Sacajawea mean?
3. How did Sacajawea get to know Toussaint Charbonneau?
4. How did Sacajawea become a part of the expedition?
5. Who was leading the expedition?
6. What was the purpose of the expedition?
7. Who did the expedition meet in the Rocky Mountains?
8. How did Sacajawea help save the expedition members?
9. What did Sacajawea obtain from the Indians for the expedition?
10. What tribute to Sacajawea is located in Portland, Oregon?

Bill Pickett Quiz Card

1. Where was Pickett born?
2. Why do you think Pickett stopped going to school in the fifth grade?
3. What did Pickett do on the Garrett King Ranch?
4. What happened the day the steer tried to run away?
5. How did Pickett make use of the incident with the steer?
6. Who did Pickett work for shortly after the turn of the century?
7. How long did Pickett perform in the Wild West Show?
8. What did Pickett do after he retired?
9. How did Pickett die?
10. What special honor did Pickett receive in 1972?

Wild Bill Hickok Quiz Card

1. What was Wild Bill Hickok's real name?
2. Where and when was Hickok born?
3. Where did he move to when he was 18 years old?
4. What was the purpose of the Free State Army?
5. Why did Hickok move to Rock Creek, Nebraska, in 1861?
6. What was the first job Hickok did for the Civil War effort?
7. What job did Hickok have in 1869?
8. What was he able to accomplish in Hays City and Abilene?
9. With what group did Hickok go east in 1872?
10. How was Hickok killed in 1876?

Annie Oakley Quiz Card

1. What was Annie's name at birth?
2. At what age did Annie first learn to shoot?
3. How did Annie meet Frank Butler?
4. What group did Annie join in 1885?
5. Who assisted Annie during her performances?
6. What kind of a trick did Annie do with a playing card?
7. What was Sitting Bull's nickname for Annie?
8. Why did Annie stop doing performances in 1901?
9. What did Annie do in 1902?
10. What did Annie do to help the war effort during World War I?

Map Study

The map below shows some famous cattle trails from the wild West. Cowboys used these trails to herd millions of cattle to market. Trace each trail with a different color. Use a reference book to identify each trail. Then make a map key that shows each color and the name of the trail it represents.

Cattle Trails

Relating the Theme

You may wish to use one or all of the following activities to supplement your own ideas about ways to integrate the *Heroes* theme into your curriculum.

Language Arts:

1. Show one or more video tapes about heroes of the wild West. Suggested videos: *Buffalo Bill* (1944), *Annie Oakley* (1935), and *Hondo* (1953). Have students take notes about the main characters and then discuss why these people are heroes.

2. Have students discuss what happened to the Native Americans who lived in the West before the settlers arrived.

Science:

1. Have students use index cards to write and illustrate reports about vegetation, such as sage brush and tumbleweed, that was found in the wild West.

2. The cattle industry was a major factor in the development of the West. Have students make a poster that shows the by-products of cattle.

Social Studies:

1. Explain that the land west of the Mississippi was explored and mapped during the Lewis and Clark Expedition. On a map of the United States, have students research and trace the route of these early explorers.

2. Have students make a chart to compare the modes of transportation used during the 1800's with those used today.

3. Have students make a time line of world events that took place during the 1800's.

Mathematics:

1. Provide copies of the map (page 62) that shows famous cattle trails. Have students use the distance scale to determine the length of each trail.

2. Have students create their own word problems using facts about the wild West.

Literature:

Tell students that the story of Pecos Bill is a tall tale. Explain what a tall tale is. Then read aloud a book about Pecos Bill. Ask students to make a chart that shows which elements of the story are real and which are fantasy.

Health:

Have students investigate which herbs were used by the pioneers for medicinal purposes.

Theater Arts:

Have students present short skits depicting cowboy life. They may want to include simple costumes and props for their skits.

Art:

1. Ask students to make a diorama that shows a scene from the wild West. You may wish to have them be sure to include a hero of the wild West.

2. Brainstorm a list of things the public would need to know if a rodeo was coming to town. Have students design a flier to advertise the imaginary rodeo.

Spotlight on History: Gold Fever

Use reference books, such as encyclopedias, to locate facts about the California Gold Rush. Write one or more facts about each topic shown in the miner's pans.

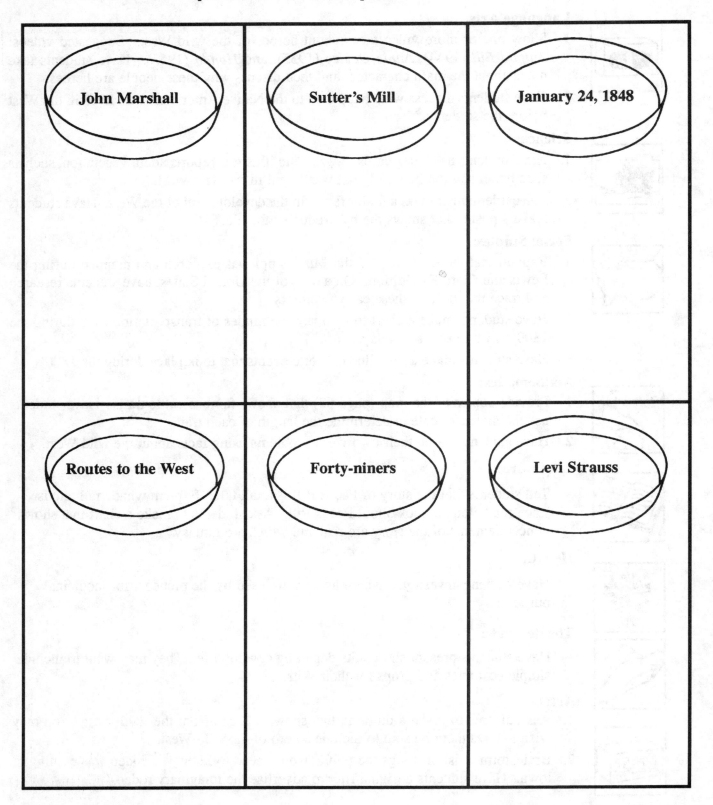

Literature Connection

Title: *Annie Oakley, Young Markswoman*   **Author:** Ellen Wilson
Publisher: Macmillan (1989) *(Canada, UK, and AUS: Macmillan)*

Summary: This biography tells about the sharpshooter, Annie Oakley. She was born to a pioneer family in 1860. Annie was always fascinated by rifles and loved to watch the men shoot. Annie's mother took a job as District Nurse and could not be home to take care of the younger children. As a result, she sent Annie to live with the Eddingtons. That summer, a farmer came and offered Annie a job helping his wife take care of their new baby. After taking the job, Annie discovered that the farmer was not sending her mother the money she earned as he had promised. Annie ran away and went back home. She began hunting for food and became an excellent shot. When she went to visit her sister in Cincinnati, she met Frank Butler, the famous trick shooter. She beat him in a shooting contest. Later they were married. Annie Oakley became famous and joined Buffalo Bill's Wild West Show. She became the star of the show and was asked to perform for the Queen of England.

Vocabulary: markswoman, hearth, nimble, trundle bed, percussion cap, solemn, varmints, ammunition, bellowed, muskrats, critters, pelt, orphan, gravely, hubbub, brambles, shabby, gobbler, crossroads, venture, clay pigeons, mischief, sharpshooter

Experiencing the Literature:
1. Have students use a variety of materials to make a model of the cabin that Annie Oakley lived in as a girl.
2. Ask students to do research to learn about clay pigeon shooting.
3. Review how to make an outline. Then have students make an outline that shows the main events in Annie Oakley's life.

Title: *Bill Pickett, Bulldogger*   **Author:** Colonel Bailey C. Hanes
Publisher: University of Oklahoma Press (1979) *(Canada: University of Oklahoma Press; UK: Eurospan; AUS: E Span)*

Summary: This story tells about the life of Bill Pickett. Bill was a mixture of African-American and Indian. He worked as a cowboy on a ranch in Oklahoma for most of his life. He is well-known for having created the rodeo event of steer wrestling. He is the first African American to be honored by the Cowboy Hall of Fame.

Vocabulary: bulldogger, impromptu, extravaganza, fraternity, progenitor, ancestral, Secessionist, aristocracy, lariats, emancipated, prominent, impoverished, literacy, heritage, lucrative, tenacious, paradoxical, desperadoes, Conquistadors, matadors, picadors, epitome, toreadors, posterity

Experiencing the Literature:
1. Ask students to write an epitaph for Bill Pickett.
2. Divide the class into cooperative learning groups. Ask students to do research about the seven different events held at rodeos.
3. Have students use a map of the United States to locate places mentioned in the story.
4. Ask students to pretend they are Bill Pickett. Have them write a speech to accept the honor of being elected a member of the Cowboy Hall of Fame.

Make a Covered Wagon

Many people traveled West using a covered wagon. Study the diagram of a covered wagon that is shown below. Then write a list of materials that you will use to make a model of the wagon. Finally, make your model.

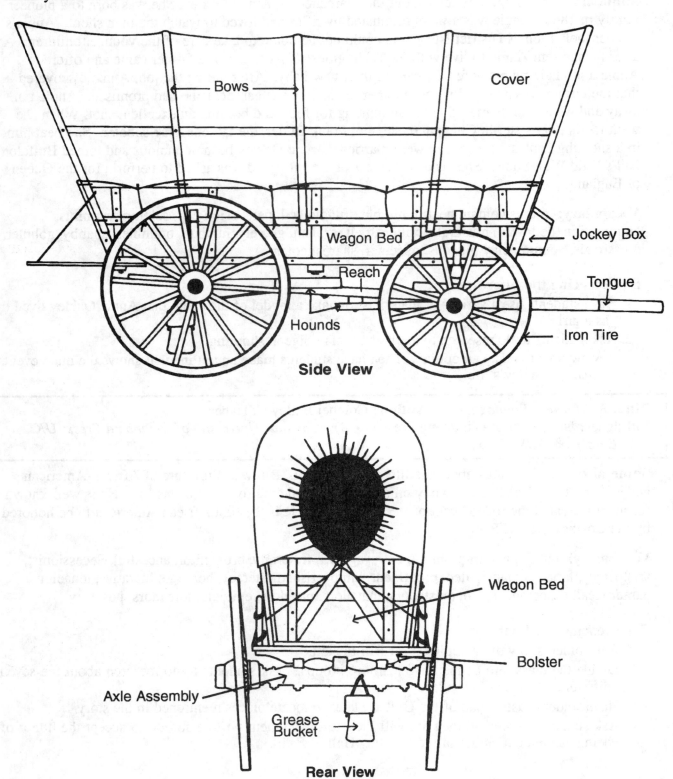

Bows

Cover

Jockey Box

Wagon Bed

Tongue

Reach

Hounds

Iron Tire

Side View

Wagon Bed

Bolster

Axle Assembly

Grease Bucket

Rear View

Cowboy Talk

Cowboys who lived in the wild West used a variety of terms to describe themselves and their work. Many of these words continue to be used today. Work with two or three other students to write a sentence using each cowboy term.

1. **amble:** to walk or ride on horseback in a slow, relaxed manner

2. **bake:** to overheat a horse by riding it too much

3. **bedroll:** the blankets, tarpaulin, raincoat, and personal items that a cowboy rolls up and ties to the rear of the saddle

4. **break:** to tame a wild horse so it can be ridden

5. **buckaroo:** another name for a cowboy

6. **cutting horse:** a horse that the cowboy has taught to take cows out of the herd one at a time

7. **dogie:** a calf that does not have a mother

8. **line rider:** a cowboy who uses a specific route to ride the range and check on the rancher's cattle and land

9. **loco weed:** a type of grass that cows eat that make them act crazy

10. **maverick:** animal that does not have a brand to identify the owner

11. **nester:** a person who comes to settle on the land

12. **norther:** a ferocious blizzard caused by cold winds from the north meeting warm winds coming off the Gulf of Mexico

13. **pull leather:** to hold on to the saddle horn when riding a wild horse

14. **six-shooter:** a pistol that shoots six bullets

15. **spread:** the land, buildings, and cattle that make up a ranch

16. **tenderfoot:** a person who does not have any experience living in the wild West

17. **vamoose:** to run away quickly

18. **whitefaces:** a type of cattle called Herefords

19. **wrangler:** a cowboy who takes care of the horses

20. **yearling:** a colt or calf that is only one year old

Research Topics

Work in cooperative learning groups to research one or more of the areas mentioned below. Share your findings with the rest of the class in any appropriate form of oral presentation.

Heroes
Bat Masterson
Wyatt Earp
Doc Holliday
Kit Carson
Tom Horn
Bill Pickett
Wild Bill Hickok
Jim Bridger
Jedediah Smith
Belle Star
Annie Oakley
David Crockett
Daniel Boone
Pat Garrett
"Buffalo Bill" Cody
Charles Goodnight
Granville Stuart
Pecos Bill
Calamity Jane
Sacajawea
Texas Rangers
Judge Roy Bean

Transportation
Wagon Trains
Railroads
Canoes
Keelboats
Steamboats

Territories
Minnesota Territory
New Mexico Territory
Utah Territory
Oregon Territory

Westward Wagon Trails
California Trail
Sante Fe Trail
Mormon Trail
Oregon Trail
Old Spanish Trail

Related Topics
Lewis and Clark Expedition
Cattle Brands
Frontier Life
Comstock Lode
Doctrine of Manifest Destiny
Cowboys
Cattle Trails
Sutter's Mill
Wells Fargo
The Pony Express
Forty-Niners
Klondike
Gold Prospecting
Native Americans
Homesteaders
Windmills
Barbed Wire
Buffalo
Range Wars
Drought
Indian Wars
Erie Canal
The Louisiana
 Purchase
Ghost Towns
Circuit Riders
Bowie Knife
Rodeos
Longhorn Cattle

68 *©1994 Teacher Created Materials, Inc.*

Bibliography

Historical Background

Adams, Andy. *The Log of a Cowboy.* University of Nebraska Press, 1964.

Anderson, Joan. *Spanish Pioneers of the Southwest.* Lodestar, 1989.

Beebe, Lucius. *American West.* Outlet Book Company, 1989.

Blumberg, Rhoda. *The Great American Gold Rush.* Bradbury, 1989.

Chrisman, Harry E. *Lost Trails of the Cimarron.* Ohio University Press, 1964.

Fowler, William W. *Women on the American Frontier.* Corner House, 1976.

Freedman, Russell. *Children of the Wild West.* Clarion Books, 1983.

The Frontiersmen. Time-Life, 1977.

Kalman, Bobbie. *Early Settler Life Series.* Crabtree Publishing Company, 1982.

Katz, William L. *Black People Who Made the Old West.* HarperCollins, 1989.

Lake, A.L. *Women of the West.* Rourke Corp., 1990.

O'Neal, Bill. *Encyclopedia of Western Gunfighters.* University of Oklahoma Press, 1980.

Parkman, Francis, Jr. *The Oregon Trail.* Viking Penguin, 1982.

The Ranchers. Time-Life, 1977.

Sabin, Francene. *Pioneers.* Troll Associates, 1985.

The Soldiers. Time-Life, 1973.

Stein, R. Conrad. *The Story of the Gold at Sutter's Mill.* Childrens, 1981.

Stein, R. Conrad. *The Story of the Lewis and Clark Expedition.* Childrens, 1978.

The Trailblazers. Time-Life, 1973.

Biographies and Autobiographies

Anderson, J. I. *I Can Read About Pecos Bill.* Troll Associates, 1977.

Blair, Gwenda. *Laura Ingalls Wilder.* Putnam Publishing Group, 1981.

Brown, Marion Marsh. *Sacagawea: Indian Interpreter to Lewis and Clark.* Childrens, 1988.

Buffalo Bill, pseud. *Buffalo Bill's True Tales.* Vistabooks, 1977.

Carson, Kit. *Kit Carson's Autobiography.* University of Nebraska Press, 1966.

Churchill, E. Richard. *Doc Holliday, Bat Masterson, Wyatt Earp: Their Colorado Careers.* Timberline Books, 1978.

Crockett, David. *Narrative of the Life of David Crockett of the State of Tennessee.* University of Tennessee Press, 1973.

Faber, Doris. *Calamity Jane: Her Life and Her Legend.* Houghton Mifflin, 1992.

Green, Carl R. *Bat Masterson.* Enslow, 1992.

Green, Carl R. *Wild Bill Hickok.* Enslow, 1992.

Levine, Ellen. *Ready, Aim, Fire! The Real Adventures of Annie Oakley.* Scholastic Inc., 1989.

Myers, John. *Doc Holliday.* University of Nebraska Press, 1973.

Peiz, Ruth. *Black Heroes of the Wild West.* Open Hand, 1989.

Stevenson, Augusta. *Buffalo Bill: Frontier Daredevil.* Macmillan, 1991.

Turner, Alford E., ed. *The Earps Talk.* Creative Texas, 1980.

Wilkie, Katharine E. *Daniel Boone: Taming the Wilds.* Chelsea House, 1991.

Zochert, Donald. *Laura: The Life of Laura Ingalls Wilder.* Avon, 1977.

Resource Books

Stenson, Elizabeth. *Early Settler Activity Guide.* Crabtree Publishing Company, 1988.

Walker, Barbara. *The Little House Cookbook.* Harper & Row, 1979.

Teacher Created Materials

282 *Thematic Unit: Westward Ho*

425 *Literature Unit: Sarah, Plain and Tall*

445 *Literature Unit: Caddie Woodlawn*

504 *Portfolios & Other Assessments*

522 *Literature Unit: Little House in the Big Woods*

906 *Newspaper and Reporting Set*

Bulletin Board Idea

Use the following bulletin board idea to introduce students to the section on Wartime Heroes. The patterns shown below make the bulletin board quick and easy to create. Begin by covering the background with butcher paper. Then use an opaque projector to enlarge and copy the patterns. You may wish to attach some toy soldiers to the bulletin board. Finally, create the title "Wartime Heroes." This bulletin board can be used to display student work or the Quiz Cards (page 77). You can create a learning/research center by placing a table with appropriate materials in front of the bulletin board.

Introduction

Wars have occurred around the world and throughout history. Wartime heroes have emerged from every war. Some of these people became heroes in battle, some by caring for the wounded, others by fighting oppression, and still others by crossing enemy lines to obtain vital information. All of the wartime heroes showed tremendous bravery. Many gave their lives performing acts of heroism. These men, women, and children have been honored with medals, memorials, statues, and books.

The outline below is a suggested plan for using the various activities presented in this section of *Heroes*. Each lesson can take from one to several days to complete. You should adapt these ideas to fit your own classroom situation.

Sample Plan

Lesson 1

- Introduce section vocabulary (page 72).
- Introduce and discuss the concept of war and wartime heroes (pages 70–72).
- Answer questions about World War I and World War II maps (page 78).
- Read and discuss the article about Crispus Attucks (page 73).
- Complete the Crispus Attucks Quiz Card (page 77).

Lesson 2

- Read and discuss the article about Andrea Castanon Ramirez Candalaria (page 74).
- Complete the Andrea Castanon Ramirez Candalaria Quiz Card (page 77).
- Choose a Relating the Theme activity (page 79).

Lesson 3

- Read and discuss the article about Harriet Tubman (page 75).
- Complete the Harriet Tubman Quiz Card (page 77).
- Begin reading a book related to the theme (page 81).
- Write a wartime story that is historical

fiction (page 80).

Lesson 4

- Read and discuss the article about Audie Murphy (page 76).
- Complete the Audie Murphy Quiz Card (page 77).
- Make a three-dimensional battle scene (page 82).
- Choose a Relating the Theme activity (page 79).
- Begin research projects (page 84).
- Continue reading a book related to the theme (page 81).

Lesson 5

- Choose a Relating the Theme activity (page 79).
- Hold a debate on wartime issues (page 83).
- Do one or more literature-related activities (page 81).
- Continue working on research projects (page 84).

Lesson 6

- Complete one or more Culminating Activities (pages 166-170).
- Share research projects (page 84).

Overview of Activities

Section Vocabulary: You may wish to introduce the following vocabulary words at the beginning of this section: militias, noncombatant, artillery, fortifications, partisans, casualties, bombardment, cryptogram, commemorate, amphibious, rations, prejudice, atomic bomb, refugee, Holocaust, surrender, liberty, allies, neutral, trenches, foxhole, guerrillas, coup, dictator, democracy, communism, constitution, overthrow, offense, defense, peace talks, tyrant, world domination, assassination.

Background Information:

- The reasons for a war can include disputes over a variety of issues, such as liberty, politics, religion, geographic boundaries, etc.
- The cost of war is always high in terms of casualties and property damage.
- The outcome of a war is not always determined by who has the greatest number of soldiers.
- Mutually assured destruction is guaranteed in a nuclear war.
- Today the media can give us a first-hand view of a war zone.

Bulletin Board Idea: This bulletin board is extremely easy to construct and will help set the stage for introducing the section on Wartime Heroes (page 70).

Articles and Discussion Questions: Four interesting articles about specific wartime heroes and related discussion questions are provided (pages 73-76).

Quiz Cards: These four cards provide questions about the articles to assess students' understanding of what they have read (page 77). Teachers may wish to make the Quiz Cards self-checking by duplicating the set of cards and placing the answers on the back.

Map Study: This activity helps develop map skills while providing background information about opposing forces during World War I and World War II (page 78). You may wish to display the maps as a border around the bulletin board for this section (page 70).

Relating the Theme: These activities connect the theme to a variety of curriculum areas, such as reading, language arts, math, science, social studies, art, music, and life skills (page 79).

Spotlight on Language Arts: Students write a wartime story that is historical fiction (page 80).

Literature Connection: Literature selections for this section are summarized and related activities are suggested (page 81).

Make a 3-D Battle Scene: This hands-on activity gives students the opportunity to make a three-dimensional battle scene (page 82).

Debate the Issues: Students work in cooperative learning groups to research and debate the issues related to a particular war (page 83).

Research Topics: These research ideas will help students better understand the heroes associated with wars throughout history (page 84). It is suggested that students work in cooperative learning groups.

Bibliography: Additional literature is suggested (page 85). The books may be used in a variety of ways, such as in a learning center, for research projects, or for book reports.

Culminating Activities: Students will pick one or more culminating activities to help them synthesize and share what they have learned (pages 166-170).

Crispus Attucks

Crispus Attucks was born sometime around 1723 in Framingham, Massachusetts. He was a slave who belonged to Deacon William Brown. When he was about 27 years old, he ran away from his master. After gaining his freedom he worked on a whaling vessel as a sailor. In 1770, Attucks returned from a whaling trip and decided to remain in Boston. Attucks realized that the colonists were not happy about conditions that were forced upon them by England who claimed ownership of the American colonies. Attucks empathized with the plight of the colonists. He understood their desperate need for freedom.

Attucks was a very charismatic person and easily inspired the colonists to action. On March 5, 1770, he took a leadership role in defying the British. Attucks led a group of unarmed colonists to the town square. There they were ringing fire bells in an effort to encourage all of the colonists to gather and speak out. Some British soldiers were present and began to argue with some of the colonists. In the process, a child was knocked down by a soldier, and the colonists became furious. Attucks grabbed the soldier's bayonet and knocked him down to the ground. At the same time someone in the crowd threw a rock at one of the soldiers. The soldiers panicked and the order to fire was given. The soldiers opened fire on the crowd of colonists. Attucks was the first to be shot. Within seconds of his death, four more patriots were killed by the soldiers. This incident, which is called the Boston Massacre, is recognized as the beginning of the American Revolution

Since the American Revolution, Crispus Attucks has been honored for his heroic deeds in several ways. African-American soldiers had a company called the "Attucks Guards" prior to the Civil War. During the years 1858 to 1870, African Americans who lived in Boston celebrated "Crispus Attucks Day." Eighteen years later, Boston's African Americans built a special memorial in Boston Common, the town square, for Crispus Attucks and the other four patriots who died on March 5, 1770.

Discussion Questions

1. What do you think Attucks' life would have been like if he had remained a sailor?

2. Why do you think Attucks supported the colonists' fight for freedom?

3. How do you think the growing tensions at the town square should have been dealt with?

Now use the Crispus Attucks Quiz Card to check your understanding of this article.

Andrea Castanon Ramirez Candalaria

Long ago, Texas was not a part of the United States. At one point in its history, it belonged to Mexico. Many Texans were unhappy about this. They wanted Texas to be its own country. Andrea Castanon Ramirez Candalaria was one of those Texans. She had been born in Mexico but moved to Laredo, Texas, when she was a young girl. At the age of 25 she moved to San Antonio.

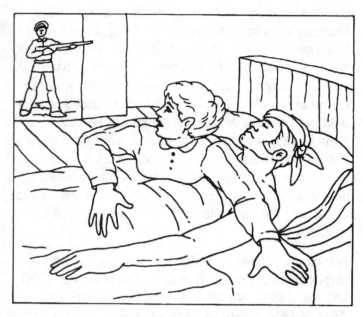

The Alamo was one of the buildings that was very familiar to Candalaria. It was a mission-fort that had been built by the Spanish back in 1718. In 1836, Candalaria had no idea that the Alamo was about to become an important part of history and a symbol to Texans who wanted an independent Texas.

Many brave Texans and other Americans came to the Alamo to help Texas win its freedom. The men of the Alamo fought bravely against the Mexican army. Candalaria was at the Alamo, too. She risked her own life to take care of the wounded. For 12 days of battle, she worked to ease the suffering of the dying patriots. One of the men she nursed was James Bowie, who was second in command. Bowie had become ill with a fever and died the day before the Alamo was captured by the Mexican soldiers. After the Mexicans took over the Alamo, they went to burn the bodies of the dead Texans.

Candalaria asked them to allow Bowie's body to be buried since he had died from an illness rather than in battle. The soldiers thought Bowie was still alive and that Candalaria was protecting him. One soldier stabbed Bowie's dead body with his sword. Candalaria was leaning over his body at the time, and she was cut by the sword on her wrist and chin. The Mexicans refused to comply with her wishes, even though it was obvious that Bowie was dead.

Only 13 brave women and children survived the Battle of the Alamo. Candalaria was one of them. She continued to live until she was 106 years old.

Discussion Questions

1. Why do you think Candalaria risked her life to stay with the dying Texans?

2. Why did the Mexican soldiers want to burn the bodies of the brave Texans?

3. How do you think this battle affected the Texans' desire for freedom? Explain your answer.

Now use the Andrea Castanon Ramirez Candalaria Quiz Card to check your understanding of this article.

Harriet Tubman

Harriet Tubman was born a slave in Dorchester County, Maryland. The exact date of her birth is unknown, but it is believed that she was born around 1820. When she was a young girl, she tried to block a doorway to stop her master from beating another slave. Her master threw an iron weight to get her to move. The weight hit her in the head, and she fell unconscious on the floor. For the rest of her life, Tubman suffered from daily blackouts that were a result of this injury.

Tubman learned that her master planned to send her further south, where she knew life would be even worse. Rather than endure the hardships of slavery any longer, she decided to escape to the north. She knew the journey would be a dangerous one. She had heard other slaves tell stories about the Underground Railroad, which was a network of roads, underground tunnels, and homes that were used to take slaves to freedom. The Underground Railroad was run by abolitionists, or people who believed that slavery was wrong. Tubman used the Underground Railroad to get to Philadelphia, Pennsylvania, where she was finally free.

Tubman got a job as a maid and worked hard to save some money. She wanted to bring her brothers and sisters to freedom. In 1851, Tubman joined the abolitionists and started leading expeditions of slaves from the south to the north. She did not worry about her personal safety. The safety of the escaping slaves was all that was important to her. Over a fifteen-year period, Tubman helped 300 slaves escape.

Tubman worked for the Union Army during the Civil War. She took jobs as a cook, nurse, and even a spy. Her heroic efforts led to the rescue of 756 slaves and the destruction of enemy property, the value of which totaled millions of dollars. Although many rewards were offered by slave masters for the capture of Harriet Tubman, she remained free. She continued to help people in need until her death on March 10, 1913.

Discussion Questions

1. How do you think Tubman's treatment as a slave affected her desire to help others?

2. Why didn't Tubman stay in the North where she was safe and free?

3. What kinds of dangers do you think escaping slaves faced while on the Underground Railroad?

Now use the Harriet Tubman Quiz Card to check your understanding of this article.

Audie Murphy

Audie Leon Murphy was born in 1924, in Kingston, Texas. When Murphy was only 17 years old, Japan sent planes to bomb the American naval base at Pearl Harbor in Hawaii. As a result, the United States became involved in World War II. One year later, it was 1942, and Murphy was old enough to enlist. He decided to help the war effort by joining the army. He proudly served in North Africa and Europe. In 1944, Murphy was appointed to the position of second lieutenant.

In 1945, his unit was stationed in France, near Colmar. On January 26, Murphy hopped on a tank destroyer that was on fire. He was able to kill fifty German soldiers with his machine gun. For this heroic action,

Murphy was given the Medal of Honor, which is the highest military award given in the United States. But his honors did not stop there. Throughout the war, Murphy showed remarkable heroism and became the most decorated American soldier during World War II.

The United States gave Murphy 24 medals, Belgium gave him one medal, and France gave him three medals.

Murphy was discharged from the army in 1945. Three years later he became an actor and started making movies. He starred in several films, including *The Red Badge of Courage,* which was released in 1951, and *To Hell and Back,* which was released in 1955. Audie Murphy tragically died in an airplane crash in 1971.

Discussion Questions

1. Why do you think Murphy was anxious to join the fighting in World War II?

2. Do you think Murphy was brave or reckless? Explain your answer.

3. How would Murphy's life have been different if World War II had not taken place?

Now use the Audie Murphy Quiz Card to check your understanding of this article.

Quiz Cards

Use the following questions to assess your students' understanding of the articles on pages 73 through 76 of this unit. Have them write their answers on notebook paper.

Crispus Attucks Quiz Card

1. What did Attucks do before working on a whaling vessel?
2. Why do you think he decided to stay in Boston?
3. What were the colonists unhappy about when Attucks decided to stay in Boston?
4. Where did Attucks go on March 5, 1770?
5. Who accompanied Attucks on March 5, 1770?
6. What did a British soldier do that made the colonists so angry?
7. What did Attucks do to the British soldier?
8. What happened after the rock was thrown at the soldiers?
9. What happened to Attucks on March 5, 1770?
10. What is this incident called, and why does it have historical importance?

Harriet Tubman Quiz Card

1. Why wasn't Harriet Tubman free to do as she pleased when she was a young girl?
2. How was Tubman injured when trying to help another slave that her master wanted to beat?
3. Why did Tubman decide to escape to the North?
4. What was the Underground Railroad?
5. Who ran the Underground Railroad?
6. Where did Tubman finally become free?
7. How and why did Tubman earn money after she became free?
8. What did Tubman do in 1851?
9. How many slaves did Tubman help free over a fifteen-year period?
10. How did Harriet Tubman's heroism make a difference during the Civil War?

Andrea Castanon Ramirez Candalaria Quiz Card

1. Where was Candalaria born?
2. Where did Candalaria move to when she was a young child?
3. When did Candalaria move to San Antonio?
4. By whom and when was the Alamo built?
5. How long did the Battle of the Alamo last?
6. What was Candalaria's job during the Battle of the Alamo?
7. Who was James Bowie?
8. How did James Bowie die?
9. What did Candalaria ask of the Mexican soldiers?
10. How many people survived the Battle of the Alamo?

Audie Murphy Quiz Card

1. Where and when was Murphy born?
2. What event happened in 1941 that changed Murphy's life?
3. What rank did Murphy get appointed to in 1944?
4. What did Murphy do near Colmar?
5. What did Murphy earn for his action near Colmar?
6. What record did Murphy hold for American soldiers during World War II?
7. How many medals did Murphy win in total?
8. When was Murphy discharged from the army?
9. What job did Murphy do three years after being discharged from the army?
10. How did Murphy die?

Map Study

Examine the two maps. The map on the left shows what Europe looked like during World War I. The other map shows what Europe looked like during World War II. Use the maps to answer the questions.

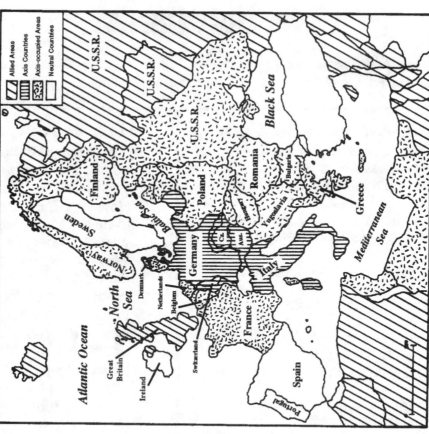

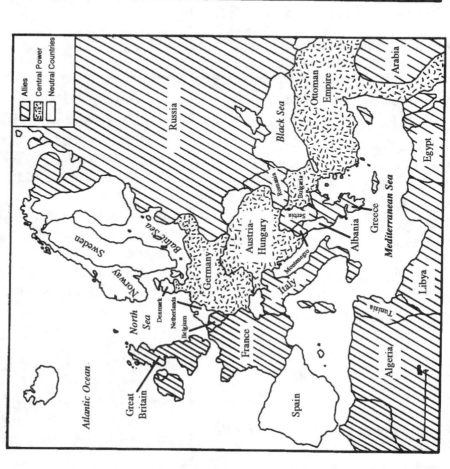

Respond

1. Who were the European Allied Countries during World War I?
2. Who were the European Central Powers during World War I?
3. Who were the European Allied Countries during World War II?
4. Who were the European Axis Countries during World War II?

Relating the Theme

You may wish to use one or all of the following activities to supplement your own ideas about ways to integrate the *Heroes* theme into your curriculum.

Language Arts:

1. Have students watch one or more video tapes about wartime heroes. Suggested videos: *The Finest Hours* (1964), *The Gallant Hours* (1960), and *The Gathering Storm* (1974). Ask students to pretend that they are movie critics and write a paragraph giving their opinion of the movie. Ask them to rate the movie from one to four stars.

2. Have students select a wartime hero. Ask students to write and present a commercial (television or radio) to honor that person. Students may wish to add sound effects or props and costumes.

3. Have students make an audio recording of a speech made by a wartime hero. Examples include: Abraham Lincoln's "Gettysburg Address" and Franklin D. Roosevelt's radio address after the bombing of Pearl Harbor. Place the recordings in a listening center.

Mathematics:

1. Have students make graphs to show statistical information, such as the number of casualties, during a war.

2. Have students look at rationing schedules from World War II. Have them determine what they could buy with a specific number of rationing points. You might also like to have students write their own word problems using the rationing schedules.

Social Studies:

1. Have students make a time line that shows the contributions of wartime heroes. Display the timeline on the classroom wall.

2. Ask students to make a chart that shows which countries have participated in the major wars.

3. Have students write a letter to a wartime hero thanking him or her.

4. Invite a veteran to come and speak to your class. Have students brainstorm a list of questions before the visitor comes.

Art:

Have students make an anti-war poster. Tell students that they should use pictures and words on their poster.

Music:

Have students listen to and sing songs that were popular during a war.

Literature:

Have students read about a wartime hero. Then have them present a skit about that hero.

Spotlight on Language Arts:
Writing Historical Fiction

Select a wartime hero. Do research and take notes about that person and the war in which he or she became a hero. Then use the space below to write a story that is historical fiction. Be sure to include some of the facts you learned while researching.

Literature Connection

Title: *Behind Rebel Lines: The Incredible Story of Emma Edmonds, Civil War Spy*
Author: Seymour Reit
Publisher: Harcourt Brace Jovanovich, Publishers (1988)

Summary: This is the true story of a woman named Emma Edmonds. She disguised herself as a man in order to fight for the Union army during the Civil War. Emma strongly supported the Northern cause and felt it was her duty to take an active role in the making of history. During the war, Emma served as Private Franklin Thompson and became a spy for the Northern army.

Vocabulary: masquerade, militias, infectious diseases, adjutant, noncombatant, bivouacs, guidons, artillery, fortifications, phrenological, parapet, prophetic, contraband, renegade, partisans

Experiencing the Literature:
1. Have students color a map of the United States to show which states were in the Union, which states were in the Confederacy, and which ones were neutral.
2. Have students role-play the adventures that Emma Edmonds had during the war.
3. Ask students to write a letter to President Lincoln asking him to allow women to fight in the Union army during the Civil War.

Title: *Navajo Code Talkers*   **Author:** Nathan Aaseng
Publisher: Walker and Company (1992)

Summary: This story describes how a group of American soldiers who were Navajos used their language as a code on the Pacific front during World War II.

Vocabulary: battalion, artillery, bombardment, cryptogram, terminology, translators, extraction, illiterate, amphibious, gibberish, ciphered, quagmire, rations, diagnostician, concealment

Experiencing the Literature:
1. Have students do research to learn more about the Navajo people.
2. Ask pairs of students invent a code with which to communicate.

Title: *Anne Frank: The Diary of a Young Girl*   **Author:** Anne Frank
Publisher: Simon and Schuster Inc. (1958)

Summary: This story is derived from the diary of a young Jewish girl named Anne Frank. It takes place in Amsterdam, Holland, during World War II. Anne and her family lived in hiding for two years. When the family was discovered by Nazi soldiers, they were sent to concentration camps. Anne died in a concentration camp in 1945, just months before the Allies freed Holland.

Vocabulary: Zionists, surreptitiously, barbarism, disposition, congenial, lavatory, rheumatism, fatalistic, hemorrhage, clandestine, tumult, capitulated, despondency, impudent, prejudiced

Experiencing the Literature:
1. Have students keep a diary. Ask volunteers to share entries from their diary.
2. Have students research the causes and effects of World War II.
3. Ask students to write a poem that commemorates Anne Frank's bravery.

Make a 3-D Battle Scene

On a piece of paper, draw a picture of a battle scene from any war. Use bright colors, especially red, to fill in the picture. Then follow the directions to make a pair of 3-D glasses.

Directions:

Step 1: Cut out the pattern parts that are shown below.

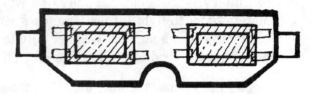

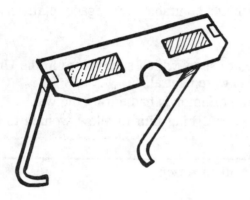

Step 2: Place the pattern parts on a piece of tagboard and trace them. Then cut out the pieces from the tagboard. Be sure to cut out the spaces for the lenses.

Step 3: Tape green cellophane to the back of the left lens and red cellophane to the back of the right lens.

Step 4: Fold back the tab on each side of the main frame.

Step 5: Tape or glue the ear pieces to the tabs on the main frame.

Step 6: Trim away any excess from the straight part first.

Step 7: Now put on your 3-D glasses and look at your drawing.

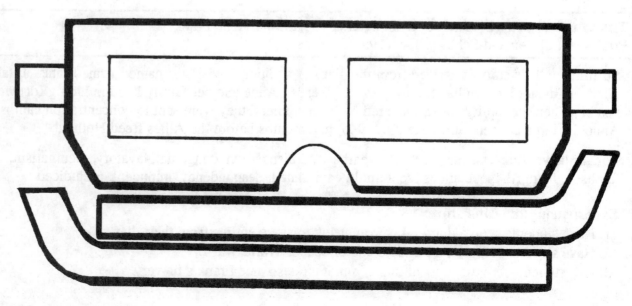

82

©*1994 Teacher Created Materials, Inc.*

Debate the Issues

Work with four or five other students to do research to find out about the issues related to a specific war.

Examples:
- Taxation without representation during the American Revolution
- Slavery during the American Civil War
- The spread of Communism during the Korean and Vietnam wars
- The use of the atomic bomb during World War II
- Boundary disputes during the Gulf War

Use the chart shown below to write facts from your research that support each side of the issue. Then divide your group in half. Have one part of your group take the "PRO" side of the issue and the other part take the "CON" side of the issue. Finally, hold a debate about the issues for the class. Use the facts you wrote on this page to help support your side of the issue.

PRO	CON

Research Topics

Work in cooperative learning groups to research one or more of the areas mentioned below. Share your findings with the rest of the class in any appropriate form of oral presentation.

American Revolutionary Heroes
John Adams
George Washington
Thomas Jefferson
James Madison
Paul Revere
Francis Scott Key

American Civil War Heroes
William Carney
Mitchel Raiders
Louisa May Alcott
Dorthea Dix
Mary Ann Bickerdyke
Clara Barton
Kady Brownell
Loreta Velazquez
Sarah Emma Edmonds
Harriet Tubman
Abraham Lincoln
Elizabeth Van Lew
Belle Boyd
Charlotte Forten
Clara Barton

World War I Heroes
Edouardo Izac
Charles Whittlesey
Alvin York
Edith Cavell
Elsie Inglis

World War II Heroes
Sadao Munemori
David Gonzales
Desmond Doss
John F. Kennedy
Winston Churchill
Mordechai Anielewicz

Anne Frank
Albert Guerisse
Andree De Jongh
Richard Bong
George Beurling
Noor Inayat Khan
Ivan N. Kozhedub
Douglas MacArthur
Odette Sansom
Audie Murphy
Nancy Wake
Ernie Pyle
Dietrich Bonhoeffer
Hector Garcia
St. Macimilian Kolbe

Vietnam War Heroes
William Dean
Lawrence Joel
Charles Rogers
John Levitow

Related Topics
Military Strategy
Weapons
Slogans
Songs
Uniforms
Technology
Aerial Photographs
Espionage
Military Satellites
Underground Bunkers
Civil Defense
Atomic Bomb
Neutron Bomb
Radiation
Economic Sanctions

Bibliography

Historical Background

Adler, David. *We Remember the Holocaust.* Holt, 1989.

Beyer, Don E. *Manhattan Project: America Makes the First Atomic Bomb.* Watts, 1991.

Bosco, Peter. *World War I.* Facts on File, 1991.

Bratman, Fred. *War in the Persian Gulf.* Millbrook, 1991.

Canon, Jill. *Civil War Heroines.* Bellerophon Books, 1989.

Carter, Alden R. *Civil War.* Watts, 1992.

Carter, Alden R. *War of 1812: Second Fight for Independence.* Watts, 1992.

Devaney, John. *America Goes to War: 1941.* Walker, 1991.

Devaney, John. *Vietnam War.* Watts, 1992.

Herda, D. J. *Afghan Rebels: The War in Afghanistan.* Watts, 1990.

Kohn, George. *Dictionary of Wars.* Doubleday, 1987.

Marrin, Albert. *Napoleon and the Napoleonic Wars.* Atheneum, 1989.

Marrin, Albert. *Spanish-American War.* Viking, 1991.

Marrin, Albert. *Struggle for a Continent: The French & Indian Wars, 1690-1760.* Macmillan 1987.

Marrin, Albert. *War for Independence: The Story of the American Revolution.* Atheneum, 1988.

McGowen, Tom. *Korean War.* Watts, 1992.

Meltzer, Milton, ed. *American Revolutionaries: A History in Their Own Words, 1750-1800.* Crowell, 1987.

Meltzer, Milton, ed. *Voices from the Civil War: A Documentary History of the Great American Conflict.* Crowell, 1989.

The Mexican War. Time-Life, 1978.

Reef, Catherine. *Buffalo Soldiers.* 21st Century, 1993.

Reef, Catherine. *Civil War Soldiers.* 21st Century, 1993.

Biographies

Davis, Burke. *Black Heroes of the American Revolution.* HBJ, 1976.

Ferris, Jeri. *Go Free or Die: A Story about Harriet Tubman.* Chelsea House, 1988.

Fritz, Jean. *Make Way for Sam Houston.* Putnam, 1986.

Fritz, Jean. *Where Was Patrick Henry on the 29th of May?* Putnam, 1980.

Longfellow, Henry Wadsworth. *Paul Revere's Ride.* Dutton, 1990.

McGovern, Ann. *Secret Soldier: The Story of Deborah Sampson.* Scholastic, 1991.

Murphy, Edward F. *Heroes of World War II.* Presidio Press, 1990.

Patterson, Lillie. *Francis Scott Key: Poet and Patriot.* Chelsea House, 1992.

Sabin, Lou. *Teddy Roosevelt, Rough Rider.* Troll Associates, 1985.

Sender, Ruth Minsky. *Holocaust Lady (Sender).* Macmillan, 1992.

Skipper, G.C. *MacArthur & the Philippines.* Childrens Press, 1982.

Stevenson, Augusta. *Molly Pitcher: Young Patriot.* Macmillan, 1986.

Sweeney, James B. *Army Leaders of World War II.* Watts, 1984.

Tregaskis, Richard. *Guadalcanal Diary.* Random, 1984.

Teacher Created Materials

142 *Patriotic Patterns and Clip Art*
290 *Thematic Unit: Civil War*
293 *Thematic Unit: Revolutionary War*
373 *Thematic Bibliography*
413 *Literature Unit: Rifles for Watie*
424 *Literature Unit: Number the Stars*
480 *American History Simulations*
481 *World History Simulations*
581 *Thematic Unit: World War II*
600 *A Trip Around the World*

Bulletin Board Idea

Use the following bulletin board idea to introduce students to the section on Sports Heroes. The patterns shown below make this three-dimensional bulletin board quick and easy to create. Begin by covering the background with butcher paper or green indoor/outdoor carpeting. The carpeting adds a unique effect because it looks like grass or Astroturf. Then use an opaque projector to enlarge the patterns. Make two copies of each pattern and cut them out. Use the patterns to create three-dimensional shapes by carefully placing the two copies of each pattern together and stapling around the edges. Be sure to leave an open space at the top so that you can add stuffing. Stuff each pattern set with newspaper. Then close the opening at the top using staples. Finally, create the title "Sports Heroes." This bulletin board can be used to display student work or the Quiz Cards (page 93). You can create a learning/research center by placing a table with appropriate materials in front of the bulletin board.

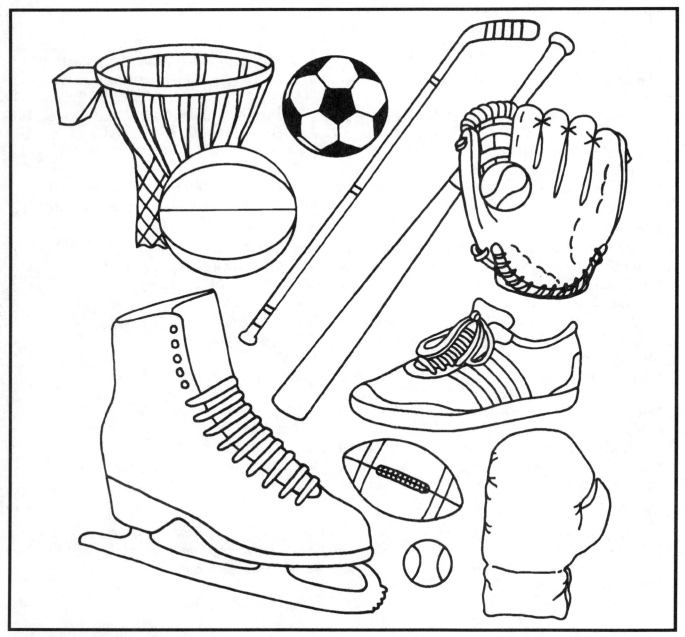

Introduction

Sports heroes have been popular throughout time. They can be found in all types of athletic events. Some participate in individual sports, while others are a part of a team. Sports heroes are men, women, and children who have extensively trained so that they can excel at a particular sport. They are in terrific physical condition and often seem to have a psychological edge. Many sports heroes have endured hardships as they climbed toward the top. All have celebrated victories, and all have learned to cope with defeat.

The outline below is a suggested plan for using the various activities presented in this section of *Heroes*. Each lesson can take from one to several days to complete. You should adapt these ideas to fit your own classroom situation.

Sample Plan

Lesson 1
- Introduce section vocabulary (page 88).
- Introduce and discuss sports and sports heroes (pages 86–88).
- Label the sites of the Olympics (page 94).
- Read and discuss the article about Jim Thorpe (page 89).
- Complete the Jim Thorpe Quiz Card (page 93).

Lesson 2
- Read and discuss the article about Wilma Rudolph (page 90).
- Complete the Wilma Rudolph Quiz Card (page 93).
- Choose a Relating the Theme activity (page 95).

Lesson 3
- Read and discuss the article about Orel Hershiser (page 91).
- Complete the Orel Hershiser Quiz Card (page 93).
- Begin reading a book related to the theme (page 97).
- Calculate sports rankings (page 96).

Lesson 4
- Read and discuss the article about Kristi Yamaguchi (page 92).
- Complete the Kristi Yamaguchi Quiz Card (page 93).
- Create a new sport (page 99).
- Choose a Relating the Theme activity (page 95).
- Begin research projects (page 100).
- Continue reading a book related to the theme (page 97).

Lesson 5
- Make sports cards (page 98).
- Choose a Relating the Theme activity (page 95).
- Do one or more literature-related activities (page 97).
- Continue working on research projects (page 100).

Lesson 6
- Complete one or more Culminating Activities (pages 166-170).
- Share research projects (page 100).

Overview of Activities

Section Vocabulary: You may wish to introduce the following vocabulary words at the beginning of this section: Olympics, standings, rankings, competition, major league, minor league, professional, amateur, coordination, stamina, endurance, flexibility, agility, arena, diamond, field, rookie, champion, physical education, foul, penalty, injury.

Background Information:

- Sports heroes have been significant role-models throughout history.
- Sports heroes have come from all around the world.
- Sports heroes show excellence in one or more athletic events.
- Competition in sports can be a team or an individual effort.
- Most people enjoy watching or participating in sporting events.
- Today the media gives a great deal of attention to sports heroes.

Bulletin Board Idea: This bulletin board is extremely easy to construct and will help set the stage for introducing the section on Sports Heroes (page 86).

Articles and Discussion Questions: Four interesting articles about specific sports heroes and related discussion questions are provided (pages 89-92).

Quiz Cards: These four cards provide questions about the articles to assess students' understanding of what they have read (page 93). Teachers may wish to make the Quiz Cards self-checking by duplicating the set of cards and placing the answers on the back.

Map Study: This activity helps develop map skills while providing background information about where the Olympics have taken place (page 94). You may wish to display the maps as a border around the bulletin board for this section (page 86).

Relating the Theme: These activities connect the theme to a variety of curriculum areas, such as reading, language arts, math, science, social studies, art, music, and life skills (page 95).

Spotlight on Math: Students calculate sports rankings (page 96).

Literature Connection: Literature selections for this section are summarized, and related activities are suggested (page 97).

Make Sports Cards: This hands-on activity gives students the opportunity to make sports cards that tell about their favorite athletes (page 98).

Create a Sport: Students work in cooperative learning groups to write a set of rules for a sport that they create (page 99).

Research Topics: These research ideas will help students better understand sports heroes (page 100). It is suggested that students work in cooperative learning groups.

Bibliography: Additional literature is suggested (page 101). The books may be used in a variety of ways, such as in a learning center, for research projects, or for book reports.

Culminating Activities: Students will pick one or more culminating activities to help them synthesize and share what they have learned (pages 166-170).

Jim Thorpe

James Francis Thorpe was a Native American who was born on May 28, 1888, in Prague, Oklahoma. Thorpe enjoyed sports when he was young. He began studying athletics in Carlisle, Pennsylvania, at the Indian Industrial School. He played football for the school and showed that he was a superb tackler, place kicker, and runner. In 1911 and 1912, he gained national recognition for himself and the school by winning all-American honors.

In 1912, Thorpe participated in the Olympic Games in Stockholm, Sweden. He won one gold medal in the pentathlon and another in the decathlon. The pentathlon, consisting of five different events, usually includes pistol shooting, fencing, swimming, horseback riding, and running. The decathlon consists of ten different events in track and field. He was the first athlete ever to win both the pentathlon and decathlon. Unfortunately, the Amateur Athletic Union told Olympic officials to take away his medals about a month after the games. The union decided that Thorpe had not been eligible to participate in the games. They claimed that Thorpe was a professional athlete because he had been paid a small amount of money for playing baseball in 1909. It was not until 1982 that this injustice was corrected by the International Olympic Committee. They put his name back on the list of Olympic champions for 1912 and gave his gold medals to his family.

One year after the Olympics, Thorpe started to play in professional baseball. For the next six years, he played for three major-league teams. In 1915, Thorpe started playing professional football. He played football for 15 years on seven different teams. In addition to playing football, in 1920 he became the first president of the American Professional Football Association, which today is called the National Football League. Many people started watching football games just to see Jim Thorpe in action. As a result, football's popularity grew enormously.

Thorpe was one of the best all-around athletes. He excelled in a variety of sports, such as running, jumping, archery, boxing, shot-putting, pole vaulting, football, handball, hockey, lacrosse, rifle shooting, swimming, and skating. Just two years before Thorpe's death in 1953, he became one of the first athletes to be chosen as a member of the National Football Foundation's Hall of Fame.

Discussion Questions

1. What qualities make Jim Thorpe a hero?

2. Do you think Thorpe should or should not have been considered a professional athlete at the 1912 Olympics? Explain your answer.

3. What would be the benefits of excelling in a variety of sports? What would be the drawbacks?

Now use the Jim Thorpe Quiz Card to check your understanding of this article.

Wilma Rudolph

Wilma Rudolph was born in Tennessee on June 23, 1940. As an infant, Rudolph suffered from double pneumonia and scarlet fever. Remarkably, she survived. A few years later, Rudolph was seriously ill again. This time she had polio. She recovered, but one of her legs was crippled by the disease. Several doctors told her parents that she would never fully regain the use of her crippled leg. Her mother refused to believe this. She took Rudolph to some doctors in Nashville. The doctors showed her mother how to massage the crippled leg. Rudolph had to go to Nashville every week for a unique water and heat therapy. When she was five years old, the doctors fitted her crippled leg with a special steel brace. She wore the brace until she was 11 years old, at which time she decided she needed to learn to walk without it.

Rudolph joined her junior high school basketball team. When she got to the ninth grade, she started running track in addition to playing basketball. She won race after race at track meets and also became a terrific basketball player. Ed Temple, a coach from Tennessee State College, was impressed when he saw Rudolph compete in the spring of 1956. He asked her to run track for the college in a summer athletic program. Rudolph agreed to go to Nashville. That summer she trained five days a week by running twenty miles a day. On the day of the national track meet, Rudolph was ready. She was victorious in all nine races that she ran.

Rudolph started her junior year in high school in the fall of 1956. Coach Temple was training her to compete in the Olympics. In October she went to Australia as a member of the United States Women's Olympic Relay Team. She won a bronze medal.

After graduating from high school, Rudolph got an athletic scholarship in order to attend Tennessee State University. She continued her training with Coach Temple. In 1960, Rudolph went to Italy for the Olympics. She came in first place in the 100-meter race, the 200-meter race, and the 400-meter relay. In the history of the Olympics, Rudolph was the first American woman to win three gold medals. Wilma Rudolph's speed was awe-inspiring in 1960. She was proclaimed the fastest woman on Earth and given the Athlete of the Year award by the Associated Press. Three years later she graduated from college and began teaching others about athletic competition.

Discussion Questions

1. How do you think Rudolph's illnesses as a child affected her?

2. Would you like to be the fastest person on Earth? Explain your answer.

3. Why do you think Rudolph went on to teach others about athletic competition?

Now use the Wilma Rudolph Quiz Card to check your understanding of this article.

Orel Hershiser

When Orel Hershiser was young, he enjoyed playing a variety of sports, such as racquetball, tennis, golf, and hockey. However, baseball was his favorite. At the age of eight, Hershiser entered a contest that was held in Yankee Stadium in New York. In the contest, he had to throw, hit, and run. He competed against boys from all across America. Hershiser came in third place.

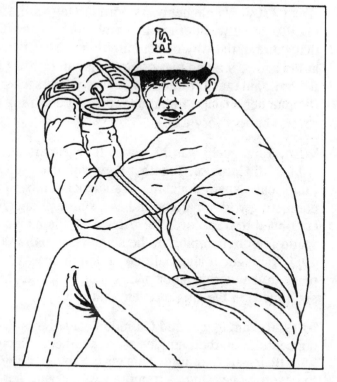

Hershiser had a great deal of difficulty playing baseball in high school and college. In high school, he started out playing, but he was cut from the team. In college, he was not allowed to join the baseball team because his grades and his playing were not good enough. Rather than give up, Hershiser worked to improve his grades and his baseball skills. His grades went up, and he increased the speed of his pitch by five miles per hour. As a result, he made the college team.

Hershiser started playing professional baseball as a pitcher for the Los Angeles Dodgers minor-league team. His playing ability was only fair, and he often felt discouraged. However, his coach, trainer, and manager felt Hershiser had potential, so they convinced him to keep working on his pitch. This is exactly what Hershiser did, and eventually he became a starring pitcher for the major leagues.

Over the next few years, Hershiser led the National League in several areas. In 1984, he pitched four shutout games. In 1985, he had the winning percentage with a record of 19–3. He pitched a record 265 innings in 1987 and another 267 innings in 1988. Hershiser's 1988 season was phenomenal. He pitched a total of 59 innings without any home runs being scored. This pitching streak broke the 1968 record of 58 scoreless innings that had been achieved by Don Drysdale. In the 1988 season, Hershiser had 23 wins and eight shutouts and was given the Cy Young Award. The Los Angeles Dodgers went on to play in the World Series that fall. They beat the Oakland A's four games to one. Hershiser was voted the Most Valuable Player of the World Series.

Discussion Questions

1. Why do you think Orel Hershiser continued to play baseball despite his mediocre record during the early years?

2. How is Orel Hershiser like other sports heroes you know? How is he different?

3. What kinds of things do you think Hershiser worried about during the 1988 season?

Now use the Orel Hershiser Quiz Card to check your understanding of this article.

Kristi Yamaguchi

Kristi Tsuya Yamaguchi was born in Hayward, California, in 1971. She was born with a clubfoot, but she did not let that stand in the way of her ambitions. She started skating at the age of six and was competing within two years. Before Yamaguchi turned ten, Christy Kjarsgaard Ness became her coach. Yamaguchi practiced skating for several hours every day.

When Yamaguchi was 12 years old, she started skating with Rudi Galindo. Together they won the 1985 national junior pairs championships. Yamaguchi enjoyed competing with a partner and as a singles skater, so she continued to train for both. At age 17, Yamaguchi was the world junior champion in the singles and pairs skating. In 1989 Yamaguchi and Galindo skated their way to fifth place in the world senior pairs event. Yamaguchi also won sixth place in the singles event that year.

In 1990, Yamaguchi and Galindo decided they wanted to concentrate on their singles careers rather than continue with their pairs skating. This gave Yamaguchi more time to devote to her singles training. As a result, her singles skating improved. She started working to make her routines more complicated. This paid off because she was able to become the world champion in figure skating in 1991 and 1992.

Yamaguchi went to Albertville, France, for the 1992 Winter Olympics. She knew that the competition was going to include many excellent skaters. She chose a routine that was technically difficult. She skated with perfection, and the judges rated her routine the highest. Yamaguchi won a gold medal. It had been 16 years since an American woman had won a gold medal in the singles event.

Discussion Questions

1. Kristi Yamaguchi started training as a skater at a very young age. What are the benefits of having a young child train as an athlete? What are the drawbacks?

2. Would you prefer to be a singles skater or a pairs skater? Explain your answer.

3. In what ways do you think Yamaguchi prepared for the 1992 Olympics?

Now use the Kristi Yamaguchi Quiz Card to check your understanding of this article.

Quiz Cards

Use the following questions to assess your students' understanding of the articles on pages 89 through 92 of this unit. Have them write their answers on notebook paper.

Jim Thorpe Quiz Card

1. When and where was Jim Thorpe born?
2. Where did people begin to realize that Thorpe was a superb tackler, place kicker, and runner?
3. How did Thorpe gain national recognition for himself and his school in 1911 and 1912?
4. In which contests did Thorpe participate in the 1912 Olympics?
5. Why were Thorpe's Olympic gold medals taken away from him?
6. What did the International Olympic Committee decide in 1982?
7. What did Thorpe do in 1913?
8. When did Thorpe begin to play professional football?
9. What football organization did Thorpe become the first president of in 1920?
10. What honor did Thorpe receive in 1951?

Orel Hershiser Quiz Card

1. What kind of sports did Orel Hershiser play when he was young?
2. Where was the contest held that Hershiser entered when he was eight years old?
3. Why wasn't Hershiser allowed to play college baseball at first?
4. What did Hershiser do to make his college baseball team?
5. For whom did Hershiser start playing professional baseball?
6. In what area did Hershiser lead the National Football League in 1984?
7. In total, how many games did Hershiser pitch during 1987 and 1988?
8. How did Hershiser break a record in 1988 that had been set twenty years earlier?
9. Who did the Los Angeles Dodgers beat in the 1988 World Series?
10. What honors did Hershiser earn in 1988?

Wilma Rudolph Quiz Card

1. What illnesses did Wilma Rudolph have as an infant?
2. How did one of Rudolph's legs become crippled?
3. What did the doctors in Nashville tell Rudolph's mother to do?
4. For how many years did Rudolph wear a brace on her crippled leg?
5. Why was Ed Temple important to Rudolph?
6. What did Rudolph do the summer of 1956?
7. How did Rudolph do in the 1956 Olympics?
8. What Olympic events did Rudolph enter in 1960?
9. What was special about Rudolph's victories at the 1960 Olympics?
10. What honor did the Associated Press give to Rudolph in 1960?

Kristi Yamaguchi Quiz Card

1. What physical problem did Yamaguchi have to overcome?
2. When did Christy Kjarsgaard Ness begin coaching Yamaguchi?
3. Who was Yamaguchi's partner in pairs skating?
4. What honor did Yamaguchi win in 1985?
5. In what year was Yamaguchi the junior singles and pairs world champion?
6. How well did Yamaguchi do in the 1989 singles skating?
7. Why was Yamaguchi able to spend more time on her singles training after 1990?
8. Which competitions did Yamaguchi win in both 1991 and 1992?
9. Where did Yamaguchi go to compete in the 1992 Olympics?
10. What award did Yamaguchi win at the 1992 Olympics, and why was this significant?

Map Study

The Olympics were inspired by games that were played in the ancient Greek city of Olympia. Use an atlas or other reference tool to locate and label the sites of the Olympic games that are listed in the box. You will probably need to enlarge the map below.

The Olympic Games—Sites and Dates

Paris, France (1900)
St. Louis, Missouri, U.S. (1904)
Athens, Greece (1906)
London, England (1908)
Stockholm, Sweden (1912)
Antwerp, Belgium (1920)
Paris, France (1924)
Amsterdam, Netherlands (1928)
Los Angeles, California, U.S. (1932)
Berlin, Germany (1936)
London, England (1948)
Helsinki, Finland (1952)

Melbourne, Australia (1956)
Rome, Italy (1960)
Tokyo, Japan (1964)
Mexico City, Mexico (1968)
Munich, Germany (1972)
Montreal, Canada (1976)
Moscow, Russia (1980)
Los Angeles, California, U.S. (1984)
Seoul, South Korea (1988)
Barcelona, Spain (1992)
Atlanta, Georgia, U.S. (1996)

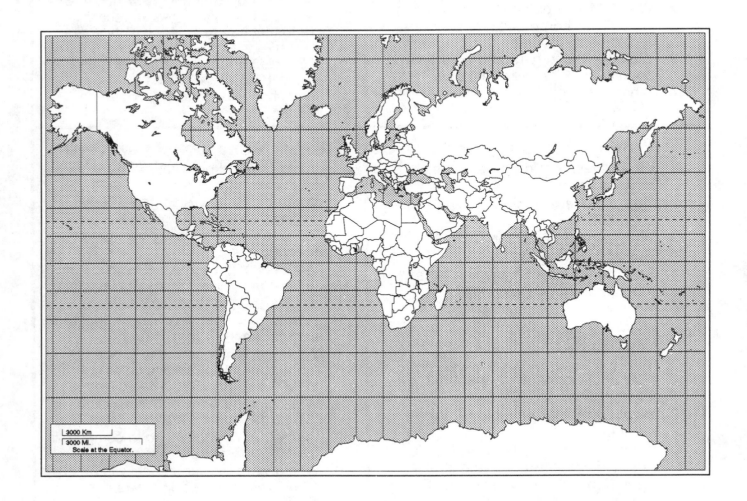

3000 Km
3000 Mi.
Scale at the Equator.

94

©1994 Teacher Created Materials, Inc.

Relating the Theme

You may wish to use one or all of the following activities to supplement your own ideas about ways to integrate the *Heroes* theme into your curriculum.

Language Arts:

1. Have students draw a cartoon strip about a sport that they enjoy. Display the cartoon strips on the bulletin board (page 86).
2. Ask students to develop a wordsearch using the names of their favorite sports heroes.

Health:

1. Discuss the nutritional value of different kinds of foods. Then have students create a menu for a restaurant that serves nutritious foods for athletes.
2. Have students write an essay persuading others to participate in sports.

Social Studies:

1. Have students create small flags using construction paper and long straight pins to represent the countries where the Olympic Games have been hosted (page 94). Ask them to indicate the year and the city on the flag. Then place the flags in a world map on a bulletin board.
2. Ask students to brainstorm a list of careers associated with sports. Examples: manager, coach, referee, goalie, quarterback, guard, etc. Have students discuss any careers that they are personally interested in pursuing.

Math:

1. Using the sports section of a newspaper, have students cut out a sports chart and explain to the class how to read it.
2. Have students conduct a poll to see which sports heroes are the most popular. Then help them show their findings in a bar graph and a circle graph. Discuss the differences in the two types of graphs.

Literature:

1. Have students read a biography or autobiography about a sports hero. Some titles are suggested in the bibliography for this section (page 101). Then ask students to give a book report about that sports hero.
2. Using the sports section of the newspaper, have students locate articles about sports heroes. Ask them to read the articles and write a summary of them. Then display the summaries on the bulletin board (page 86).

Art:

1. Have students use papier-mâché to make models of sporting equipment, such as a bat, a football, and a ski. Use the models to decorate the classroom by suspending them from the ceiling.
2. Have students make a collage of sports heroes using newspaper and magazine pictures that they cut and paste.

Physical Education:

Have students teach a sport to a group of younger children.

Spotlight on Math: Sports Rankings

The sports pages of a newspaper often show a variety of sports statistics. One example of the types of statistics shown is the team standings in the United States National Basketball Association for their particular conference rank. Use the chart below to calculate the rankings of the basketball teams that are listed. The wins and losses are given. First calculate their percentages and then rank them. The champion with the best record for either division gets #1 rank and the champion of the other division gets the #2 rank. All other rankings go in order of highest percentage to the lowest percentage. The first one has been done for you.

Remember, to find the percentage, add the wins and losses to get the total number of games. Divide the number of wins by the total number of games to get your percentage.

WESTERN CONFERENCE

PACIFIC DIVISION

Teams	Wins	Losses	Percentage	Ranking
Lakers	18	14	.563	6TH
Clippers	17	16		
Sacramento	13	17		
Seattle	22	8		
Phoenix	23	5		
Portland	20	10		

MIDWEST DIVISION

Teams	Wins	Losses	Percentage	Ranking
Dallas	2	27		
Utah	21	10		
Houston	15	16		
San Antonio	18	13		
Denver	8	22		
Minnesota	6	23		

Literature Connection

Title: *The Random House Book of Short Stories* **Selected by:** L.M. Schulman
Publisher: Random House (1990) *(Canada and AUS: Random House; UK: Random Century House)*

*Special Note: This book contains stories that describe real life. Therefore, it includes subject matter and language that you might not feel is appropriate for your students. Please pre-read the book and use it at your discretion.

Summary: This is a compilation of 16 short stories about sports. The stories are written by a variety of well-known authors, such as James Thurber, Ernest Hemingway, Jack London, and William Faulkner. Each author describes a sporting event from a unique perspective. The sporting events include baseball, tennis, pool, horse-racing, boxing, karate, football, skiing, and hunting. These stories allow the reader to experience these sporting events and the emotions related to each participant's triumph or defeat.

Vocabulary: exhibition, midget, vestibule, mockery, prodigy, tournament, entrusted, capricious, steeplechase, unconscious, karate, meditation, choreography, cue ball, opponents, ricochet, outfielders, junta, eligible, aspiring, compensation, solar plexus, scrimmage, pennants, turnstile, doubleheader, half-nelson, endurance, synchronized

Experiencing the Literature:

1. Have students write a story that could be added to the book.
2. Have students make a chart that shows examples of formal and informal language.
3. Ask students to describe the traits of different characters in the book.

Title: *Roberto Clemente*   **Author:** Thomas W. Gilbert
Publisher: Chelsea House Publishers (1991) *(Canada: Nelson, UK: Letterworth Press; AUS: CIS Publishers)*

Summary: This is the life story of Roberto Clemente, who was born in Puerto Rico in 1934 to a working-class family. He loved to play baseball from the time he was a child. When he was 19 years old, he joined the Brooklyn Dodgers. Then, in 1954, Clemente became a member of the Pittsburgh Pirates. He was a superior batter and pitcher. During his 18 major league seasons, Clemente won four National League batting titles, was voted the National League's Most Valuable Player in 1966, and became the World Series Most Valuable Player in 1971. In 1972, he was killed in an airplane crash while attempting to take emergency supplies to people in Nicaragua who were the victims of an earthquake. After his death, Clemente was elected to the Hall of Fame for baseball players.

Vocabulary: profoundly, literary, adversity, exaggeration, humiliated, pensively, figuratively, unorthodox, perennial, arch-rivals, obligation, sophisticated, disillusioned, intransigent, ordeal, denunciation, controversial, uncontroverted, predicament, exemplified

Experiencing the Literature:

1. Have students use an atlas to draw a map of Puerto Rico and label the place names mentioned in the book.
2. Ask students to list Clemente's batting averages for his major-league career.
3. Have students write a paragraph explaining why Clemente deserved to be a member of baseball's Hall of Fame.

Make Sports Cards

Use the space below to make sports cards for your favorite sports heroes. Cut out the cards shown below. Fill out the information on the back of the card. Then draw the hero's picture on the front of the card.

Name:

Position:

Team:

Date of Birth:

Place of Birth:

Background Information:

Career Highlights:

Name:

Position:

Team:

Date of Birth:

Place of Birth:

Background Information:

Career Highlights:

Name:

Position:

Team:

Date of Birth:

Place of Birth:

Background Information:

Career Highlights:

Name:

Position:

Team:

Date of Birth:

Place of Birth:

Background Information:

Career Highlights:

Create a Sport

In this activity, you will get to create your own sport. It can be based on a sport that already exists or it can be something that is completely new and different. Begin by listing any equipment that you will need. Then write the step-by-step directions for how to play your sport. Be sure to give your sport a name. Finally, draw a picture of people playing your sport on the back of this page.

Equipment:

Name of Sport:

Directions:

Research Topics

Work in cooperative learning groups to research one or more of the people mentioned below. Share your findings with the rest of the class in any appropriate form of oral presentation.

Gymnasts
Mary Lou Retton
Kurt Thomas
Olga Korbut
Nadia Comaneci
Nikolai Andrianov
Peter Vidmar

Baseball Players
Roberto Clemente
Babe Ruth
Lou Gehrig
Hank Aaron
Rickey Henderson
Roy Campanella
Sandy Koufax
Bob Gibson
Willie Mays
Jackie Robinson

Football Players
Walter Payton
Joe Montana
Jim Plunkett
Brian Piccolo
Joe Namath
Terry Bradshaw
Jim Brown
Randall Cunningham
Jim Thorpe
Bob Hayes
Emmitt Smith

Basketball Players
Larry Bird
Michael Jordan
Sheryl Swoopes
Bill Russell
Wilt Chamberlain
Oscar Robertson

Hockey Players
Jacque Plante
Gordie Howe
Wayne Gretzky

Tennis Players
Chris Evert
Arthur Ashe
Billie Jean King
Jimmy Conners
Althea Gibson
Michael Chang
Boris Becker
Steffi Graf

Water Sports
Dawn Fraser
Sammy Lee
Greg Louganis
Pablo Morales
Gerard D'Aboville
Tracie Ruiz
Lynn Cox
Janet Evans

Skaters
Scott Hamilton
Kristi Yamaguchi
Dorothy Hamill
Kurt Browning
Eric Heiden
Bonnie Blair

Boxers
Wilfredo Benitez
Muhammad Ali (Cassius Clay)
Joe Frazier
Henry Armstrong
Jack Johnson
Sugar Ray Leonard

Runners
Terry Fox
Kip Keino
Jackie Joyner-Kersey
Gail Devers
Carl Lewis
Jesse Owens
Wilma Rudolph

Bibliography

Background Information
Arnold, Caroline. *Olympic Summer Games*. Watts, 1991.
Arnold, Caroline. *Olympic Winter Games*. Watts, 1991.
Arnold, Caroline. *Pele: The King of Soccer*. Watts, 1992.
Arnold Caroline. *Soccer*. Watts, 1991.
Barrett, Norman. *Football*. Watts, 1988.
Barrett, Norman. *Scuba Diving*. Watts, 1988.
Barrett, Norman. *Windsurfing*. Watts, 1987.
Benagh, Jim. *Basketball: Startling Stories Behind the Records*. Sterling, 1991.
Berger, Melvin. *Sports*. Watts, 1983.
Blackstone, Margaret. *This Is Baseball*. Holt, 1993.
Brown, Fern G. *Special Olympics*. Watts, 1992.
Coombs, Charles Ira. *All-terrain Bicycling*. Holt, 1987.
Dieterich, Michele. *Skiing*. Lerner, 1991.
Garber, Angus G. *Champions: The Greatest Sports Legends of All Time*. BDD Promo Books, 1990.
Great Sports Performances. Capstone Press, 1989.
Helmer, Diane Star. *Belles of the Ballpark*. Millbrook, 1993.
Hot Air Ballooning. Capstone Press, 1989.
Knudson, R. Rozanne, comp. *American Sports Poems*. Orchard, 1988.
Leder, Jane Mersky. *Learning How, Karate*. Bancroft-Sage, 1992.
Leder, Jane Mersky. *Learning How, Skateboarding*. Bancroft-Sage, 1991.
Schulman, L.M., ed. *The Random House Book of Sports Stories*. Random, 1990.
Sports Illustrated Staff. *Best of Sports Illustrated*. Oxmoor House, 1990.
Sullivan, George. *Racing Indy Cars*. Cobblehill, 1992.
Wood, Tim. *Ice Skating*. Watts, 1990.
Wood, Tim. *Motorcycling*. Watts, 1989.

Biographies
Brandt, Keith. *Lou Gehrig: Pride of the Yankees*. Troll Associates, 1986.
Coffey, Wayne R. *Jim Thorpe*. Blackbirch, 1993.
Coffey, W. *Wilma Rudolph*. Blackbirch, 1993.
Dell, Pamela. *Michael Chang: Tennis Champion*. Childrens, 1992.
Dolan, Ellen M. *Susan Butcher & Iditarod Trail*. Walker, 1993.
Gallagher, Mark. *Mickey Mantle*. Chelsea House, 1991.
Greene Carol. *Jackie Robinson: Baseball's First Black Major-Leaguer*. Childrens, 1990.
Greene, Carol. *Roberto Clemente: Baseball Superstar*. Childrens, 1991.
Gutman, Bill. *Jennifer Capriati: Teenage Tennis Star*. Millbrook, 1993.
Hahn, James & Hahn, Lynn. *Patty! The Sports Career of Patricia Berg*. Macmillan, 1981.
Knapp, Ron. *Sports Great Isiah Thomas*. Enslow, 1992.
Lipsyte, Robert. *Free To Be Muhammad Ali*. Harper, 1978.
McKissack, Pat. *Jesse Owens: Olympic Star*. Enslow, 1992.
Raber, Thomas R. *Wayne Gretzky: Hockey Great*. Lerner, 1991.
Van Riper, Guernsey. *Babe Ruth: One of Baseball's Greatest*. Macmillan, 1986.

Teacher Created Materials
144   *How to Manage Your Whole Language Classroom*
417   *Literature Unit: In the Year of the Boar and Jackie Robinson*
504   *Portfolios & Other Assessments*
906   *Newspaper and Reporting Set*

Bulletin Board Idea

Use the following bulletin board idea to introduce students to the section on Heroes of Science & Invention. The pattern shown below makes the bulletin board quick and easy to create. Begin by covering the background with butcher paper. Then use an opaque projector to enlarge and copy the pattern. Finally, create the title "Heroes of Science & Invention." This bulletin board can be used to display student work or the Quiz Cards (page 109). You can create a learning/research center by placing a table with appropriate materials in front of the bulletin board.

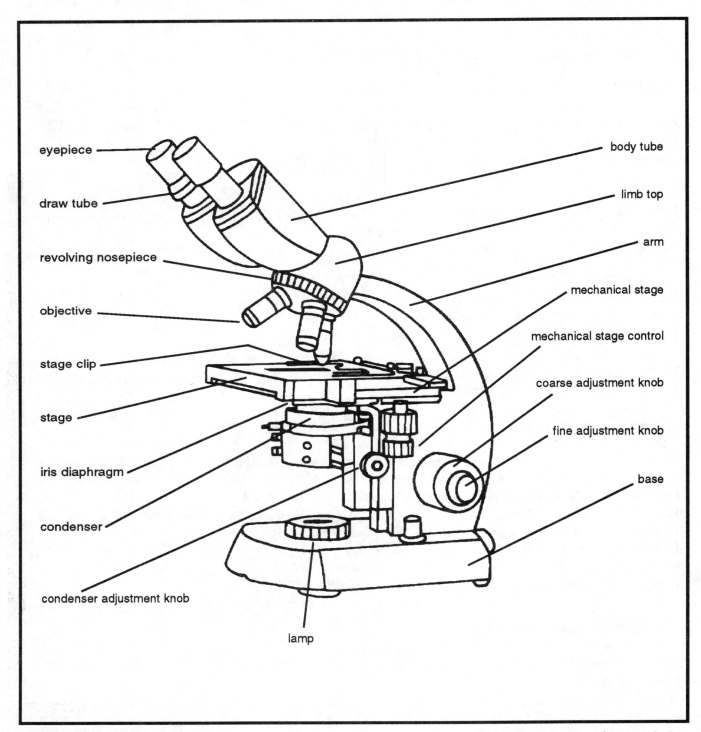

Introduction

Science is the study of things that occur naturally. It is usually broken down into three areas: life science, earth science, and physical science. Through scientific discovery, students learn to use process skills. This allows them to see the relationship between concepts and principles in science. It also gives them a chance to clearly understand key concepts that can later be applied to other situations.

Inventions are all around us. Some are the by-products of scientific experimentation, while others are the creations of unique problem solvers. Not all inventions are brand new ideas. Many inventions are the result of innovation. An innovation is an extension of an existing scientific discovery, idea, or invention. There are several reasons why inventions are made. Some inventions are intended to make work easier for people. Some are intended to fill a need. Others are made to solve a problem.

The outline below is a suggested plan for using the various activities presented in this section of *Heroes*. Each lesson can take from one to several days to complete. You should adapt these ideas to fit your own classroom situation.

Sample Plan

Lesson 1

- Introduce section vocabulary (page 104).
- Introduce and discuss the study of science and inventions (pages 102–104).
- Read and discuss the article about George Washington Carver (page 105).
- Complete the George Washington Carver Quiz Card (page 109).
- Label a map that shows where scientific discoveries and inventions were made (page 110).

Lesson 2

- Read and discuss the article about Madame C.J. Walker (page 106).
- Complete the Madame C.J. Walker Quiz Card (page 109).
- Choose a Relating the Theme activity (page 111).

Lesson 3

- Read and discuss the article about Marie Curie (page 107).
- Complete the Marie Curie Quiz Card (page 109).
- Begin reading a book related to the theme (page 113).
- Record the growth of a plant (page 112).

Lesson 4

- Read and discuss the article about Albert Einstein (page 108).
- Complete the Albert Einstein Quiz Card (page 109).
- Learn how to use the scientific method (page 115).
- Choose a Relating the Theme activity (page 111).
- Begin research projects (page 116).
- Continue reading a book related to the theme (page 113).

Lesson 5

- Make one or more peanut butter recipes (page 114).
- Choose a Relating the Theme activity (page 111).
- Do one or more literature-related activities (page 113).
- Continue working on research projects (page 116).

Lesson 6

- Complete one or more Culminating Activities (pages 166-170).
- Share research projects (page 116).

Overview of Activities

Section Vocabulary: You may wish to introduce the following vocabulary words at the beginning of this section: calculation, equations, theories, observation, hypotheses, experiment, property, law, characteristic, trait, principle, classification, microscope, hardware, software, Fahrenheit, Celsius, energy, atoms, molecules, ecosystem, prototype, patent, diagram, innovation, trademark.

Background Information:

- Inventions and scientific discoveries have been made throughout history.
- People from all around the world have contributed to science and invention.
- Inventions are made to fill a need or to solve a problem.
- Many inventions come from scientific discovery or are an adaptation of other inventions.
- Science is divided into three areas: life science, earth science, and physical science.

Bulletin Board Idea: This bulletin board is extremely easy to construct and will help set the stage for introducing the section on Heroes of Science & Invention (page 102).

Articles and Discussion Questions: Four interesting articles about specific heroes of science and invention and related discussion questions are provided (pages 105-108).

Quiz Cards: These four cards provide questions about the articles to assess students' understanding of what they have read (page 109). Teachers may wish to make the Quiz Cards self-checking by duplicating the set of cards and placing the answers on the back.

Map Study: This activity helps develop map skills while providing background information about where some scientific discoveries and inventions were made (page 110). Students should use the map for reference throughout their study of heroes of science and invention.

Relating the Theme: These activities connect the theme to a variety of curriculum areas, such as reading, language arts, math, science, social studies, art, music, and life skills (page 111).

Spotlight on Science: Students record the growth of a plant (page 112).

Literature Connection: Literature selections for this section are summarized, and related activities are suggested (page 113).

Peanut Butter Recipes: This hands-on activity gives students the opportunity to make a peanut butter recipe (page 114).

Using the Scientific Method: Students work in cooperative learning groups to discover how to use the scientific method (page 115).

Research Topics: These research ideas will help students learn more about the heroic work of scientists and inventors (page 116). It is suggested that students work in cooperative learning groups.

Bibliography: Additional literature is suggested (page 117). The books may be used in a variety of ways, such as in a learning center, for research projects, or for book reports.

Culminating Activities: Students will pick one or more culminating activities to help them synthesize and share what they have learned (pages 166-170).

George Washington Carver

George Washington Carver was born in Missouri in 1864. The Civil War was still being fought when he was born. Carver was a slave, as were his parents. His father was killed in an accident, and his mother was abducted by night raiders, people who stole and sold slaves. Carver was owned by Moses and Susan Carver. The couple raised him even after slavery was abolished.

As a young child, Carver learned a variety of household chores, such as sewing, knitting, candle-making, and cooking. He was very curious about plants and began learning everything he could about them. Carver learned to read and write from his adoptive parents. He did not receive any formal education until he was 11 years old. At that time, he moved to Neosho to go to a school for African-American children. Carver held many different jobs to work his way through school.

In 1890, Carver enrolled in Simpson College in Iowa. He was the first African-American student to go to this college. One year later, Carver decided to attend Iowa State Agricultural College. Carver studied agriculture and earned bachelor's and a master's degrees by 1896. After graduating from college, Carver became a faculty member at Tuskegee Institute in Alabama. This school was for African-American students who were interested in industrial and agricultural careers. Soon Carver became the head of the agricultural department at Tuskegee and also directed an agricultural station for the state. In his laboratory, Carver did research to find ways to conserve the soil and grow more crops. He educated farmers in Alabama and other states by writing articles, giving lectures and demonstrations, and by taking exhibits from place to place.

By 1914, Carver became the head of the research department at Tuskegee. After about four years he began concentrating on the study of peanuts. He discovered more than 300 ways to use peanut plants. Some of the products he developed included ink, soap, milk, face powder, and plastic. As a result, peanuts became an important cash crop for southern farmers.

Carver received many honors for his work in agriculture. In 1916, he became a fellow of London's Royal Society of Arts. In 1921, he was asked to speak before a committee in Congress. In 1923, he earned the Springarn Medal for his work in agricultural chemistry. In 1939, he was awarded the Theodore Roosevelt Medal. In 1951, eight years after Carver's death, the George Washington Carver National Monument was built on part of the farm where he had been born.

Discussion Questions

1. Why were some of the schools George Washington Carver attended only for African-American students?

2. Why do you think Carver chose to study peanuts?

3. In what ways was Carver a hero?

Now use the George Washington Carver Quiz Card to check your understanding of this article.

Madame C.J. Walker

Madame C.J. Walker was born in Louisiana in 1867. Her name at birth was Sarah Breedlove. Her parents, Owen and Minerva Breedlove, had been slaves before the Civil War. Walker's parents became sharecroppers after the war. The family worked together in the cotton fields from sunup until sundown. Living conditions were miserable, and Walker experienced prejudice many times in her young life.

After her parents died, Walker, her sister, and her brother-in-law moved to Mississippi. Walker's brother-in-law was extremely abusive. At the age of 14, Walker finally escaped her problems at home by marrying Moses McWilliams. After four years of marriage, they had a baby girl. When Walker was twenty years old, her husband was murdered. Faced with raising a two-year-old by herself, she moved to St. Louis, Missouri, where she had family who could help her. She earned money by doing laundry and cooking for others. She worked hard to make sure her daughter went to school even though she had never had the opportunity to go.

One day, Walker realized that she, like other African-American women, was experiencing hair loss due to the tightly wrapped hairstyle that was popular at that time. She developed a special medicine that promoted hair growth. The medicine was made by mixing existing medicines with some secret ingredients. Walker's concoction worked and became very popular. She went on to invent five different hair-care products. Then she moved in with her sister-in-law in Denver, Colorado. Walker, her sister-in-law, and her nieces put the hair-care products into jars and sold them by going door to door. About six months after starting the business, Walker married a newspaper man named C.J. Walker, whom she later divorced. She retained the name Madame C.J. Walker and put all of her energy into making the business a huge success. Eventually Walker had so many orders that she had her own factories and laboratories built. She became the first African-American woman to become a millionaire. Until her death in 1919, Walker frequently donated large sums of money to social causes and education.

Discussion Questions

1. What would be the benefits of having a million dollars? What would be the problems?

2. Do people who work to earn a large amount of money view things differently than those who are born into a rich family? Explain your answer.

3. What kind of qualities made Madame C.J. Walker a success?

Now use the Madame C.J. Walker Quiz Card to check your understanding of this article.

Marie Curie

Marie Curie was born in 1867, in Warsaw, Poland. She was called Marie Sklodowska at birth. Her family encouraged education, but they could not afford to send her to college. Curie and her sister, Bronya, decided to help put each other through school. Curie earned money as a governess for a wealthy Warsaw family to pay for her sister's education. After five years, it was finally Curie's turn to go to school. She joined her sister in Paris. Curie studied at Sorbonne University. She was very frugal so she could afford to continue her education. In 1893, Curie earned her degree in physics and graduated first in her class. About a year after graduating, she met Pierre Curie, who was also a physicist. They fell in love and were married in 1895.

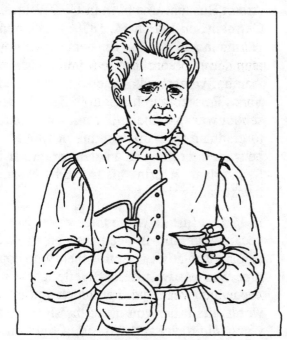

Money was tight for the young couple. However, they were still able to conduct experiments in their little shed. They were both dedicated to learning more about radioactivity. They discovered uranium ore was extremely radioactive because it contained two elements that were previously unknown. The Curies named these elements radium and polonium. In 1903, Marie and Pierre Curie and a French physicist named Antoine Henri Becquerel, who was credited with having discovered natural radioactivity, were awarded the Nobel Prize in physics.

In 1906, Pierre Curie was killed in a car accident. Deeply saddened by the loss of her husband, Marie Curie knew that she had to continue the work that they had started together. She did additional experiments on radium and polonium to discover their chemical properties. As a result of Curie's discovery and subsequent research of radium and polonium, she was given the Nobel Prize in chemistry in 1911.

Curie died in 1934 from a disease that was the result of her prolonged exposure to radiation. However, before she died she was able to see the practical use of the work she had done. Many patients' lives were saved when the diseases they were suffering from were treated using radiation therapy.

Discussion Questions

1. Why did Curie and her sister take turns going to school?

2. Why didn't Curie take special safety precautions when working with radioactive materials?

3. How do you think Curie felt when she realized the benefits that her research would have on some people's lives? Explain your answer.

Now use the Marie Curie Quiz Card to check your understanding of this article.

Albert Einstein

Albert Einstein was born in Ulm, Württemburg, Germany, on March 14, 1879. His parents were Hermann and Paulina Einstein. As a boy, Einstein attended public school in Munich, Germany, and Aarau, Switzerland. He continued his education at the Swiss Polytechnic Institute in Zurich. Even though school was extremely difficult for Einstein, he managed to graduate from the Institute in 1900. Two years later he started working as a patent examiner in Bern, Switzerland. During his free time Einstein enjoyed investigating science.

In 1905, Einstein wrote three major papers for which he became famous. In one paper, he wrote about the theory of relativity. In this theory he concluded that time was relative. He believed that the passing of time depended on the speed at which you traveled. In other words, the faster you move the slower time passes. If you could travel at the speed of light, time would actually stop. Many people are familiar with $E=mc^2$, the formula Einstein used to explain this idea.

In a second paper, Einstein described the idea for a photoelectric cell. He explained that electrons were released when photons of light energy collided with atoms in a metal. Photoelectric cells are used for products such as movies and television. In a third paper, Einstein described the atomic theory of matter. This theory stated that any tiny particles suspended in a gas or liquid moved irregularly.

Einstein worked as a professor in theoretical physics at several different universities from 1909 until the 1920's. In 1921, Einstein won the Nobel Prize for his work in physics. At the end of the 1920's, he started working on a theory to combine electromagnetism with gravitation. He spent 25 years working on this idea but was never able to formulate a theory.

In 1933, Einstein went to visit England and the United States. While he was away from Germany, the Nazi government seized all of his property and refused to let him back into the country because he was Jewish. As a result of the situation with his homeland, he became a staff member at the Institute for Advanced Study in Princeton, New Jersey, and worked there until his death on April 18, 1955.

Discussion Questions

1. Why were the things that Einstein wrote about important to the scientific community?

2. What would be some of the benefits of traveling at the speed of light? What might be some of the problems you would encounter?

3. How would you feel if your government seized your property and refused to let you back into your native country while you were abroad?

Now use the Albert Einstein Quiz Card to check your understanding of this article.

Quiz Cards

Use the following questions to assess your students' understanding of the articles on pages 105 through 108 of this unit. Have them write their answers on notebook paper.

George Washington Carver Quiz Card

1. What major event in United States history was taking place at the time George Washington Carver was born?
2. What happened to Carver's natural parents?
3. How did Carver learn to read and write?
4. Where was the first school Carver attended?
5. From where did Carver receive his degrees in agriculture?
6. What job did Carver take after graduating from college?
7. In what ways did Carver try to educate southern farmers?
8. What position did Carver hold at Tuskegee in 1914?
9. Why did peanuts become an important cash crop in the South?
10. Where is the George Washington Carver National Monument located?

Marie Curie Quiz Card

1. When and where was Marie Curie born?
2. Why did Curie work as a governess before going to college?
3. From which school did Curie earn her degree in physics?
4. Who was Pierre Curie?
5. Where did Curie and her husband conduct their experiments on radioactivity?
6. What did Curie discover about uranium ore?
7. What did Curie name the unknown parts of uranium ore?
8. What two awards did Curie earn for her work with radioactive materials?
9. What was the cause of Marie Curie's death?
10. What practical benefit did Curie see from her research?

Madame C.J. Walker Quiz Card

1. What was Madame C.J. Walker's name when she was born?
2. What job did Walker and her parents do after the Civil War?
3. When did Walker move to Mississippi?
4. How did Walker escape from her abusive brother-in-law?
5. Why do you think it was so important to Walker that her daughter get an education?
6. Why did Walker move to St. Louis, Missouri?
7. How did Walker decide to make a medicine for balding African-American women?
8. Who helped Walker prepare her hair-care products?
9. From whom did Madame C.J. Walker get her name?
10. Why do you think Walker donated money to social causes and education?

Albert Einstein Quiz Card

1. Where did Albert Einstein attend public school when he was young?
2. When did Einstein graduate from the Swiss Polytechnic Institute?
3. What kind of job did Einstein have in 1902?
4. What is Einstein's theory of relativity?
5. What mathematical formula did Einstein use to explain his theory of relativity?
6. What was Einstein's idea for the photoelectric cell?
7. What was Einstein's atomic theory of matter?
8. What honor did Einstein receive in 1921?
9. Why did Einstein remain in New Jersey in 1933?
10. How do you think Einstein was able to achieve so much in his lifetime even though he was not a good student?

Map Study

Use an almanac to learn about inventions and scientific discoveries that have been made around the world. Fill in the chart below using information from the almanac. Then use an atlas to locate the country where those discoveries or inventions were made. Color and label those countries on the map. The first one has been done for you.

Invention/Discovery	Date	Inventor/Discoverer	Country
Balloon	1783	Montgolfier	France

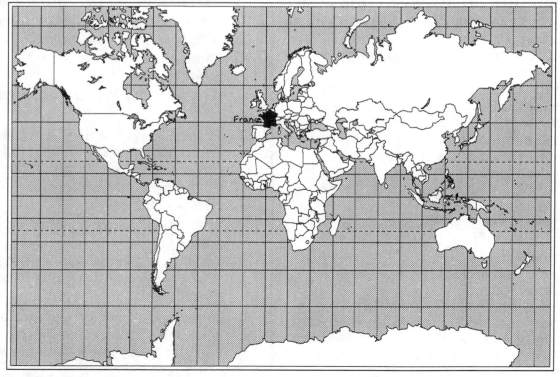

Relating the Theme

You may wish to use one or all of the following activities to supplement your own ideas about ways to integrate the *Heroes* theme into your curriculum.

Language Arts:

1. Have students watch a video about a real or fictional scientist or inventor and write a short biographical sketch about the main character in the story. Suggested videos include: *Young Einstein* (1988); *Madame Curie* (1943); *Edison, the Man* (1940); *Young Tom Edison* (1940); *The Story of Louis Pasteur* (1936); *Ford: The Man and the Machine* (1987).

2. Have students select an invention, such as the telephone or automobile. Ask them to write an essay about what their life would be like without this particular invention.

Science:

Have students work in cooperative learning groups to conduct simple experiments. See the bibliography (page 117) for a suggested list of books that include experiments.

Social Studies:

1. Using an almanac, have students make a list of the names of Nobel Prize winners for the past ten years.

2. Have students debate the positive and negative aspects of a controversial invention, such as nuclear energy. Students will need to do research about the topic before they are able to debate any issue.

Math:

1. List some simple scientific formulas, such as $E = mc^2$ (energy = mass times the speed of light squared) or $E = IR$ (voltage = current X resistance), on the chalkboard. Ask students to do research to find out who discovered the formula and what it means.

2. Write the word "googolplex" on the chalkboard. Have students use a dictionary to find its meaning.

Literature:

1. Using library resources, ask student groups to make a short bibliography of science books that are available at your school.

2. Read aloud to the class a biography or autobiography about a scientist or an inventor. Generate a discussion about the character traits of this person. Ask students to focus on what makes that person unique.

Life Skills:

1. Explain to students that recipes have ingredients and step-by-step instructions just like a science experiment does. Provide some simple recipes for students. Allow time for students to follow one or more of the recipes. After students have had some experience using recipes, you may also wish to have them write their own.

2. Have students pretend that they are inventors. Ask them to make a poster that shows a diagram of an invention that they would like to design. You may also wish to have students make a model of their invention. It does not have to be a working model. Then allow students to explain their invention to the class.

Spotlight on Science: Plant Growth

In this activity, you will plant some seeds and keep a record of their growth.

Materials:
- seeds (bean or radish seeds grow quickly)
- potting soil
- paper cups (or a planter)
- ruler

Procedure:

Step 1: Put potting soil in the paper cups.

Step 2: Plant two or three seeds. If you are using packaged seeds follow the directions on the package. Otherwise, place the seeds about an inch (2.5 cm) below the top of the soil.

Step 3: Water the seeds, making sure not to overwater them. Place them in a place where they can get some sunlight for at least part of the day.

Step 4: Continue to water the seeds as needed.

Step 5: Observe the plants as they grow. Use the space below to keep a record of the observations you make every two or three days. Begin by recording the date and writing down exactly what you see. Then use your ruler to take measurements as your plants grow. Draw a sketch to show what your plants look like.

Record of Observations
Date: _____

Record of Observations
Date: _____

Record of Observations
Date: _____

Record of Observations
Date: _____

Literature Connection

Title: *Levi Strauss: The Blue Jeans Man* **Author:** Elizabeth Van Steenwyk
Publisher: Walker and Company (1988) *(Canada: Thomas Allen & Son; UK and AUS: Baker and Taylor Int.)*

Summary: This biography describes the life of Levi Strauss. When Strauss was a young man, he left his home in Germany and sailed to America. In 1853, during the gold rush, he moved to California. He planned to work as a peddler selling the miners a variety of goods, such as tools, pots, pans, canvas, scissors, thread, needles, and broadcloth. Strauss realized that the miners needed heavy-duty pants for their work. As a result, he created work pants made out of tent canvas. He bought the idea to use rivets to connect pockets to the work pants. This is how blue jeans, which remain popular today, were invented.

Vocabulary: broadcloth, merchandise, bigotry, tuberculosis, emigration, immigrants, kosher, catastrophic, Gentiles, prejudice, intuitive, desperadoes, entrepreneurs, intercontinental, magistrates, ominous, synagogues, memoirs, philanthropy, ostracism, oblivion, sentiments, capitalism, unanimously, barricades, monopoly, refurbish

Experiencing the Literature:
1. Have students discuss ways to fight bigotry and prejudice.
2. Ask students to make an advertisement for the jeans Levi Strauss wanted to sell to the miners.
3. Have students do research to learn more about the great earthquake and fire that devastated San Francisco in 1906.

Title: *Dr. An Wang: Computer Pioneer*   **Author:** Jim Hargrove
Publisher: Childrens Press (1993) *(Canada: Riverwood Publishers; AUS: Franklin Watts)*

Summary: This biography tells about the life of Dr. An Wang. Dr. Wang was born in Shanghai, China, on February 7, 1920. In 1945, Dr. Wang left China to study applied physics at Harvard University in the United States. Dr. Wang worked hard to develop a company, called Wang Laboratories, that made innovative electronic machines. In the 1960's, Wang Labs became a huge success with its line of electronic calculators. In the 1970's, Dr. Wang's company made computers that were used by businesses all around the world. Wang Labs was stiff competition for some of the largest computer businesses in the world. The company's prosperity continued in the 1980's. Dr. Wang died of cancer in 1990. Over the next couple of years, Wang Labs, like so many computer companies, experienced economic problems due to staggering losses. The company had to declare bankruptcy, and it was broken apart and sold.

Vocabulary: corporations, innovation, bankruptcy, programmers, entrepreneur, Communists, compulsory, radio transmitters, starvation, atrocities, circumstances, electromechanical, generated, silicon, receptacles, digital, rotational, patent, matrix, McCarthyism, transistor, circuit, logarithms, juggernaut, philanthropy

Experiencing the Literature:
1. Tell students that Dr. Wang's company made inventive electronic calculators. Explain that an abacus was the first counting machine. Have students make an abacus.
2. Have students do research to learn about the history of computers.
3. Have students use a world map to label the places where Dr. Wang lived and worked.

Peanut Butter Recipes

George Washington Carver found that there were many uses for peanuts when he researched them. In this activity, you will work with two or three other students to make two recipes that use peanuts. Be sure to observe kitchen safety rules at all times and work under the supervision of an adult. Always wash your hands and collect everything you need before you begin.

Peanut Butter Candy

Ingredients:
- 3 ounces (100 g) peanut butter
- 1 stick of margarine
- 1 pound (450 g) powdered sugar
- 1 tablespoon (15 mL) vanilla extract
- food coloring (optional)

Directions:

Step 1: In a mixing bowl, stir together the margarine, peanut butter, and sugar.

Step 2: Stir in the vanilla extract.

Step 3: Place the mixture on a cutting board and roll it with your hands.

Step 4: You may wish to add food coloring to your mixture. If you do, be sure to add it one drop at a time. A little bit goes a long way!

Step 5: Use your hands to mold the mixture into different shaped candies. Once this is done, your candies are ready to eat.

Now use a cookbook to find another recipe that uses peanuts. Write the recipe on the card below. Then make the recipe, and share your final product with some friends.

Ingredients:

Directions:

Using the Scientific Method

When studying science, you should follow a step-by-step process. The steps in this process are shown in the flowchart. Study the flowchart. Then use the steps in the flowchart to complete the experiment shown at the bottom of the page.

Make Your Observations: Record all of the things that you see. Observations may take place over a period of time.

State Your Hypothesis: Tell what you think will happen and explain what you believe the reasons are for this outcome.

Test Your Hypothesis: Conduct experiments so you can gather more data, or information. If possible, have a control group for which all of the conditions stay exactly the same.

Collect Your Data: Write down any data that you get during your experiment. This data can take the form of descriptions, lists of words or numbers, charts, graphs, and sketches.

Draw Your Conclusions: Examine your data to see if it supports your conclusion. If it does not, you might need to rethink your hypothesis.

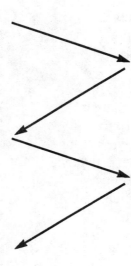

Now use the scientific method to complete this experiment.

In this experiment you will test the effects of acid rain on plant growth. Grow your seeds according to the directions shown on page 112. You may wish to grow additional seeds for this experiment.

Materials:

- 3 or more plants
- 3 labeled watering bottles
- vinegar
- water
- baking soda

Directions:

Step 1: Label the watering bottles as plain water, vinegar (acid), and baking soda (base).

Step 2: Pour plain water in one of the watering bottles.

Step 2: Pour vinegar in a second watering bottle until it is about three-fourths full. Fill with water and mix to dilute the vinegar.

Step 3: Make a mixture of baking soda and water in the third watering bottle.

Step 4: Write a number on each cup of your plants.

Step 5: Every time you water your plants, do the following:
Water plant #1 with plain water.
Water plant #2 with the diluted vinegar.
Water plant #3 with the baking soda and water mixture.

Step 6: Observe and measure the growth of your plants over a period of time.

What conclusion can you draw from this experiment?

Research Topics

Work in cooperative learning groups to research one or more of the areas mentioned below. Share your findings with the rest of the class in any appropriate form of oral presentation.

Nobel Prize Winners
Dr. Linus Carl Pauling
Madame Marie Curie
Pierre Curie
Antoine Henri Becquerel
Professor Frederick Sanger
Professor John Bardeen
Professor Francis Peyton Rous
Professor Sir William Lawrence
Sir William Henry Bragg
Theodore William Richards
Dr. Chen Ning Yang
Dr. Tsung-Dao Lee
Dr. Chien-shuing Wu

Other Heroes
Louis Braille
Alexander Graham Bell
Leonardo da Vinci
Archimedes
Pythagoras
Jan Baptist Van Helmont
John Mayow
Joseph Priestley
Henry Cavendish
Otto von Guericke
Paul Cailletet
Simon Ohm
Karl Ferdinand Braun
Heinrich Geissler
Wilhelm Konrad Rontgen
Robert Watson-Watt
Paul McCready
Jacques Garnerin

Earth Science
Landforms
Oceans
Weather
Solar System

Careers in Science
Biologist
Zoologist
Archaeologist
Physicist
Ecologist
Meteorologist
Audiologist
Computer Programmer
Computer Technician
Geologist
Oceanographer
Anthropologist
Geologist
Horticulturist
Entomologist

Related Topics
Compass
Magnifying Glass
Microscope
Telescope
Process Skills
Experiments
Control Group

Life Science
Plants
Animals
Ecology

Physical Science
Matter
Work and Energy
Electricity
Magnetism
Light
Sound

Bibliography

Experiments and Background Information

Broekel, R. *Experiments with Air.* Childrens Press, 1988.

Broekel, R. *Experiments with Straws & Paper.* Childrens Press, 1988.

Burt, McKinley, Jr. *Black Inventors of America.* National Book, 1969.

Challand, Helen. *Activities in the Physical Sciences.* Childrens Press, 1984.

Challand, Helen. *Experiments with Electricity.* Childrens Press, 1986.

Donovan, Richard X. *Black Scientists of America.* National Book Co., 1990.

Endacott, Geoff. *Discovery and Inventions.* Viking, 1991.

Gallant, Roy A. *Macmillan Book of Astronomy.* Macmillan, 1991.

Gallant, Roy A. *Young Person's Guide to Science: Ideas that Changed the World.* Macmillan, 1990.

Gardner, Robert. *Energy Projects for Young Scientists.* Watts, 1987.

Gardner, Robert. *Famous Experiments You Can Do.* Watts, 1990.

Gardner, Robert. *Kitchen Chemistry: Science Experiments to Do at Home.* Julian Messner, 1988.

Gardner, Robert. *Science in Your Backyard.* Julian Messner, 1987.

Kent, Zachary. *The Story of the Television.* Childrens Press, 1990.

Kettlekamp, Larry. *High Tech for the Handicapped: New Ways to Hear, See, Talk, and Walk.* Enslow, 1991.

Parker, Steve. *Random House Book of How Things Work.* Random, 1992.

Simon, Seymour. *How To Be an Ocean Scientist in Your Own Home.* Harper, 1988.

Sipiera, Paul P. *I Can Be a Physicist.* Childrens Press, 1991.

Ward, Alan. *Experimenting with Nature Study.* Chelsea House, 1991.

Williams, Brian. *Random House Book of 1001 Wonders of Science.* Random House, 1990.

Wulffson, D. *Invention of Ordinary Things.* Lothrop, 1981.

Zubrowski, Bernie. *Blinkers and Buzzers: Building and Experimenting with Electricity and Magnetism.* Morrow, 1991.

Zubrowski, Bernie. *Messing Around with Baking Chemistry.* Little, 1981.

Zubrowski, Bernie. *Wheels at Work: Building and Experimenting with Models of Machines.* Morrow, 1986.

Biographies

Freedman, Russell. *Wright Brothers: How They Invented the Airplane.* Holiday, 1991.

Greene Carol. *Jacques Cousteau: Man of the Oceans.* Childrens Press, 1990.

Greene Carol. *Thomas Alva Edison: Bringer of Light.* Childrens Press, 1985.

Kaye, Judith. *Life of Alexander Fleming.* 21st Century, 1993.

Kent, Zachary. *The Story of Henry Ford and the Automobile.* Childrens Press, 1993.

Kudlinski, Kathleen V. *Rachel Carson: Pioneer of Ecology.* Viking, 1988.

Lafferty. Peter. *Albert Einstein.* Watts, 1992.

McGovern. Ann. *Shark Lady: The Adventures of Eugenie Clark.* Four Winds, 1978.

McKissack, P. *Madam C.J. Walker: Self-made Millionaire.* Enslow, 1992.

Parker, Steve. *Marie Curie and Radium.* Harper, 1992.

Tames, Richard. *Alexander Graham Bell.* Watts, 1990.

Tames, Richard. *Gugleilmo Marconi.* Watts, 1990.

Tames, Richard. *Louis Pasteur.* Watts, 1990.

Teacher Created Materials

Bulletin Board Idea

Use the following bulletin board idea to introduce students to the section on Space Heroes. The patterns shown below make the bulletin board quick and easy to create. Begin by covering the background with butcher paper. Next use an opaque projector to enlarge and copy the patterns. Use glitter in a variety of colors to make the rings around the planet. Then add stars to the background using glow-in-the-dark paint. Finally, create the title "Space Heroes." This bulletin board can be used to display student work or the Quiz Cards (page 125). You can create a learning/research center by placing a table with appropriate materials in front of the bulletin board.

118   ©1994 Teacher Created Materials, Inc.

Introduction

On October 4, 1957, the space age officially began when the Soviets launched the first artificial satellite, Sputnik I, to orbit the Earth. Four years later the Soviets achieved another first when they launched a spacecraft with their cosmonaut, Yuri A. Gagarin, to orbit the Earth. Alan B. Shepherd, Jr., was the first American astronaut to go into space in May, 1961, and John H. Glenn, Jr., was the first American astronaut to orbit the Earth in February, 1962. On July 20, 1969, the first person walked on the moon. That person was the American astronaut, Neil A. Armstrong. Since those early expeditions, advanced technology has allowed space travel to improve. Today, astronauts use the space shuttle system. A space shuttle can hold up to seven crew members in addition to a payload. The benefit of using a space shuttle is that it is reusable, meaning it can make many flights.

The outline below is a suggested plan for using the various activities presented in this section of *Heroes*. Each lesson can take from one to several days to complete. You should adapt these ideas to fit your own classroom situation.

Sample Plan

Lesson 1
- Introduce section vocabulary (page 120).
- Introduce and discuss space and space travel (pages 118-120).
- Explore a map of the Earth's moon (page 126).
- Read and discuss the article about Benjamin Banneker (page 121).
- Complete the Benjamin Banneker Quiz Card (page 125).

Lesson 2
- Read and discuss the article about Neil Armstrong (page 122).
- Complete the Neil Armstrong Quiz Card (page 125).
- Choose a Relating the Theme activity (page 127).

Lesson 3
- Read and discuss the article about Christa McAuliffe (page 123).
- Complete the Christa McAuliffe Quiz Card (page 125).
- Begin reading a book related to the theme (page 129).
- Use physics to make a balloon rocket (page 128).

Lesson 4
- Read and discuss the article about Mae C. Jemison (page 124).
- Complete the Mae C. Jemison Quiz Card (page 125).
- Learn about the history of space flight (page 131).
- Choose a Relating the Theme activity (page 127).
- Begin research projects (page 132).
- Continue reading a book related to the theme (page 129).

Lesson 5
- Make a model of the space shuttle (page 130).
- Choose a Relating the Theme activity (page 127).
- Do one or more literature-related activities (page 129).
- Continue working on research projects (page 132).

Lesson 6
- Complete one or more Culminating Activities (pages 166-170).
- Share research projects (page 132).

Overview of Activities

Section Vocabulary: You may wish to introduce the following vocabulary words at the beginning of this section: galaxy, nebula, cosmos, crater, astronaut, cosmonaut, artificial satellite, orbit, space shuttle, NASA, module, solid rocket boosters, cargo compartment, liquid nitrogen, liquid oxygen, countdown, pressurized suit, radiation, ions, weightlessness, escape velocity, heat shield, stage, rendezvous, propellant, reentry.

Background Information:

- The first U.S. manned space flight orbited around Earth in May, 1961.
- Astronauts from the U.S. began exploring the moon in July, 1969.
- Astronauts from the U.S. and cosmonauts from the former Soviet Union went on their first space mission together in 1975.
- The space shuttle *Challenger* exploded in January, 1986, and all of the crew members were killed.
- The U.S. hopes to establish a permanent moon-base by the year 2010.

Bulletin Board Idea: This bulletin board is extremely easy to construct and will help set the stage for introducing the section on Space Heroes (page 118).

Articles and Discussion Questions: Four interesting articles about specific space heroes and related discussion questions are provided (pages 121-124).

Quiz Cards: These four cards provide questions about the articles to assess students' understanding of what they have read (page 125). Teachers may wish to make the Quiz Cards self-checking by duplicating the set of cards and placing the answers on the back.

Map Study: This activity helps develop map skills while providing background information about the surface of the Earth's moon (page 126).

Relating the Theme: These activities connect the theme to a variety of curriculum areas, such as reading, language arts, math, science, social studies, art, music, and life skills (page 127).

Spotlight on Physics: Students do a physics experiment by making a balloon rocket (page 128).

Literature Connection: Literature selections for this section are summarized and related activities are suggested (page 129).

Make a Model of the Space Shuttle: This hands-on activity gives students the opportunity to make a model of the space shuttle based on a diagram (page 130).

The History of Space Flight: Students work in cooperative learning groups to find out about the history of space flight (page 131).

Research Topics: These research ideas will help students better understand space and the heroes who study it and work in it (page 132). It is suggested that students work in cooperative learning groups.

Bibliography: Additional literature is suggested (page 133). The books may be used in a variety of ways, such as in a learning center, for research projects, or for book reports.

Culminating Activities: Students will pick one or more culminating activities to help them synthesize and share what they have learned (pages 166-170).

Benjamin Banneker

Benjamin Banneker was born in Baltimore County, Maryland, on November 9, 1731. His grandmother was an Englishwoman who had come to America as an indentured servant, and his grandfather was an African who had been brought to America as a slave. Banneker's grandmother had four children. Mary, the oldest, married Robert, a freed slave. Benjamin Banneker was the son of Mary and Robert.

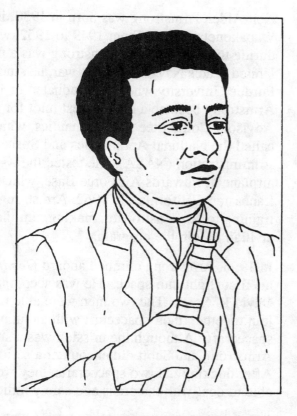

Banneker learned to read and write from his grandmother while living on the family's tobacco farm. He received a basic education from a school that was run by Quakers. Banneker's thirst for knowledge was enormous, and he read and studied anything he could. When he was in his twenties, he became fascinated by clocks and decided to build one. He used a pocket watch and a picture as his models. Historians believe that Banneker made the first mechanical clock in America. Reportedly the clock kept excellent time for fifty years. In 1781, Banneker turned his attention to studying the stars. A friend who died left Banneker some telescopes, as well as some books about astronomy. Banneker taught himself about astronomy and began work on an almanac. In the almanac, he wrote his predictions of eclipses and patterns of weather from information that he gathered about the sun, moon, and stars. Banneker published his almanac every year for ten years. Banneker's almanacs were amazingly accurate, and they became popular.

In 1790, President George Washington asked Banneker to work for the federal government as a surveyor and astronomer. Banneker proudly accepted the position. As part of his job, Banneker helped to plan the federal district for the government, known as Washington, D.C.

Discussion Questions

1. Why do you think Banneker's grandmother taught him how to read and write?

2. Why would an accurate almanac be helpful to people?

3. How would Banneker's life have been different if he had never been given the telescopes and books about astronomy?

Now use the Benjamin Banneker Quiz Card to check your understanding of this article.

Neil Armstrong

Neil Alden Armstrong was born in 1930, in Wapakoneta, Ohio. From 1949 to 1952, which was during the Korean War, Armstrong was a pilot for the United States Navy. After the war, he studied at Purdue University where he graduated in 1955. Then Armstrong became a civilian test pilot for the National Advisory Committee for Aeronautics, which today is called the National Aeronautics and Space Administration (NASA). He tested the X-15 rocket airplane at Edwards Air Force Base, which is located in Lancaster, California. In 1962, Armstrong started training to be an astronaut, making him the first civilian to join the program.

In 1966, Armstrong climbed aboard *Gemini 8* to make his first flight into space. He was accompanied by David R. Scott. The two men were able to dock, or join together, their spacecraft with an unmanned spacecraft. Although the mission was a success, Armstrong and Scott did encounter a serious problem. After docking the two spacecrafts, they went into a violent roll. Fortunately, Armstrong and Scott were able to deal with the crisis and safely return to Earth.

In July 1969, Armstrong was chosen as the commander of the *Apollo 11* mission. Armstrong and Edwin E. Aldrin, Jr., landed on the moon with the lunar module, while fellow-astronaut Michael Collins orbited the moon in the command module. People from all around the world watched as Armstrong made history on July 20, 1969, by being the first person to walk on the moon.

Armstrong retired from NASA in 1971 to become an aerospace engineering professor at the University of Cincinnati. In 1980, he started working as the chairman of a company that sold equipment used to drill for oil. In 1986, Armstrong was asked to help investigate the *Challenger* space shuttle disaster.

Discussion Questions

1. What characteristics made Neil Armstrong a good candidate for the astronaut program?

2. What would be exciting about space travel? What kinds of dangers might you encounter?

3. How do you think Armstrong felt about being the first person to walk on the moon? Explain your answer.

Now use the Neil Armstrong Quiz Card to check your understanding of this article.

Christa McAuliffe

Christa McAuliffe was born in Boston, Massachusetts, in 1948. Her name at birth was Sharon Christa Corrigan. In 1970, she graduated from Framingham State College with a bachelor's degree. That same year, she married Steven McAuliffe. Later the couple had two children. In 1978, McAuliffe graduated from Bowie State College with a master's degree in the field of education. Four years later, she was living in Concord, New Hampshire, and began to teach social studies at Concord High School.

The National Aeronautics and Space Administration (NASA) wanted to send a teacher into space, so they asked for applications. The response was overwhelming. NASA had more than 11,000 teachers interested in going into space who applied for the position. However, only one teacher could be chosen. NASA had a difficult time deciding which teacher to send. Finally, they selected McAuliffe to go on a space mission with the astronauts. This was quite an honor for McAuliffe, and she was very proud that she was going to be the first teacher in space.

McAuliffe decided the best way to remember everything about her experiences would be to keep a diary. She started the diary by writing about how she was chosen for the mission. She planned to write about the journey itself and then conclude by describing her feelings about the entire experience.

On January 28, 1986, McAuliffe boarded the space shuttle *Challenger* with six astronauts. The *Challenger* mission started off like so many other shuttle missions. However, not long after take-off the *Challenger* exploded, and all seven crew members on board were killed. Everyone was stunned and saddened by this disaster. People around the world mourned the loss of these heroes. The sacrifice that Christa McAuliffe made is not forgotten. Scholarships have been established in her name, and libraries and schools have been named after her.

Discussion Questions

1. Why do you think NASA wanted to send a teacher into space?

2. Do you think NASA should continue sending people into space in spite of the risks? Explain your answer.

3. Would you want to take a trip into space? Explain your answer.

Now use the Christa McAuliffe Quiz Card to check your understanding of this article.

Mae C. Jemison

Mae C. Jemison is the daughter of Charlie and Dorothy Jemison. She was born in Decatur, Alabama, on October 17, 1956. When Jemison was three years old her family moved to Chicago. Jemison's parents encouraged her to pursue the things that interested her. As a result, Jemison enjoyed learning about anthropology, archaeology, and astronomy.

Jemison graduated from high school in 1973 and attended Stanford University with a National Achievement Scholarship. She graduated with a bachelor's degree in chemical engineering and another bachelor's degree in Afro-American studies. In 1977, Jemison started going to medical school at Cornell University. Two years later, Jemison got special funding from the International Travelers Institute to study health conditions in Kenya. She also organized a health and law fair in New York City that same year. Jemison graduated from medical school in 1981. Within the next year, she completed her residency and began to work as a general practitioner. In 1983, Jemison went to West Africa as a medical officer in the Peace Corps. After two years, she came back to the United States and worked for a health maintenance organization (HMO) located in Los Angeles, California.

Jemison started working as an astronaut for NASA (National Aeronautics and Space Administration) in 1987. She trained to be a mission specialist and was chosen to be a member of the crew on a space shuttle mission in 1992. This mission made Jemison the first African-American woman in space. This was a joint mission, with some of the crew members from the United States and others from Japan. Jemison and the other crew members performed important experiments related to life science, materials processing, and the effects of gravity.

Discussion Questions

1. How do you think Jemison was able to accomplish so many different types of things?

2. Why does the United States embark on joint space missions with other countries, such as Japan?

3. Why are experiments conducted in space?

Now use the Mae C. Jemison Quiz Card to check your understanding of this article.

Quiz Cards

Use the following questions to assess your students' understanding of the articles on pages 121 through 124 of this unit. Have them write their answers on notebook paper.

Benjamin Banneker Quiz Card

1. From where did Benjamin Banneker's grandparents come?
2. Who taught Banneker how to read and write?
3. What models did Banneker use to make his clock?
4. Why does Banneker's clock interest historians?
5. How did Banneker learn about the stars?
6. In what type of book did Banneker publish his astronomical observations?
7. What kind of predictions did Banneker make using information he had obtained by observing the sun, moon, and stars?
8. Who asked Banneker to work for the federal government?
9. What position did Banneker hold in the federal government?
10. How do you think Banneker felt about helping to plan Washington, D.C.?

Christa McAuliffe Quiz Card

1. Where and when was Christa McAuliffe born?
2. From which college did McAuliffe earn her bachelor's degree?
3. From which college did McAuliffe earn her master's degree?
4. What job did McAuliffe have in Concord, New Hampshire?
5. How many teachers applied to go on a space shuttle mission?
6. How was McAuliffe going to document her experiences in the space program?
7. Why do you think McAuliffe wanted to document her experiences?
8. On what date did McAuliffe's mission on the *Challenger* begin?
9. What happened to the *Challenger?*
10. How is Christa McAuliffe's sacrifice remembered?

Neil Armstrong Quiz Card

1. When and where was Neil Armstrong born?
2. What event was occurring when Armstrong was a Navy pilot?
3. Where did Armstrong go to school after being in the Navy?
4. Who did Armstrong work for after graduating from the university?
5. What job did Armstrong do at Edwards Air Force Base?
6. On which spacecraft did Armstrong take his first flight into space?
7. What problem did Armstrong and Scott encounter while on their mission?
8. When did Armstrong go on the *Apollo 11* mission?
9. How did Armstrong make history during the *Apollo 11* mission?
10. How was Armstrong associated with the space program in 1986?

Mae C. Jemison Quiz Card

1. How did Jemison's parents encourage her when she was young?
2. How did Jemison pay for her education at Stanford University?
3. In which fields did Jemison earn her bachelor's degrees?
4. Why did Jemison go to Kenya?
5. Where did Jemison go to medical school?
6. What type of job did Jemison have in the Peace Corps?
7. What job did Jemison do before she started working for NASA?
8. What job did Jemison train for with NASA?
9. In what way was Jemison's trip into space considered a first?
10. What kind of experiments did Jemison and the other crew members perform?

Map Study

Study the maps of the moon. The map on the top shows the near side of the moon. The map on the bottom shows the far side of the moon. Use the grid coordinates shown in the map key to locate and label places on these maps.

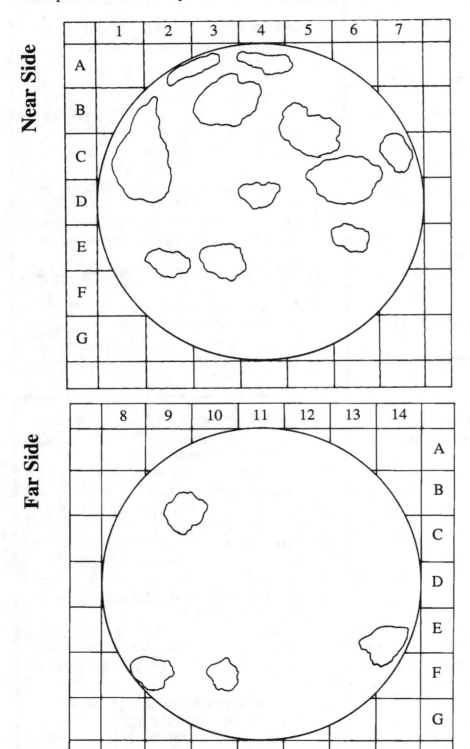

Map Key

Bay of Dew	A	2
Central Bay	D	4
Eastern Sea	E	14
Moscow Sea	B	9
Ocean of Storms	C	1
Sea of Clouds	E	3
Sea of Cold	A	4
Sea of Crises	C	7
Sea of Ingenuity	F	10
Sea of Moisture	E	2
Sea of Nectar	E	6
Sea of Rains	B	3
Sea of Serenity	B	5
Sea of Tranquility	C	6
Southern Sea	F	8

Relating the Theme

You may wish to use one or all of the following activities to supplement your own ideas about ways to integrate the *Heroes* theme into your curriculum.

Language Arts:

1. Have students make a pictionary using terminology that relates to space exploration, such as laser, space shuttle, and satellite.

2. Have students write a persuasive paragraph telling whether they think people should or should not explore other planets.

3. Have students imagine that they are on a spaceship that has landed on the moon. Ask them to write seven or eight journal entries describing their experience and how they feel about it.

Science:

1. Have students create a chart that compares science fiction with science fact.

2. Explain that the galaxy that is the closest neighbor to our own Milky Way galaxy is around the star Alpha Centauri. Have students use library resources to do a report on Alpha Centauri.

3. Ask students to work with three or four other students to make a list of facts about the moon.

Social Studies:

1. In the near future, the United States hopes to set up a colony on Earth's moon. Ask students to brainstorm a list of laws that could be used by settlers on the moon that could ensure safety and promote productivity, while guaranteeing them the same rights and freedoms that they have on Earth.

2. Have students design a base that could be used by humans to live on another planet or on Earth's moon.

Math:

1. Explain that using present technology, it takes astronauts three days and three nights to travel from the Earth to the moon. The moon is approximately 238,857 miles (382,171 km) from the Earth. Have student calculate the speed of travel based on this information.

2. Have students make a chart that shows statistical information about the planets in our solar system.

Literature:

Have students read *2001: A Space Odyssey* (NAL, 1968) and *Two Thousand Ten: Odyssey Two* (Ballantine, 1987) by Arthur C. Clarke. Then have them watch the videos of these stories. Discuss how the movie and book versions are the same and how they are different.

Art:

Have students create a model of the solar system.

Spotlight on Physics: Making a Balloon Rocket

In this physics activity, you will make a balloon rocket.
Here are the materials you will need.

- long balloon
- string or yarn
- large straw with a short piece cut off
- tape
- measuring tape

Follow these directions to make your balloon rocket.

Step 1: Place the string or yarn through the longer piece of straw. Attach the string or yarn to each side of the room.

Step 2: Blow up the balloon. Do not let the air out. You may wish to use something to clamp the neck of the balloon closed.

Step 3: Tape the longer piece of straw to the balloon, making sure not to let the air out.

Step 4: Place the shorter piece of straw into the neck of the balloon and tape it into place.

Step 5: Stand at one end of the room and let the air out of the balloon. As the air rushes out, the balloon should travel along the string or yarn.

Step 6: Launch your balloon rocket three times. Use the measuring tape to see how far your balloon rocket moves each time. Record your measurements below.

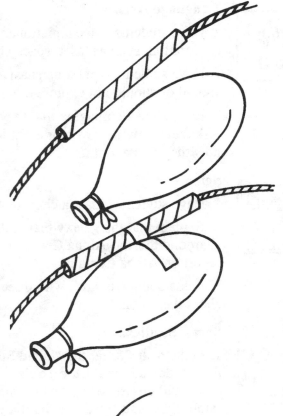

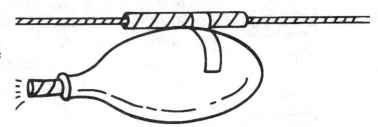

Distance 1: _____

Distance 2: _____

Distance 3: _____

Literature Connection

Title: *Sally Ride, Astronaut: An American First*   **Author:** June Behrens
Publisher: Childrens Press (1984) *(Canada: Riverwood Publishers; AUS: Franklin Watts)*

Summary: This book is a biography about Sally Ride. She was born in Los Angeles, California, in 1951. Ride went to Stanford University, where she received one bachelor's degree in English and another in astrophysics. She continued her study of astrophysics and went on to earn master's and doctoral degrees. In 1978, she was chosen to be part of NASA's astronaut training program. In 1983, Ride became the first American woman to fly in space when she served as the mission specialist aboard the space shuttle *Challenger*.

Vocabulary: pioneer, flight deck, cargo bay, satellites, astrophysics, applicants, simulated, parachute harness, determination

Experiencing the Literature:

1. Have students investigate the career field of astrophysics. If possible, invite an astrophysicist to speak to your class.

2. Ask students to pretend that it is 1983. Have them write a letter to persuade NASA that Sally Ride should be a member of the crew aboard *Challenger*.

3. Have students make a mural that shows Sally Ride in training to be an astronaut.

4. Ask students to write an adventure story about being an astronaut.

Title: *Space Challenger, The Story of Guion Bluford*   **Authors:** Jim Haskins and Kathleen Benson
Publisher: Carolrhoda Books, Inc. (1984) *(Canada: Nelson Canada, Grolier; AUS: Stafford Books)*

Summary: This story is about Guion (Guy) Bluford, the first African-American astronaut to travel in space. After earning a Ph.D. in aerospace engineering and laser physics, Bluford decided to apply for the astronaut program. He was accepted and started studying to be an astronaut. In 1984, Bluford was a mission specialist on the third flight of the space shuttle *Challenger*.

Vocabulary: simulator, vibration, inquisitiveness, aerospace engineer, artificial satellites, segregation, discrimination, laser physics, dissertation, velocity, applicants, aerodynamics, eligible, ascents, orbital, asteroid, immersion, dwarfism, dehydrated, deployment, electrodes

Experiencing the Literature:

1. Have students brainstorm a list of careers associated with space exploration. Then have them take a poll to find out how many students are interested in pursuing each career. Ask students to use the information from the poll to make a bar graph.

2. Divide the class into cooperative learning groups. Have students do research to find out about the contributions of other African Americans to the space program. Ask the groups to give an oral presentation after completing the research.

3. Have students brainstorm a list of qualities they think would be important for an astronaut to have.

4. Ask students to pretend to be Bluford. Have them write a story about the 1984 *Challenger* mission from Bluford's perspective.

Make a Model of the Space Shuttle

Have you ever wondered what it would be like to fly aboard the space shuttle? Study the diagram of the space shuttle that is shown below. Then make a model of the space shuttle. On the back of this page, write a paragraph that describes how you made your model.

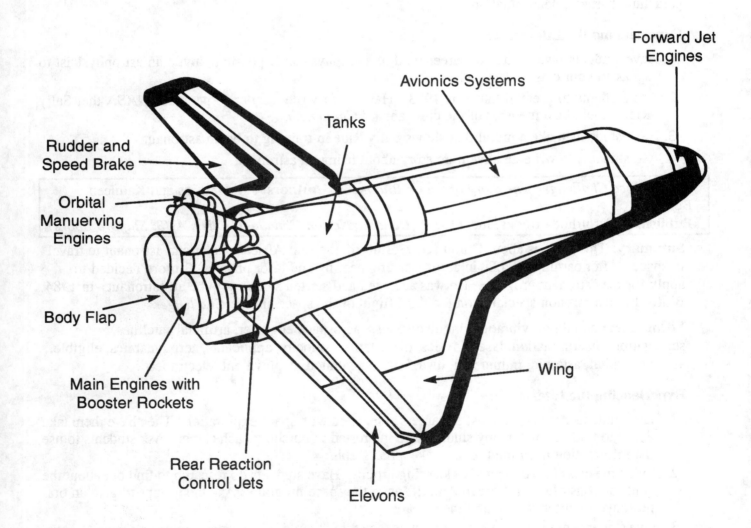

The History of Space Flight

Work with three or four other students to learn about the history of space flight. Write information about each type of launch.

1. **Mercury - Atlas** _____

   _____

   _____

   _____

2. **Titan 2** _____

   _____

   _____

3. **Saturn 5** _____

   _____

   _____

   _____

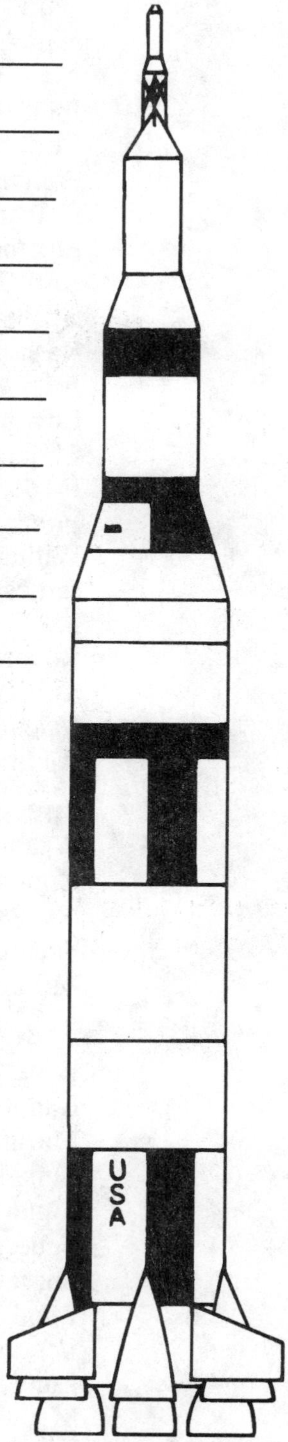

4. **Space Shuttle** _____

   _____

   _____

   _____

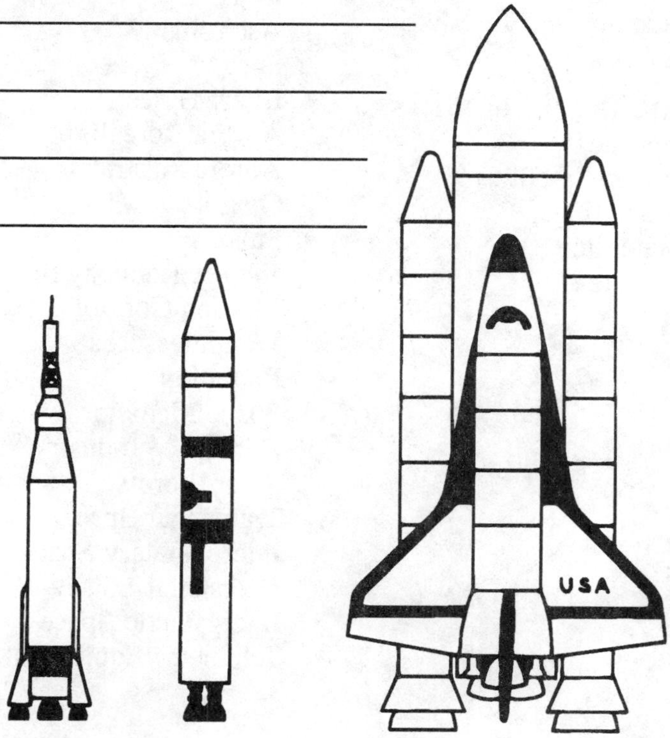

Research Topics

Work in cooperative learning groups to research one or more of the areas mentioned below. Share your findings with the rest of the class in any appropriate form of oral presentation.

Astronauts and Cosmonauts
Mae C. Jemison
Sally Ride
Guion (Guy) Bluford
Neil Armstrong
Alan B. Shepard, Jr.
John H. Glenn, Jr.
Christa McAuliffe
Franklin Chang-Diaz
Katherine Johnson
Eugene A. Cernan
Karl G. Henize
Bruce McCandless
Kathryn Sullivan
John Watts Young
Edwin Eugene Aldrin, Jr.
Thomas Patten Stafford
Frederick Gregory
Frank Borman
William A. Anders
James A. Lovell, Jr.
Michael Collins
Robert L. Crippen
Yuri Gagarin
Valentia Vladinirovna Tereshkova
Aleksey A. Leonov

Types of Artificial Satellites
Weather Satellites
Communication Satellites
Navigation Satellites
Scientific Satellites
Military Satellites

Space Probes
Luna 2
Ranger 4
Mariner 4
Luna 9
Luna 10
Venera 4
Surveyor 5
Zond 5
Venera 7
Luna 16
Mars 3
Mariner 9
Pioneer 10
Pioneer-Saturn
Mariner 10
Venera 9
Viking 1
Viking 2
Voyager 2
Voyager 1
Pioneer Venus 1
Pioneer Venus 2
Venera 11
Venera 12
Venera 13
Giotto
Magellan

Related Topics
Light Year
Meteors and Meteorites
Halley's Comet
Comets
The Sun
Solar Eclipse
Lunar Eclipse
Asteroids
Stars
Black Holes
Aurora Borealis
Aurora Australis
Quasars
Pulsars
John F. Kennedy Space Center
Mission Control
Weightlessness
Radiation
Space Medicine
Aerospace Industry
Solar Storms
Translunar Space
Interplanetary Space
Interstellar Space
Intergalactic Space
Telemetry Equipment

132   ©1994 Teacher Created Materials, Inc.

Bibliography

Abbott, David. *The Biographical Dictionary of Scientists: Astronomers.* P. Bedrick Books, 1984.

Apfel, Necia H. *Astronomy Projects for Young Scientists.* Prentice Hall, 1984.

Asimov, Isaac. *Ancient Astronomy.* Dell, 1991.

Berliner, Don. *Distance Flights.* Lerner Publications, 1990.

Borman, Frank & Serling Robert J. *Countdown: An Autobiography.* Morrow, 1988.

Branley, Franklyn M. *From Sputnik to Space Shuttle: Into the New Space Age.* HarperCollins, 1986.

Briggs, Carole S. *Women in Space: Reaching the Last Frontier.* Lerner, 1988.

Cassutt, Michael. *Who's Who in Space: The First Twenty-Five Years.* G.K. Hall, 1987.

Collins, Michael. *Carrying Fire: An Astronaut's Journey.* Bantam, 1989.

Cross, Wilber. *Space Shuttle.* Childrens Press, 1985.

Darling, David. *Could You Ever Fly to the Stars?* Macmillan, 1990.

DeOld, Alan & Judge, Joseph W. *Space Travel: A Technological Frontier.* Davis Mass, 1990.

Dewaard, John. *History of NASA: America's Voyage to the Stars.* S&S Trade, 1984.

Dickinson, Terence. *Exploring the Night Sky: The Equinox Astronomy Guide for Beginners.* Camden House, 1989.

Embury, Barbara & Crouch, Tom D. *The Dream is Alive: A Flight of Discovery Aboard a Space Shuttle.* HarperCollins, 1990.

Ferris, Jeri. *What Are You Figuring Now?: A Story About Benjamin Banneker.* Carolrhoda, 1988.

Goldsmith, Donald. *Astronomers.* St. Martin, 1991.

Hurwitz, Jane & Hurwitz, Sue. *Sally Ride: Shooting for the Stars.* Fawcett, 1989.

Joels, Kerry M. *The Official Young Astronaut Handbook.* Bantam, 1987.

Kent, Zachary. *The Story of the Challenger Disaster.* Childrens Press, 1986.

Lauber, Patricia. *Seeing Earth from Space.* Orchard Books Watts, 1990.

Long, Kim. *Astronaut Training Book for Kids.* Dutton, 1990.

MacKinnon, Douglas & Baldanza, Joseph. *Footprints: The Twelve Men Who Walked on the Moon Reflect on Their Flights.* Acropolis, 1989.

Radlauer, Ruth & Young, Carolyn. *Voyagers One & Two: Robots in Space.* Childrens Press, 1987.

Scott, Catherine D., ed. *Aeronautics & Space Flight.* Haworth Press, 1985.

Simon, Seymour. *How To Be a Space Scientist in Your Own Home.* HarperCollins, 1982.

Sullivan, George. *The Day We Walked on the Moon: A Photo History of Space Exploration.* Scholastic, 1990.

Taylor, L.B., Jr. *Space: Battleground of the Future?* Watts, 1988.

Trefil, James S. *Living in Space.* Macmillan, 1981.

Vogt, Gregory. *An Album of Modern Spaceships.* Watts, 1987.

Vogt, Gregory. *The Space Shuttle.* Millbrook Press, 1991.

Williams, Brian. *Pioneers of Flight.* Steck-Vaughn, 1990.

Wolfe, Tom. *The Right Stuff.* Bantam, 1983.

Teacher Created Materials
144 *How to Manage Your Whole Language Classroom*
145 *Portfolio Assessment for Your Whole Language Classroom*
373 *Thematic Bibliography*
502 *Write All About It: 4, 5, 6*
503 *Write All About It: 6, 7, 8*
906 *Newspaper and Reporting Set*

Bulletin Board Idea

Use the following bulletin board idea to introduce students to the section on Medical Heroes. The patterns shown below make the bulletin board quick and easy to create. Begin by covering the background with butcher paper. Use an opaque projector to enlarge and copy the patterns. Then create the title "Medical Heroes." This bulletin board can be used to display student work or the Quiz Cards (page 141). You can create a learning/research center by placing a table with appropriate materials in front of the bulletin board.

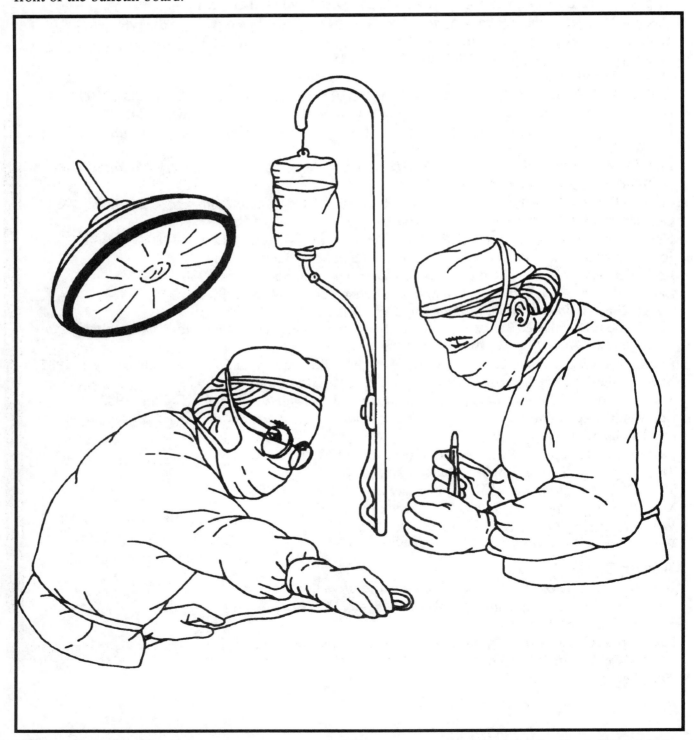

Introduction

Medical heroes are the doctors, nurses, researchers, and other specialists who have made a difference in the field of medicine. These heroes come from cultures all around the world and have made contributions throughout history. They have worked long hours trying to cure the ill and comfort the dying. Some of these people risked their personal health to improve the quality of life for others. Some even gave their life for this cause. Many medical heroes have been honored for their efforts. Some have received very special awards, such as the Nobel Prize.

The outline below is a suggested plan for using the various activities presented in this section of *Heroes*. Each lesson can take from one to several days to complete. You should adapt these ideas to fit your own classroom situation.

Sample Plan

Lesson 1
- Introduce section vocabulary (page 136).
- Introduce and discuss medical heroes (pages 134-136).
- Label a map to show where some of the medical discoveries were made (page 142).
- Read and discuss the article about Henry Ingersoll Bowditch (page 137).
- Complete the Henry Ingersoll Bowditch Quiz Card (page 141).

Lesson 2
- Read and discuss the article about Florence Nightingale (page 138).
- Complete the Florence Nightingale Quiz Card (page 141).
- Choose a Relating the Theme activity (page 143).

Lesson 3
- Read and discuss the article about Daniel Hale Williams (page 139).
- Complete the Daniel Hale Williams Quiz Card (page 141).
- Begin reading a book related to the theme (page 145).
- Keep a daily health log (page 144).

Lesson 4
- Read and discuss the article about Jane Cooke Wright (page 140).
- Complete the Jane Cooke Wright Quiz Card (page 141).
- Choose a Relating the Theme activity (page 143).
- Begin research projects (page 148).
- Continue reading a book related to the theme (page 145).

Lesson 5
- Make a diagram of body systems (pages 146-147).
- Choose a Relating the Theme activity (page 143).
- Do one or more literature-related activities (page 145).
- Continue working on research projects (page 148).

Lesson 6
- Complete one or more Culminating Activities (pages 166-170).
- Share research projects (page 148).

Overview of Activities

Section Vocabulary: You may wish to introduce the following vocabulary words at the beginning of this section: anesthesia, antibiotic, bacteria, virus, X-rays, blood type, vaccination, coma, transfusion, toxin, electrocardiograph, genes, sterilization, reflex, hemoglobin, syringe, influenza, infection, plasma, inoculation, malnutrition, immunity.

Background Information:

- Primitive medicine depended on magic and sorcery to prevent and cure illness.
- The use of a shaman, or medicine man, is a common practice in primitive medicine.
- Medical practices in Egypt at around 2500 B.C. are considered to be most like modern medicine in that doctors defined the illness, described its symptoms, described the physical examination, indicated the choice of therapy, and gave a prognosis.
- Hippocrates, an ancient Greek, wrote a physicians' code of conduct which was used to create the Hippocratic Oath that all doctors take when they graduate from medical school.
- Advances in science and technology have triggered advances in medicine.

Bulletin Board Idea: This bulletin board is extremely easy to construct and will help set the stage for introducing the section on Medical Heroes (page 134).

Articles and Discussion Questions: Four interesting articles about specific medical heroes and related discussion questions are provided (pages 137-140).

Quiz Cards: These four cards provide questions about the articles to assess students' understanding of what they have read (page 141). Teachers may wish to make the Quiz Cards self-checking by duplicating the set of cards and placing the answers on the back.

Map Study: This activity helps develop map skills while providing background information about the location of specific medical discoveries (page 142). Students should use the map for reference throughout their study of medical heroes.

Relating the Theme: These activities connect the theme to a variety of curriculum areas, such as reading, language arts, math, science, social studies, art, music, and life skills (page 143).

Spotlight on Health: Students use a daily log to keep track of their health habits (page 144).

Literature Connection: Literature selections for this section are summarized and related activities are suggested (page 145).

Make a Diagram of Body Systems: This hands-on activity gives students the opportunity to make an diagram with acetate overlays to show different body systems (pages 146-147).

Research Topics: These research ideas will help students better understand medical heroes (page 148). It is suggested that students work in cooperative learning groups.

Bibliography: Additional literature is suggested (page 149). The books may be used in a variety of ways, such as in a learning center, for research projects, or for book reports.

Culminating Activities: Students will pick one or more culminating activities to help them synthesize and share what they have learned (page 166-170).

Henry Ingersoll Bowditch

Henry Ingersoll Bowditch was born on August 9, 1808, in Salem, Massachusetts. His father was a famous mathematician named Nathaniel Bowditch, and his mother was Mary. Bowditch went to private school when he was young. When his family moved to Boston in 1823, he attended Public Latin School. Bowditch went on to study at Harvard College where he graduated in 1828. He was not sure what he wanted to do with his life, so he decided to enter Harvard Medical School. In 1832, Bowditch graduated with a degree in medicine. During his internship at Massachusetts General Hospital, Bowditch discovered that he really enjoyed the field of medicine.

Bowditch traveled to Europe in order to study medicine in France. While in Paris, he had the opportunity to work with some of the finest French physicians. They taught him to make close observations and use inductive reasoning. They inspired him to be deeply committed to the study of medicine. After spending a year in France, Bowditch went to study medicine in England. However, he did not feel that the English were as advanced in the field of medicine as the French. As a result, he returned to France for one more year of study.

In 1834, Bowditch went home to Boston where he started a medical practice. He was extremely opposed to slavery and joined the work of the abolitionists. He helped many slaves escape to the North and spoke out against fugitive slave laws. In 1861, the Civil War was being fought, and Bowditch volunteered to be a doctor for Union soldiers who were fighting in Virginia. He worked hard to convince the Senate to institute an army ambulance corps so that wounded soldiers could be taken off of the battlefield.

Bowditch also struggled to improve public health in the 1860's by making people more aware of how tuberculosis was being spread. He helped to create many health boards that were used to monitor public health. He personally served on many of these boards. In 1879, he became the president of the American Medical Association. Until his death on January 14, 1892, Bowditch spoke out about many public health issues and encouraged women to pursue a career in medicine.

Discussion Questions

1. Why did Bowditch decide to go to Europe to study medicine?

2. Why did Bowditch think it was important to have an army ambulance corps?

3. Why do you think Bowditch cared about public health issues?

Now use the Henry Ingersoll Bowditch Quiz Card to check your understanding of this article.

Florence Nightingale

In 1854, a nurse named Florence Nightingale was determined to make a difference during the Crimean War. Nightingale organized a group of nurses to care for wounded British soldiers. She and the other nurses boarded a ship in England and set sail for a hospital in Scutari, Turkey. When they arrived at the hospital, the nurses saw that it was surrounded by mud and trash. However, the worst was yet to come. Upon entering the hospital, Nightingale and her nurses could not believe the deplorable conditions these soldiers had to endure. Everything in the hospital was dirty and falling apart. Rats moved about freely. Soldiers who were sick or injured lay on bed after bed. But there were not enough beds to go around, so many other soldiers were on the floor. The hospital had few or no supplies. The soldiers often went without food and medicine. There was not enough clothing, blankets, or equipment.

The hospital's doctors and staff did not welcome the nurses. They felt the nurses would be more trouble than they were worth. They would not allow the nurses to help the soldiers. The nurses were not given any supplies except for a daily pint of water intended for drinking and washing.

Every day more sick and wounded soldiers arrived at the hospital from the battlefield. Conditions got increasingly worse, and the stench of human refuse filled the air. The situation seemed hopeless. But Nightingale was more determined than ever to make the hospital a better place. Against army regulations, she went to Constantinople to purchase supplies. She made sure the orderlies cleaned and scrubbed everything in the hospital. She had the patients' clothes washed regularly. She managed to obtain money that was raised in England to buy additional supplies. Not only did Nightingale attend to all these administrative duties, she also spent countless hours caring for the sick and dying. The doctors were inspired by her dedication, and the soldiers felt that she was an angel of mercy. Nightingale ensured the survival of many soldiers who might otherwise have died.

In 1856, after the war had ended, Nightingale went home to England. She was honored as a hero for her work in the Crimea. Once home, Nightingale's commitment to helping others continued. She worked to improve the quality of army and civilian hospitals.

Discussion Questions

1. What kinds of problems do you think nurses encounter working in a war zone?

2. What do you think made Florence Nightingale risk her own life to ease the suffering of others?

3. How do you think morale affected the survival rate of the sick and wounded soldiers?

Now use the Florence Nightingale Quiz Card to check your understanding of this article.

Daniel Hale Williams

Daniel Hale Williams was an African American who was born in Hollidaysburg, Pennsylvania, on January 18, 1856. His mother was Sarah Ann Williams, and his father was Daniel Williams, Jr., a barber and abolitionist. When Williams was eleven years old his father died, and he became an apprentice for a shoemaker in Baltimore. It was at this job that Williams learned to sew. Later, he worked as a barber, a dock worker, and a deckhand on boats. At the age of 17, Williams moved to Wisconsin, worked in a barbershop, and went to Jefferson High School. Unfortunately, he became ill and had to quit school. Things started to look up for Williams when he learned how to play the bass, and he joined a band. The band was invited to give concerts throughout Wisconsin. Finally, Williams had the opportunity to go back to school, so he attended Dr. Haire's Classical Academy. For a short time after graduating, he worked in a law office. However, he found the work very boring and decided to become an apprentice for a physician named Dr. Henry Palmer.

In 1880, Williams started medical school at Chicago Medical College. He was particularly interested in surgery, a field that was relatively new at that time. It took Williams three years to complete medical school. After graduating, he opened his own medical office, he became a physician for an orphanage, and he was a surgeon for a couple of different companies.

During this period of history, many African Americans did not receive the same health care as other people. In addition, their educational opportunities, especially in the field of medicine, were severely limited. As a result, Williams worked to establish Provident Hospital and a school for nurses that would accept people of any race and never turn anyone away.

One day in 1893, a man was rushed to Provident Hospital. This man was an African American named James Cornish. During a fight, he had been stabbed in the chest with a knife, and his heart had been cut. Williams knew he had to perform heart surgery even though it had never been tried before. He carefully sewed up Cornish's heart. The surgery was a huge success, and Williams saved Cornish's life.

Discussion Questions

1. Why do you think Daniel Hale Williams was interested in doing surgery even though it was a new field in medicine and techniques were primitive?

2. How might James Cornish have been treated if he had gone to a different hospital?

3. What do you think would have happened if James Cornish had died in spite of the surgery?

Now use the Daniel Hale Williams Quiz Card to check your understanding of this article.

Jane Cooke Wright

Jane Cooke Wright was born on November 20, 1919, in New York City. Her grandfather, step-grandfather, and father were all famous doctors. As Wright grew up she went to private schools. After graduating from high school, she earned a scholarship to go to Smith College. She graduated from there with a bachelor's degree in 1942. It was no surprise to her family when Wright decided to pursue a career in medicine. She attended New York Medical College. In 1945 Wright graduated from medical school with honors. For the rest of 1945 and throughout 1946, she was an intern and completed her assistant residency at Bellevue Hospital. She worked an additional two years at Harlem Hospital doing her residency in internal medicine.

In 1949, Wright found employment as a physician at a school and at Harlem Hospital. In that same year, she started working as a clinician at Harlem Hospital's Cancer Research Foundation. Wright performed experiments to see how drugs affected tumors. This research helped advance chemotherapy treatment for cancer patients.

During the 1960's, Wright was a professor of surgery and an associate dean. She created a research program to study cancer, heart disease, and stroke. She also worked on the president's commission that was dedicated to studying and treating these diseases. Over the years, Wright has received many honors for her outstanding work in the field of medical research. She has been given awards from colleges and research foundations and frequently has been asked to give lectures at these institutions. Wright has been on the covers of magazines that include articles about her contributions to clinical research. She has also been the recipient of several honorary degrees.

Discussion Questions

1. What qualities do you think make a person a medical hero?

2. Why is medical research important?

3. Would you be interested in doing medical research? Explain your answer.

Now use the Jane Cooke Wright Quiz Card to check your understanding of this article.

Quiz Cards

Use the following questions to assess your students' understanding of the articles on pages 137 through 140 of this unit. Have them write their answers on notebook paper.

Henry Ingersoll Bowditch Quiz Card

1. Who was Henry Ingersoll Bowditch's father?
2. From which college did Bowditch graduate in 1828?
3. When did Bowditch discover that he really liked the field of medicine?
4. Why didn't Bowditch stay in England to study medicine?
5. What did Bowditch do when he returned to Boston in 1834?
6. How did Bowditch try to help slaves?
7. How did Bowditch help the Union soldiers during the Civil War?
8. Why did Bowditch want an army ambulance corps?
9. What kind of issues did Bowditch speak out on until his death?
10. Why do you think Bowditch encouraged women to enter the field of medicine?

Daniel Hale Williams Quiz Card

1. What kind of work did Daniel Hale Williams's father do?
2. What important skill did Williams learn as an apprentice for a shoemaker?
3. Why did Williams have to drop out of Jefferson High School?
4. What did Williams do after he worked in a law office?
5. Where did Williams attend medical school?
6. What area of medicine was Williams particularly interested in?
7. What jobs did Williams do after graduating from medical school?
8. What was special about Provident Hospital?
9. What happened to James Cornish?
10. What did Williams have to do to save James Cornish's life?

Florence Nightingale Quiz Card

1. In which war was Florence Nightingale a nurse?
2. Where was the hospital for British soldiers located?
3. What did the outside of the hospital look like?
4. What problems did the nurses find inside the hospital?
5. How did the doctors and staff at the hospital react to the arrival of the nurses?
6. Where did Nightingale go to buy supplies for the hospital?
7. What did Nightingale do to improve conditions at the hospital?
8. How did the doctors and soldiers come to view Nightingale as a result of her hard work?
9. How was Nightengale received when she returned home?
10. What did Nightingale do after returning home to England?

Jane Cooke Wright Quiz Card

1. Where and when was Jane Cooke Wright born?
2. Who were the doctors in Wright's family?
3. From which school did Wright earn her bachelor's degree?
4. Where did Wright go to medical school?
5. What did Wright do at Bellevue Hospital in 1945 and 1946?
6. What did Wright do at Harlem Hospital?
7. Where did Wright find her first job as a physician?
8. What kind of research did Wright do at Harlem Hospital's Cancer Research Foundation?
9. How did Wright's clinical research help patients?
10. What kind of a research program did Wright create in the 1960's?

Map Study

Medical heroes can be found in all parts of the world. Read about some of these people and their contributions in the box shown below. Use a reference book, such as an atlas, to locate the places where these contributions were made. Then color these places on the map. Finally, next to each place, write the number to show which hero is from that place. The first one has been done for you.

1. In France, in 1878, Louis Pasteur discovered the staphylococcus microbes.

2. In the United States, in 1893, Daniel Hale Williams performed the first open-heart surgery.

3. In Germany, in 1895, Wilhelm Konrad Roentgen invented X-rays.

4. In Czechoslovakia, in 1914, Dr. Elschwig performed the first transplant of a cornea.

5. In Connecticut, in 1919, Barbara McClintock discovered that genes can change positions on chromosomes.

6. In Sweden, in 1958, Ake Senning implanted the first pacemaker.

7. In Australia, in 1978, Graeme Clark invented the bionic ear for the hearing impaired.

8. In Belgium, in 1983, Claude Veraart developed glasses for the visually impaired that have small earplugs and can be used to hear ultrasound bouncing off of obstacles.

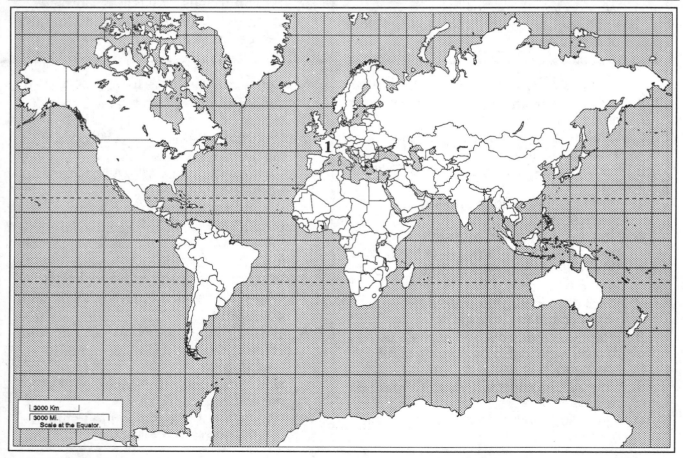

Relating the Theme

You may wish to use one or all of the following activities to supplement your own ideas about ways to integrate the *Heroes* theme into your curriculum.

Language Arts:

1. Show one or more videos about medical heroes. Suggested videos: *Nurse Edith Cavell* (1939) and *Young Dr. Kildare* (1938). Discuss the videos.

2. Have students create a pictionary of medical terms.

Science:

1. Show students how to prepare slides for a microscope. Then have students use a microscope to look at different kinds of cells. Ask them to write an essay about the similarities and differences among the cells. Display the essays on the bulletin board (page 134).

2. Discuss with students how to make a diagram and have them make one of the human eye or ear. Allow students time to share their diagram with the class.

Social Studies:

1. Plan a field trip to a local hospital or health clinic. Before going on the field trip, help students brainstorm a list of questions that they would like to ask. After returning to school, discuss what the students have learned.

2. Divide the class into cooperative learning groups. Have students do research to find out about health care in other countries. Ask students to share their information with the class.

3. Have students brainstorm a list of tools that medical professionals use. Then have them discuss the purpose of each tool.

Mathematics:

Have students brainstorm a list of expenses that a hospital or health clinic might have as you write the suggestions on the chalkboard. Then have students create a budget for that hospital or clinic. Ask what was easy about creating the budget and what was difficult.

Physical Education:

Have students create health stations around the room. Some suggested topics for the health stations include: nutrition, exercise, ways to deal with stress, and first aid. Students should include illustrations and information in the stations.

Life Skills:

1. Have students brainstorm a list of medical careers. Then take a poll to see how many people are interested in each career. You may wish to have students make a graph of the poll results.

2. Have students measure personal medical information, such as their height, weight, pulse rate at rest, and pulse rate after exercise. Then have them make a chart and record this information.

Art:

Divide the class into cooperative learning groups. Have students make a mural that shows medical heroes in action.

Health:

Have students learn first aid from a trained professional.

Spotlight on Health: A Daily Log

How healthy are your habits? Do you eat the right foods? Do you get enough exercise? Do you take time to do activities that are fun and relaxing? In this activity you will learn the answers to these questions. Use the top of this page to keep a record of your activities, such as exercise and leisure time activities. Tell what the physical and/or mental benefits are of each activity.

ACTIVITY CHART

Date: _____

Start Time	End Time	Activity	Benefit

Use the bottom of this page to keep a record of the foods you eat. Write the number of calories for each food. You can find information about calories in a cookbook.

MEALS	FOODS	CALORIES
Breakfast		
Lunch		
Dinner		
Snack		

TOTAL CALORIES: _____

Literature Connection

Title: *Alexander Fleming*   **Author:** Richard Tames
Publisher: Franklin Watts (1990) *(Canada: Gage Distributors; UK: Baker and Taylor Int.; AUS: Franklin Watts Australia)*

Summary: This is the life story of Alexander Fleming, a medical researcher. Fleming was born in 1881 outside of Ayrshire, Scotland. After the death of his father in 1901, he decided to go to medical school to become a doctor. He studied at St. Mary's Hospital Medical School. Fleming became a surgeon by 1909. During World War I, he studied bacteriology. After the war, he lectured about bacteriology at St. Mary's and continued to do medical research. In 1928, Fleming accidentally discovered the antibiotic penicillin. It was not until World War II that the value of penicillin was recognized. In 1945, Alexander Fleming was given the Nobel Prize for Medicine.

Vocabulary: inhabitants, assertive, immunizing, infectious diseases, inoculation, pathologist, compulsory, bacterial cultures, infantry regiment, ingenuity, contaminants, translucent, opaque, degeneration, bacteriologist, biochemist, meticulously, abscesses, gangrene, extracted

Experiencing the Literature:

1. Have students perform some experiments with molds on fruit or bread.
2. Provide students with copies of an almanac. Have them work in groups to make a chart that shows the discoverer and discovery dates of 15 types of medicine.
3. Have students pretend that they are a soldier during World War II whose life was saved by using penicillin. Have them write a letter to Alexander Fleming thanking him for this miracle drug.
4. Ask students to work in pairs. Have students conduct an interview by having one pretend to be a reporter and the other pretend to be Alexander Fleming.

Title: *Clara Barton: Founder, American Red Cross*   **Author:** Leni Hamilton
Publisher: Chelsea House (1988) *(Canada: Nelson; UK: Letterworth Press; AUS: CIS Publishers)*

Summary: This is the biography of Clara Barton. Barton was born in Massachusetts in 1821. When she was a young woman, she worked as a teacher. She moved to New Jersey and worked to create the first public school there. In 1853, Barton moved to Washington, D.C., and became a Patent Office clerk. After the Civil War began, she started an organization for helping soldiers. Barton made sure that supplies were sent to the soldiers. She risked her life to take care of wounded soldiers on the battlefield. She also searched for missing soldiers. The organization Barton started became known as the American Red Cross. The Red Cross continues to be active today and helps people who are victims of war and natural disasters.

Vocabulary: grim reaper, infirmary, bloodletting, deliberations, unanimous, impropriety, stamina, fraternal, consternation, languishing, indispensable, alliance, philanthropist, ascension, rehabilitation, rheumatic fever, sanitarium, predominant, integrity, famine, epidemics

Experiencing the Literature:

1. Invite someone from your local chapter of the American Red Cross to speak to your class.
2. Have students work in groups to paint a mural that shows a scene from Barton's life.
3. Ask students to write an advertisement asking people to be Red Cross volunteers.
4. Have students pretend to be Clara Barton and write diary entries describing the Civil War.

Make a Diagram of Body Systems

In this activity you will make a diagram that allows you to view four body systems at one time.

Materials: scissors, glue, posterboard, marker with a fine point, paper clips, a sheet of acetate as large as this page (Acetate is a thin, clear plastic. A sheet of overhead transparency works well for this.)

Procedure:

Cut out the box that shows the skeletal system and glue it down on a piece of posterboard that is the same size. Cut three pieces of acetate. Each needs to be the same size as the boxes on this page and the next. Paper clip the acetate over each of the other body systems. Use the marker to carefully trace the body systems on the acetate. After tracing the body systems, remove the acetate from the original. Then, place each piece of acetate over the skeletal system, taking care to line up the outline of the body each time.

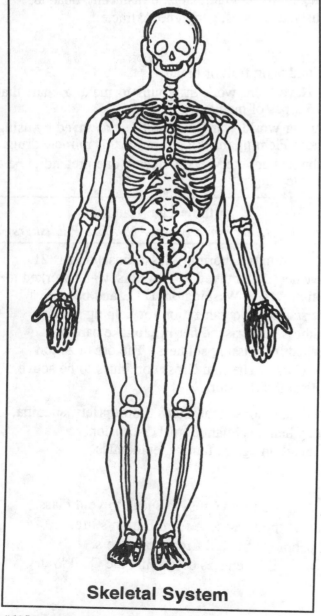

Skeletal System

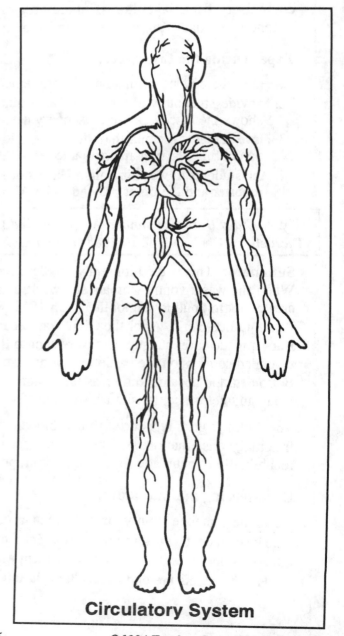

Circulatory System

Make a Diagram of Body Systems *(cont.)*

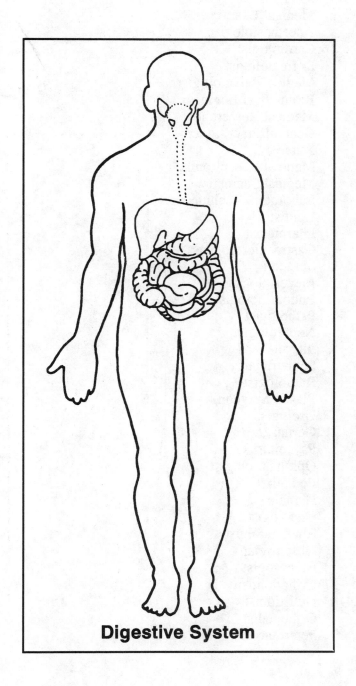

Digestive System

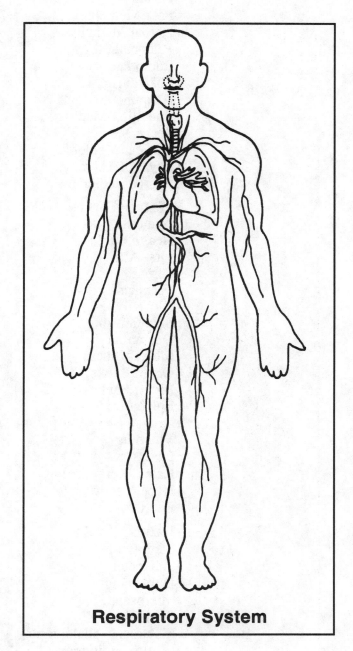

Respiratory System

Research Topics

Work in cooperative learning groups to research one or more of the areas mentioned below. Share your findings with the rest of the class in any appropriate form of oral presentation.

Types of Medicine
Biofeedback
Genetics
Folk Medicine
Herbal Medicine
Paleopathology
Radiotherapy
Shamanism
Acupuncture
Radiation Medicine
Space Medicine
Nuclear Medicine
Physical Therapy
Sports Medicine

Related Topics
Anatomy
Health Care
First Aid
Disease
Vaccines
Alchemy
Skin Grafting
Quarantine
Mental Illness
Organ Banks
Blood Banks
Epidemics
Drugs
Vitamins
Lasers
Radial Keratotomy
Hyperactivity
Red Cross

Medical Tools
Stethoscope
Telemeter
Ultrasound
Microscope
Petri Dish
Electroencephalograph
Electrocardiograph
X-rays
Sphygmomanometer
Surgical Instruments

Medical Careers
Allergist
Medical Examiner
Anesthesiologist
Cardiologist
Dermatologist
Medical Technologist
Biomedical Engineer
Medical Researcher
General Practitioner
Nurse
Medical Receptionist
Medical Secretary
Laboratory Technician
Dentist
Pharmacist
Gastroenterologist
Surgeon
Bacteriologist
Endocrinologist
Pathologist
Nephrologist
Internist
Pediatrician
Radiologist
Plastic Surgeon
Urologist
Geriatrics
Psychiatrist
Ophthalmologist
Podiatrist
Hematologist
Oncologist
Rheumatolgist
Obstetrician
Neurologist
Orthodontist
Nutritionist
Orthopedist
Veterinarian

Bibliography

Background Information

Arnold, Caroline. *Genetics: From Mendel to Gene Splicing.* Watts, 1986.

Bakay, Louis. *Neurosurgeons of the Past.* C.C. Thomas, 1987.

Berger, Melvin. *Disease Detectives.* HarperCollins, 1978.

Bourdillon, Hilary. *Women as Healers: The History of Women & Medicine.* Cambridge University Press, 1989.

Bryan, Jenny. *Heath & Science.* Watts, 1988.

Calder, Ritchie. *The Wonderful World of Medicine.* Doubleday, 1969.

Cosner, Sharon. *War Nurses.* Walker and Company, 1988.

Cowen, David L. & Helfand, William H. *Pharmacy: An Illustrated History.* Mosby, 1991.

Cryz, Stanley. *Immunotherapy & Vaccines.* VCH Publications, 1991.

DeStefano, Susan. *Focus on Medicines.* 21st Century, 1991.

Dietz, David. *All about Great Medical Discoveries.* Random House, 1960.

Eberson, Frederick. *Profiles: Giants in Medicine.* Valkyrie Publishing House, 1980.

Edelstein, L. *The Hippocratic Oath.* Ares, 1979.

Fisher, Leonard Everett. *Colonial Americans: The Doctors.* Franklin Watts, 1968.

Fraser, K. & Tatchell, J. *You & Your Fitness & Health.* EDC, 1987.

Harner, Michael J. *The Way of the Shaman.* Harper, 1990.

Heidel, William A. *Hippocratic Medicine.* Ayer, 1981.

International Who's Who in Medicine. Taylor & Francis, 1987.

Krementz, Jill. *How it Feels to Live with a Physical Disability.* Little Simon, 1992.

Levin, Beatrice. *Women & Medicine: Pioneers Meeting the Challenge.* Media Publications, 1989.

Nuland, Sherwin B. *Doctors: The Biography of Medicine.* Random House, 1989.

Sammons, Vivian O. *Blacks in Science and Medicine.* Hemisphere Publications, 1989.

Simon, Nissa. *Good Sports: Plain Talk About Health and Fitness for Teens.* Carolrhoda, 1990.

Skolnick, Georgette B. *To Be a Doctor: A Health Education Workbook.* GBS Publications, 1982.

Witty, Margot. *A Day in the Life of an Emergency Room Nurse.* Troll Associates, 1980.

Biographies

Crawford, Gail & Renna, Giani. *Albert Schweitzer.* Silver Burdett, 1990.

Crofford, Emily. *Frontier Surgeons: A Story About the Mayo Brothers.* Carolrhoda Books, 1989.

Ferris, Jeri. *Native American Doctor: The Story of Susan LaFlesche Picotte.* Carolrhoda Books, 1991.

Gaffney, Timothy. *Jerold Petrofsky: Biomedical Pioneer.* Childrens Press, 1984.

Greene, Carol. *Elizabeth Blackwell: First Woman Doctor.* Childrens Press, 1991.

Greene, Carol. *Louis Pasteur: Enemy of Disease.* Childrens Press, 1990.

Hamilton, Leni. *Clara Barton.* Chelsea House, 1988.

Jones, David E. *Sanapia: Comanche Medicine Woman.* Waveland Press, 1984.

Pepper, William. *The Medical Side of Benjamin Franklin.* Argosy, 1970.

Schleichert, Elizabeth. *The Life of Dorthea Dix.* 21st Century, 1992.

Tames, Richard. *Alexander Fleming.* Watts, 1990.

Tames, Richard. *Florence Nightingale.* Watts, 1991.

Weeks, Nora. *The Medical Discoveries of Edward Bach, Physician.* Keats, 1979.

Wolfe, Rinna. *Charles Richard Drew, M.D.* Troll Associates, 1986.

Teacher Created Materials

144 *How to Manage Your Whole Language Classroom*
145 *Portfolio Assessment for Your Whole Language Classroom*
220 *Body Basics*
235 *Thematic Unit: The Human Body*

Bulletin Board Idea

Use the following bulletin board idea to introduce students to the section on Heroes of Social Causes. The patterns shown below make the bulletin board quick and easy to create. Begin by covering the background with butcher paper. Then use an opaque projector to enlarge and copy the patterns. Finally, create the title "Heroes of Social Causes." As students study this section of the unit, you may wish to have them draw or cut out pictures of other heroes of social causes to add to the bulletin board. This bulletin board can be used to display student work or the Quiz Cards (page 157). You can create a learning/research center by placing a table with appropriate materials in front of the bulletin board.

Introduction

Heroes of social causes have come from all around the world with a variety of social and cultural backgrounds. These unique individuals appear throughout history. They are deeply moved by the suffering or injustice that they see in the world around them. They are dedicated to a cause and attempt to make the world a better place, without concern for their own safety. Heroes of social causes are not looking for personal glory or recognition, but rather they seek the satisfaction of knowing that they have put forth their best efforts to help others. These heroes are honored in many ways, such as through shrines, sculptures, special holidays, and books.

The outline below is a suggested plan for using the various activities presented in this section of *Heroes*. Each lesson can take from one to several days to complete. You should adapt these ideas to fit your own classroom situation.

Sample Plan

Lesson 1

- Introduce section vocabulary (page 152).
- Introduce and discuss heroes of social causes (pages 150-152).
- Use an environmental map (page 158).
- Read and discuss the article about Mother Teresa (page 153).
- Complete the Mother Teresa Quiz Card (page 157).

Lesson 2

- Read and discuss the article about Cesar Chavez (page 154).
- Complete the Cesar Chavez Quiz Card (page 157).
- Choose a Relating the Theme activity (page 159).

Lesson 3

- Read and discuss the article about Martin Luther King, Jr. (page 155).
- Complete the Martin Luther King, Jr., Quiz Card (page 157).
- Begin reading a book related to the theme (page 161).
- Write a newspaper article (page 160).

Lesson 4

- Read and discuss the article about Corazon Aquino (page 156).
- Complete the Corazon Aquino Quiz Card (page 157).
- Make a Directory of Social Organizations (page 163).
- Choose a Relating the Theme activity (page 159).
- Begin research projects (page 164).
- Continue reading a book related to the theme (page 161).

Lesson 5

- Make a mural (page 162).
- Choose a Relating the Theme activity (page 159).
- Do one or more literature-related activities (page 161).
- Continue working on research projects (page 164).

Lesson 6

- Complete one or more Culminating Activities (pages 166-170).
- Share research projects (page 164).

Overview of Activities

Section Vocabulary: You may wish to introduce the following vocabulary words at the beginning of this section: starvation, famine, poverty, illiteracy, aid, rights, responsibilities, gross national product (GNP), resources, unions, martyr, leader, epidemic, development, civil liberties, suffrage, philanthropy, humanitarianism, environment, ecology, activist.

Background Information:

- Every day millions of men, women, and children go hungry.
- The first leader to achieve a major revolution by non-violent resistance was Gandhi.
- The term "third world countries" refers to the underdeveloped nations of the world.
- The International Bank for Reconstruction and Development helps member countries develop a stronger economic base.
- The United Nations, an international organization, works for world peace and security. It was formed in 1945.
- The World Health organization was established in 1948.

Bulletin Board Idea: This bulletin board is extremely easy to construct and will help set the stage for introducing the section on Heroes of Social Causes (page 150).

Articles and Discussion Questions: Four interesting articles about specific heroes of social causes and related discussion questions are provided (pages 153-156).

Quiz Cards: These four cards provide questions about the articles to assess students' understanding of what they have read (page 157). Teachers may wish to make the Quiz Cards self-checking by duplicating the set of cards and placing the answers on the back.

Map Study: This activity helps develop map and chart skills while providing background information about environmental issues (page 158).

Relating the Theme: These activities connect the theme to a variety of curriculum areas, such as reading, language arts, math, science, social studies, art, music, and life skills (page 159).

Spotlight on Language Arts: Students write a front page newspaper article about a hero who has fought for a social cause (page 160).

Literature Connection: Literature selections for this section are summarized and related activities are suggested (page 161).

Make a Mural: This hands-on activity gives cooperative learning groups the opportunity to create a mural that depicts a hero fighting for a social cause (page 162).

Create a Directory of Social Organizations: Students make a miniature phone directory for organizations and agencies that do work for social causes (page 163).

Research Topics: These research ideas will help students better understand social causes and the heroes who fight for them (page 164). It is suggested that students work in cooperative learning groups.

Bibliography: Additional literature is suggested (page 165). The books may be used in a variety of ways, such as in a learning center, for research projects, or for book reports.

Culminating Activities: Students will pick one or more culminating activities to help them synthesize and share what they have learned (pages 166-170).

Mother Teresa

Mother Teresa was born in Albania, on August 27, 1910. Her name at birth was Agnes Gonxha Bojaxhiu. When she was 18 years old, she joined the Roman Catholic Order of the Sisters of Our Lady of Loreto, located in Ireland. She studied to be a nun in Dublin, Ireland, and Darjeeling, India. She took her religious vows in 1937. At that time, she went to Calcutta, India, and became the principal of a Catholic high school. Mother Teresa was concerned about all of the people she saw suffering in the city slums. She asked the church if she could work with Calcutta's poverty stricken people.

In 1948, Mother Teresa was given permission to learn how to be a nurse so she could begin a ministry for the poor and sick in India. She started the Order of the Missionaries of Charity, which is a group of Roman Catholic women who dedicate their lives to helping the poor. Then she became a citizen of India and went to live in the slums with the people she hoped to help. As people heard about Mother Teresa's compassion and dedication, many came to assist her.

Mother Teresa has accomplished many things through her hard work. She opened the first school in the slums of Calcutta. She organized clinics for people who were blind, frail, or crippled. In 1952, Mother Teresa opened a home called "Pure Heart" for people who were penniless and dying. Three years later, she created an orphanage that cared for babies that had been abandoned. In 1957, Mother Teresa oversaw the construction of a colony called "Town of Peace" for people who had leprosy.

Mother Teresa knew there were people suffering in other parts of the world. As a result, beginning in 1960, she decided the work of the Missions of Charity should be extended to other countries, such as Venezuela, Italy, Tanzania, Australia, Jordan, and England. Mother Teresa has been honored in many ways for her missionary work. In 1963, the government in India gave her an award called the Padmashri. In 1971, Pope Paul presented her with the Pope John XXIII Peace Prize. She was the first ever to receive this award. In 1979, she won the Nobel Peace Prize. To this day, in spite of her age and failing health, Mother Teresa remains dedicated to the cause of helping people who are in desperate need.

Discussion Questions

1. What qualities make Mother Teresa a hero of social causes?

2. Where do you think the help of someone like Mother Teresa is needed? Explain your answer.

3. What would be the hardest part about working with people who are desperately poor? What would be the most rewarding part of this work?

Now use the Mother Teresa Quiz Card to check your understanding of this article.

Cesar Chavez

Cesar Chavez was born in 1927. His birthplace was a farm in the Yuma, Arizona, area. When Chavez was a boy, his parents had financial problems and had to give up the farm. Chavez's parents became migrant workers in California. Migrant workers faced many hardships as they moved from farm to farm in search of employment. Chavez's family was no exception to this. Because his family was always on the move, Chavez didn't have a home, he had very little clothing, he frequently went hungry, and he never got to stay in one school for very long. As Chavez grew up working in the fields, he realized that farm workers toiled for long hours under miserable conditions and received very little pay. He also knew that his family, like so many other Mexican Americans, were the victims of discrimination. Chavez wanted to do something that would make a difference in the lives of the farm workers, many of whom were Mexican Americans.

For many years Chavez worked for an agency in California called the Community Service Organization. The purpose of this agency was to help migrant workers. Then, in 1962, Chavez became an organizer for a labor union. He motivated farmers to use nonviolent methods, such as strikes and protests, to improve their working conditions and pay. Chavez created the National Farm Workers Association. This labor union included people who picked grapes in California. Four years later, Chavez's union became a part of the United Farm Workers Organizing Committee (UFWOC). Some of the grape growers agreed to let the union bargain on behalf of the farm workers, but others would not. As a result, Chavez asked Americans to boycott, or refuse to buy, grapes. This action was successful, and the majority of the grape growers began to work with the union. After that Chavez led other boycotts that resulted in positive changes. In the 1970's, the UFWOC changed its name to the United Farm Workers of America (UFW), but its purpose has remained the same. Chavez continued to be committed to the cause of improving working conditions for farm workers until his death in 1993.

Discussion Questions

1. How is a migrant farm worker's life different from yours? How is it similar?

2. What are some things you can do to fight against discrimination?

3. Why do you think labor unions can be an effective way to cause change?

Now use the Cesar Chavez Quiz Card to check your understanding of this article.

Martin Luther King, Jr.

"I have a dream that my four children will one day live in a nation where they will not be judged by the color of their skin but by the content of their character."

Martin Luther King, Jr., was born in Atlanta, Georgia, on January 15, 1929. His mother was a teacher, and his father was a minister. When King was young, he loved to read. He was an excellent student and graduated from high school at the age of 15. He continued his education by attending Morehouse College. In 1948, he earned a bachelor's degree. He studied theology at Crozer Theological Seminar in Chester, Pennsylvania, and received a Bachelor of Divinity degree in 1951. Then he attended Boston University, where he earned a Ph.D. in 1955.

While working on his doctorate, King became a minister. In the mid-1950's, he spoke out against the discrimination that many African Americans faced. For example, during this period of time African Americans were forced, by law, to sit in the back of city buses. One day an African American named Rosa Parks was arrested in Montgomery, Alabama, for refusing to sit in the back of a bus. As a result, King urged people to stop riding that city's buses until the law was changed. When the African Americans refused to ride the buses, the city suffered a serious loss of income. The boycott was very effective and led to the desegregation of city buses all over the United States.

King was a charismatic leader of the civil rights movement. He told his followers to use nonviolent methods to force the government to change unfair and discriminatory laws. In 1963, he organized the March on Washington to make people aware of the need for equality. King often suffered abuse as a result of his beliefs. Sometimes he was arrested, and other times he was beaten. But King persevered. He knew many people, such as President John F. Kennedy, who believed in his cause. King and his followers were determined to have a Civil Rights Act passed in Congress. In 1964, the Civil Rights Act became law, and King was awarded the Nobel Peace Prize for his work. King continued to protest against racism for four more years. In 1968, the world lost one of its greatest heroes of social causes when Martin Luther King, Jr. was assassinated.

Discussion Questions

1. Why did King believe that change should be brought about by nonviolent protest?

2. What risks do protesters take when they fight for a cause? What benefits do they achieve?

3. Why do you think Martin Luther King, Jr., will be remembered throughout history as a hero of social causes?

Now use the Martin Luther King, Jr., Quiz Card to check your understanding of this article.

Corazon Aquino

Corazon Aquino was born in 1933, in the Philippines, with the name Corazon Cojuangco. When she was young, she went to school in Manila as well as parochial school in the United States. She attended Mount St. Vincent College, which is located in New York City. After graduating in 1953, she became a law student at Manila's Far Eastern University. One year later, she married Benigno Simeon Aquino, Jr.

Aquino's husband was very active in politics. He held several government positions and became a leader of the Liberal party in the Philippines. This party opposed the actions of President Ferdinand Marcos. In 1983, Aquino's husband was murdered. Aquino strongly believed that the government was responsible for the death of her husband.

After her husband's death, Aquino began working to have members of the Liberal party elected to the legislature. In the 1984 election, her hard work paid off because one-third of the legislature was from the Liberal party. Two years later, Marcos wanted a presidential election so that he could declare himself the winner once again. However, Aquino spoke out against Marcos and inspired people to vote for a change. Marcos claimed the victory, but the military and the people of the Philippines rebelled. They supported Aquino and wanted her to be their president. Marcos fled the Philippines, and Aquino took her place as the first woman president of the Philippines.

Aquino began to reorganize the government. She gave the country a new constitution and held elections for the legislature in 1987. The economy improved, but some people felt that Aquino's government was not doing enough. In 1989, some of those who were opposed to Aquino tried to take over the government. Approximately 100 people died in the fighting, but Aquino prevailed and remained the president of the Philippines.

Discussion Questions

1. Do you think Corazon Aquino would have become president if her husband had lived?

2. Why do you think it was difficult for people to oppose the existing government?

3. Would you like to be the president of a country? Explain your answer.

Now use the Corazon Aquino Quiz Card to check your understanding of this article.

Quiz Cards

Use the following questions to assess your students' understanding of the articles on pages 153 through 156 of this unit. Have them write their answers on notebook paper.

Mother Teresa Quiz Card
1. Where did Mother Teresa study to be a nun?
2. What job did Mother Teresa have after taking her religious vows?
3. What did the church give Mother Teresa permission to do in 1948?
4. What is the purpose of the Order of the Missionaries of Charity?
5. Why do you think Mother Teresa became a citizen of India?
6. What was the purpose of the home called "Pure Heart"?
7. What was the name of the leper colony Mother Teresa oversaw the construction of?
8. How did the work of the Missions of Charity change beginning in 1960?
9. What award did the government of India give Mother Teresa?
10. What awards were given to Mother Teresa in the 1970's?

Martin Luther King, Jr., Quiz Card
1. Where and when was Martin Luther King, Jr., born?
2. How old was King when he graduated from high school?
3. From which school did King earn his Ph. D.?
4. How did King get the city buses desegregated?
5. How did King want his followers to change unfair laws?
6. What event did King lead in 1963?
7. Why was King beaten and arrested at times?
8. Who was one of the important politicians who supported King's cause?
9. When did King win the Nobel Peace Prize?
10. What event happened in 1968?

Cesar Chavez Quiz Card
1. When and where was Cesar Chavez born?
2. What did Chavez's parents do after they lost the farm?
3. As many farm workers moved from place to place to find jobs, what kind of hardships did they face?
4. In what ways do you think Mexican American farm workers were discriminated against?
5. What did Chavez do to help migrant workers before he started a union?
6. What was the name of the union Chavez created in 1962?
7. What was the purpose of the union Chavez created in 1962?
8. Why did Chavez ask Americans to boycott grapes?
9. What happened as a result of the grape boycott?
10. What did the United Farm Workers Organizing Committee (UFWOC) change its name to in the 1970's?

Corazon Aquino Quiz Card
1. Where did Corazon Aquino go to school when she was young?
2. What school did she attend before becoming a law student?
3. Where did Aquino attend law school?
4. What was one purpose of the Liberal party in the Philippines?
5. How did the murder of Aquino's husband influence her political life?
6. What happened in the 1984 legislative elections?
7. What stopped Marcos from becoming the president of the Philippines in 1986?
8. What are two things that Aquino did to reorganize the government?
9. What happened in 1989?
10. How do you think Aquino felt when some rebels tried to take over the government?

Map Study

Heroes of social causes sometimes work to improve the environment. This map of the United States shows how each state rates on environmental issues. Use the information presented in the map to fill out the chart.

Map of Ratings on Environmental Issues

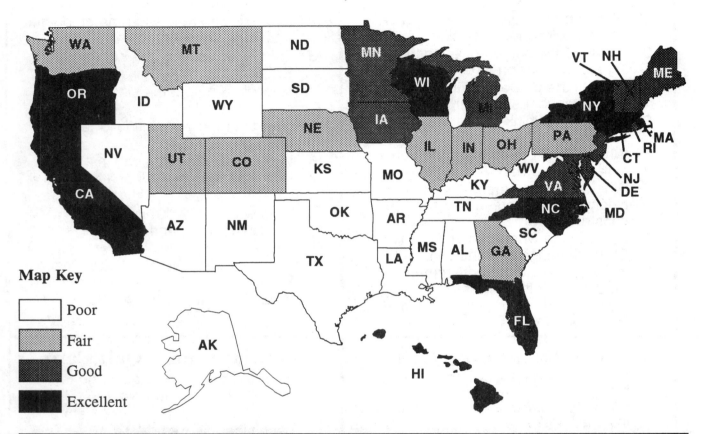

Map Key

- Poor
- Fair
- Good
- Excellent

CHART OF RATINGS ON ENVIRONMENTAL ISSUES			
Poor	**Fair**	**Good**	**Excellent**

Locate your state on the map or on the chart. What is its rating on environmental issues?

Relating the Theme

You may wish to use one or all of the following activities to supplement your own ideas about ways to integrate the *Heroes* theme into your curriculum.

Language Arts:

1. Have students trace their footprints on construction paper and cut them out. On the footprints have students write short biographical sketches about heroes of social causes. Laminate the footprints and tape them onto the floor around the classroom. On the floor near the doorway, tape a laminated sign that says, "Follow in the footsteps of the world's greatest heroes of social causes!"

2. Have students brainstorm a list of social problems. Then have them pick a social problem and write a report about how they think that problem could be solved.

3. Ask students to research and write a report on a contemporary hero of a social cause.

Science:

Explain that today there are many environmental problems, such as destruction of the rain forests, water pollution, and global warming, that need to be addressed. Have students make a poster that calls attention to an environmental problem.

Social Studies:

1. Have students brainstorm a list of things that they can do about social problems that exist in their community. For example, students might suggest that they could sponsor a food drive or start a recycling project.

2. Invite a guest speaker from a local agency or business that deals with social issues. If this is not possible, have students write letters requesting information from the agencies or businesses.

Math:

1. Divide the class into cooperative learning groups. Have each group pretend that they have one million dollars to give away to worthy causes. Have students make an itemized planning sheet that shows to whom they would make a donation and how much they would give.

2. Have students use an almanac to find out how many people have lived below the poverty line for the past five years. Ask them to illustrate this information in a bar graph.

Art:

Have students create a mural after viewing one or more of the following videos: *King, the Martin Luther King Story* (1978); *A Woman Called Golda* (1982); *Abe Lincoln in Illinois* (1940); *Eleanor, First Lady of the World* (1982); and *Gandhi* (1982).

Literature:

Have students read a book about a social hero. Then ask them to present a book report to the class.

Spotlight on Language Arts:
A Newspaper Article

Look at some front-page articles in a newspaper. Front-page articles are about important people and current events. Notice how these articles answer questions, such as who, what, when, where, how, and why. Pretend that you are a newspaper reporter. You have been asked to write a front-page article about a hero of a social cause. Select the hero that you want to write about. You can use one of the heroes named as a research topic on page 164 or you can pick one of your own. Do some research to learn more about the hero you have chosen. Then write a front-page article about that hero. No matter which hero your article is about, write about that person as if you have just witnessed his or her heroic deeds.

Today's News

_____ , 19 _____

_____   _____
_____   _____
_____   _____
_____   _____
_____   _____
_____   _____
_____   _____
_____   _____
_____   _____
_____   _____
_____   _____
_____   _____
_____   _____
_____   _____
_____   _____
_____   _____
_____   _____

Literature Connection

Title: *Susan B. Anthony, Woman Suffragist*   **Author:** Barbara Weisberg
Publisher: Chelsea House Publishers (1988) *(Canada: Nelson; UK: Letterworth Press; AUS: CIS Publishers)*

Summary: This book describes the dedication and courage of Susan B. Anthony, who fought for women's rights during the 1800's. Anthony was born in 1820, in Massachusetts. When she grew up, she began to speak publicly against alcohol and slavery. She came to the realization that women would never be able to cause social change unless they had the power to vote. For fifty years, she worked tirelessly to inform people throughout America that women should have equal rights. Anthony died in 1906 before her dream of voting rights for women was fulfilled. However, it finally became a reality when the Nineteenth Amendment to the Constitution was passed in 1920.

Vocabulary: prophetic, charismatic, enfranchise, controversial, tangible, legacies, dilemma, inherently, mortified, naturalized citizens, servitude, indictment, despotism, crusade, propriety, abolition, temperance, eradication, pandemonium, degradation

Experiencing the Literature:

1. Obtain copies of the voter's registration form. Have students fill out the form.
2. Have students hold a mock election for class president.
3. Discuss with students why the right to vote is important. Ask what it would be like if they did not have this right.
4. Have students do research to learn about voting rights in other countries.

Title: *Lincoln: A Photobiography*   **Author:** Russell Freedman
Publisher: Houghton & Mufflin (1987) *(Canada: Thomas Allen & Son; UK: Gallanoz Services; AUS: Jackarana Wiley)*

Summary: This photobiography combines historical photographs with a text that describes the life of Abraham Lincoln. The book allows the reader to see how Lincoln rose above his humble beginnings to become the president of the United States. It traces his legal and political career. Lincoln shows his courage of conviction as he struggles to hold the country together during the Civil War. The book concludes with the events surrounding Lincoln's assassination and the funeral tribute that followed.

Vocabulary: eloquent, melancholy, superstitious, abolitionist, preeminently, epidemic, candidacy, impassioned, obstacle, precedents, temperamental, sophisticated, intensity, nomination, resolutions, anecdotes, propriety, tyranny, manacled, inalienable, allegiance, supremacy, inauguration, sovereign, emancipation, proclamation, court martial, retribution

Experiencing the Literature:

1. Have students research the American Civil War and its causes.
2. Ask students to use craft sticks to make a model of the cabin in which Lincoln was born.
3. Have students summarize Lincoln's viewpoint on slavery in their own words.
4. Have students pretend to be Abraham Lincoln. Ask them to deliver one of Lincoln's speeches to the class.

Make a Mural

Work with three or four other students to choose four heroes of social causes. Use the space below to plan a mural that shows these heroes in action. Your mural can include pictures and words. Then use butcher paper to make your mural.

Directory of Social Organizations

Write the information in the boxes below to create your own directory of local organizations that benefit social causes. Use as many copies of this page as needed. Then, cut out the boxes. Next, make a cover for your directory. Finally, use staples to bind your directory together. After your directory is complete, you may wish to call some of the organizations and ask for additional information about the work that they do.

Name of Organization: **Address:** **Telephone:** **Purpose of Organization:** **Additional Information:**	**Name of Organization:** **Address:** **Telephone:** **Purpose of Organization:** **Additional Information:**
Name of Organization: **Address:** **Telephone:** **Purpose of Organization:** **Additional Information:**	**Name of Organization:** **Address:** **Telephone:** **Purpose of Organization:** **Additional Information:**

Research Topics

Work in cooperative learning groups to research one or more of the areas mentioned below. Share your findings with the rest of the class in any appropriate form of oral presentation.

Missionaries and Humanitarians
Mother Teresa
Junípero Serra
Father Joseph Damien de Veuster
Albert Schweitzer
Audrey Hepburn
Dr. Lena Edwards
Gladys Aylward
David Brainerd
Sir Wilfred Grenfell
Bartolomé de Las Casas
David Livingstone
Mary Slessor
John Williams
Captain August Martin
Samuel Ajayi Crowther

Revolutionaries
Emiliano Zapata
Toussaint L'Ouverture
José de San Martín
Bernardo O'Higgins
Maccabees
Edward Bangs
John Adams
George Washington
Simón Bolívar
Thomas Jefferson
Thomas Paine

Abolitionists
Charlotte Forten
John Brown
Frederick Douglass
Horace Greeley
Harriet Beecher Stowe
Sojourner Truth
Harriet Tubman

Civil Rights Leaders
Marcus Garvey
Martin Luther King, Jr.
Coretta Scott King
Booker T. Washington
Clarence Darrow
Eleanor Roosevelt
Lucretia Mott
Anna Dickinson
Rosa Parks
Barbara Jordan
Thurgood Marshall
Rodolfo Gonzales
Mohandas Gandhi
Benazir Bhutto

Women's Rights
Dr. Anna Shaw
Carrie Chapman
Nellie Letitia McClung
Susan B. Anthony
Elizabeth Cady Stanton
Alice Paul
Sarah and Angelina Grimké
Lucy Stone
Belva Lockwood
Carrie Chapman Catt
Jeannette Rankin

Ecologists and Environmentalists
Rachel Carson
Theodore Roosevelt
Chico Mendes
David Brower
John Muir

Organizations
UNICEF
ACTION US
VISTA
Alcoholics Anonymous
Salvation Army
Red Cross
Peace Corps
Amnesty International
Greenpeace
Save the Children Fund
Red Crescent
Sisters of Charity
Society of Friends (Quakers)
Missionaries of Charity
Oxfam
Sierra Club
Environmental Protection Agency
World Wildlife Fund

Bibliography

Adler, David A. *Martin Luther King, Jr.: Free at Last.* Holiday, 1986.

Adler, David A. *Our Golda, The Story of Golda Meir.* Viking, 1984.

Baines, Rae. *Gandhi: Peaceful Warrior.* Troll Associates, 1990.

Crawford, Gail & Renna, Giani. *Albert Schweitzer.* Silver Burdett, 1990.

DeStefano, Susan. *Chico Mendes: Fight for the Forest.* 21st Century, 1992.

DeStefano, Susan. *Theodore Roosevelt: Conservation President.* 21st Century, 1993.

De Varona, Frank. *Benito Juárez: President of Mexico.* Millbrook, 1993.

De Varona, Frank. *Simón Bolívar: Latin American Liberator.* Millbrook, 1993.

Ferris, Jeri. *Go Free or Die: A Story about Harriet Tubman.* Carolrhoda, 1989.

Ferris, Jeri. *Walking the Road to Freedom: A Story About Sojourner Truth.* Carolrhoda, 1988.

Foster, Leila Merrell. *The Story of Rachel Carson and the Environmental Movement.* Childrens Press, 1990.

Fox, Mary Virginia. *Chief Joseph of the Nez Percé Indians: Champion of Liberty.* Childrens Press, 1992.

Fradin, Dennis B. *Hiawatha: Messenger of Peace.* McElderry, 1992.

Freedman, Russell. *Lincoln: A Photobiography.* Clarion, 1987.

Hovde, Jane. *Jane Addams.* Facts on File, 1989.

Hunter, Nigel. *Gandhi.* Watts, 1987.

Kaye, Tony. *Lech Walesa.* Chelsea House, 1989.

Kent, Zachary. *Andrew Johnson: Seventeenth President of the United States.* Childrens Press, 1989.

Kent, Zachary. *The Story of John Brown's Raid on Harpers Ferry.* Childrens Press, 1988.

Kent, Zachary. *The Story of the Peace Corps.* Childrens Press, 1990.

Leoper, John J. *Crusade for Kindness: Henry Bergh and the ASPCA.* Atheneum, 1991.

Lepthien, Emilie U. *Corazon Aquino: President of the Philippines.* Childrens Press, 1987.

McAuley, Karen. *Eleanor Roosevelt.* Chelsea House, 1987.

McKissack, Pat. *Jesse Jackson: A Biography.* Scholastic, 1989.

McKissack, Pat. *Ralph J. Bunche: Peacemaker.* Enslow, 1991.

McKissack, Pat. *The Story of Booker T. Washington.* Childrens Press, 1991.

Meltzer, Milton. *Thomas Jefferson: The Revolutionary Aristocrat.* Watts, 1990.

Parks, Rosa. *Rosa Parks: My Story.* Dial, 1992.

Patrick, Diane. *Coretta Scott King.* Watts, 1991.

Pond, Mildred. *Mother Teresa.* Chelsea House, 1992.

Powledge, Fred. *We Shall Overcome: Heroes of the Civil Rights Movement.* Scribners, 1993.

Russell, Sharman. *Frederick Douglass.* Chelsea House, 1988.

Stevenson, Augusta. *Molly Pitcher: Young Patriot.* Macmillan, 1963.

Tames, Richard. *Nelson Mandela.* Watts, 1991.

Teacher Created Materials

112 *Great Americans*

288 *Thematic Unit: Explorers*

316 *Literature & Critical Thinking*

373 *Thematic Bibliography*

502 *Write All About It: 4, 5, 6*

503 *Write All About It: 6, 7, 8*

504 *Portfolios & Other Assessments*

906 *Newspaper and Reporting Set*

Outline

In this unit, you have studied many different types of heroes. You can organize the information that you learned by making an outline. Use the outline form on this page to tell about some of the heroes you have studied. After A. and B., write the names of two individuals who fit in the group of heroes shown by the main heading. Then use phrases to write two facts about each hero after 1. and 2.

I. Superheroes
   A.
      1._____
      2._____
   B.
      1._____
      2._____

II. Ancient Greek Heroes
   A.
      1._____
      2._____
   B.
      1._____
      2._____

III. Medieval Heroes
   A.
      1._____
      2._____
   B.
      1._____
      2._____

IV. Heroes of the Wild West
   A.
      1._____
      2._____
   B.
      1._____
      2._____

V. Wartime Heroes
   A.
      1._____
      2._____
   B.
      1._____
      2._____

VI. Sports Heroes
   A.
      1._____
      2._____
   B.
      1._____
      2._____

VII. Heroes of Science & Invention
   A.
      1._____
      2._____
   B.
      1._____
      2._____

VIII. Space Heroes
   A.
      1._____
      2._____
   B.
      1._____
      2._____

IX. Medical Heroes
   A.
      1._____
      2._____
   B.
      1._____
      2._____

X. Heroes of Social Causes
   A.
      1._____
      2._____
   B.
      1._____
      2._____

A Time Line

In this culminating activity, you will work with three or four other students to make a time line that shows when different heroes lived. The time line on this page is broken down into one-hundred-year increments. Write the names of heroes that belong in each century with a brief description of each hero's contribution. Then carefully cut out the time line strips. Use glue or tape to join the pieces of the time line. When you are finished, display your time line on a classroom wall.

1200 B.C.	400 B.C.	A.D. 400	A.D. 1200
1100 B.C.	300 B.C.	A.D. 500	A.D. 1300
1000 B.C.	200 B.C.	A.D. 600	A.D. 1400
900 B.C.	100 B.C.	A.D. 700	A.D. 1500
800 B.C.	A.D. 1	A.D. 800	A.D. 1600
700 B.C.	A.D. 100	A.D. 900	A.D. 1700
600 B.C.	A.D. 200	A.D. 1000	A.D. 1800
500 B.C.	A.D. 300	A.D. 1100	A.D. 1900

Book Report

In this culminating activity, you will read a biography, autobiography, or fictional story about a hero. Then develop a report about that book to present to the class. You may use one of the ways suggested below or create your own idea. After you have finished giving your report, allow time for other students to ask you questions about the hero and his or her contribution.

- **See What I Read?**

  This report is a visual one. Create a display that shows the contribution that the hero made, or make a drawing or sculpture of the hero. Then use your display, drawing, or sculpture to describe the hero and his or her contribution.

- **Guess Who or What!**

  This report is similar to the game "Twenty Questions." The reporter gives a series of general-to-specific clues about a hero described in the book. Other students try to guess which hero is being described.

- **Coming Attraction!**

  Pretend that the book you have read is about to be made into a movie, and you have been chosen to design the promotional poster. Include the title and author of the book, the name of the hero if it is not mentioned in the title, the name of the contemporary actor who will play that hero, a drawing of a scene from the book, and a paragraph synopsis of the story.

- **Literary Interview**

  This report is done in pairs. One student pretends to be the hero in the story. The other student will play the role of a television or radio interviewer, providing the audience with insights into the hero's personality and life. It is the responsibility of the partners to create meaningful questions and appropriate responses.

- **Letter to a Hero**

  In this report, you may write a letter to the hero of the book. You may wish to thank that person for his or her dedication or ask him or her questions about the heroic contribution that was made. Be sure to include information that you learned from the book in the letter.

- **Role-Playing**

  This report is one that lends itself to a group project. Work with three or four other students to role-play a scene from the book. You may wish to use costumes and props that will help the scene come to life. After performing the scene, explain why it is an important part of the story.

- **Make a Photo Album**

  Draw a series of pictures to represent photographs, showing important events in the story. Then make an album for your pictures.

- **Add Yourself to the Story**

  Rewrite your favorite part of the story, adding yourself as one of the people who knew that hero. Be sure to include conversations that take place between you and the hero.

A Patchwork Quilt

In this culminating activity, you will work with two or three other students to make a patchwork quilt that tells about the different types of heroes you have studied in this unit.

Here is what you will need to make your patchwork quilt.
- two sheets of butcher paper—each sheet: 2 feet x 2 feet (61 cm x 61 cm)
- 16 construction paper squares—each square: 6 inches x 6 inches (15 cm x 15 cm)
- colorful scraps or pieces of construction paper
- glue

Here are the directions for making your patchwork quilt.

Step 1: Pick 16 heroes that you want to tell about on your quilt. On each quilt square, you will draw a picture of a hero and write a short description of his or her contribution. Use the space below to plan what your quilt will look like.

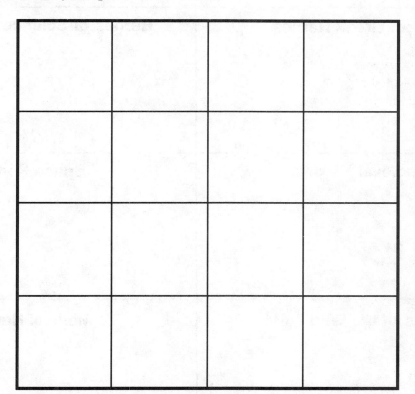

Step 2: Glue the two sheets of butcher paper together. This will make the back of your quilt and the middle layer, which is called the interlining. Allow the glue to dry.

Step 3: Decorate each construction paper square by drawing a picture of a hero and writing a brief description of that person's contribution.

Step 4: Lay your squares on the interlining according to the plan you made above. Glue the squares down onto the interlining. Allow the glue to dry.

Step 5: Display your patchwork quilt on a wall or bulletin board.

Heroes' Day

Divide the class into cooperative learning groups and have a "Heroes' Day." Have students brainstorm to make a list of activities they could use to tell other students about the different types of heroes. Then have students make the necessary preparations for the "Heroes' Day." Finally, have students invite other classes to participate in this event.

Superheroes	Sports Heroes
Ancient Greek Heroes	**Heroes of Science & Invention**
Medieval Heroes	**Space Heroes**
Heroes of the Wild West	**Medical Heroes**
Wartime Heroes	**Heroes of Social Causes**

Answer Key

Page 13

Spider-Man Quiz Card

1. Spider-Man's real identity is Peter Parker, the freelance photographer.
2. Spider-Man was raised by his Aunt May and Uncle Ben.
3. Spider-Man was bitten by a spider that had been exposed to huge amounts of radiation.
4. Spider-Man is strong and agile like a spider and is able to cling to any surface, including walls and ceilings. He also has spider-sense, which is an instinctive feeling of danger.
5. Spider-Man decided to devote his life to fighting crime because his uncle was killed by a burglar.
6. The web-shooter is used to trap criminals and to attach a swing-line to tall buildings so Spider-Man can get to high places.
7. The beacon is used to startle criminals.
8. Spider-Man wears the beacon and a camera in his belt.
9. Spider-Man sells photographs of his adventures to a daily newspaper.
10. Answers will vary.

Spider-Woman Quiz Card

1. Spider-Woman doesn't reveal her identity because she wants to protect the people that she cares about from being harmed by her enemies.
2. No one knows how Spider-Woman got her special powers.
3. Spider-Woman has extraordinary strength, endurance, and agility, and she can move her body like a spider, climbing up walls and across ceilings.
4. Spider-Woman's intuition is described as average because she is not able to sense danger any better than the ordinary person.
5. Spider-Woman uses her psychic ability to create a web.
6. The web is multidirectional and expands outward from Spider-Woman.
7. The web becomes increasingly weaker the farther away it is from Spider-Woman, and a criminal can easily break loose.
8. A criminal could escape by breaking the web.
9. If Spider-Woman loses consciousness, she cannot create or maintain a web.
10. Spider-Woman is a relatively new superhero.

Superman Quiz Card

1. Superman was born on the planet Krypton.
2. Superman had to leave Krypton because the gravitational forces became unstable and the planet was about to explode.
3. Jonathan and Martha Kent adopted Superman and named him Clark.
4. Superman moved to Metropolis when he grew up.
5. Superman works as a reporter for a newspaper called *The Daily Planet* when he is Clark Kent.
6. Clark uses a telephone booth to change into his Superman costume.
7. Superman flies at incredible speeds, leaps over tall buildings, and picks up heavy objects. He has freezing cold breath, X-ray vision, and supersensitive hearing.
8. Lead is a problem for Superman because he cannot see through it.
9. Exposure to kryptonite, especially if it's green, causes Superman to become powerless.
10. Superman was first introduced to the public in 1938 in a comic strip published as a magazine.

Storm Quiz Card

1. A mutant is human, but the DNA has been changed in some radical way that results in that person having special powers. A mutant is considered to be higher on the evolutionary scale than an ordinary person.
2. Most people are afraid of mutants because they have tremendous power.
3. Storm became an orphan because her parents were killed in an air raid.
4. Storm grew up in the streets of Cairo, Egypt.
5. Storm leads the X-Men.
6. She uses the wind to fly and to throw her enemies in all directions.
7. Storm uses her agility to escape if captured.
8. Storm's endurance is important because she has only average physical strength and must use her endurance to outlast her enemies.
9. If Storm loses control of the weather, the effects are devastating. The area experiencing the storm will suffer massive destruction.
10. An enemy could cause the end of a weather disturbance by knocking Storm unconscious.

Page 16

Answers may vary. Possible outline:

The Spider
I. Physical appearance
  A. Body
    1. Two small sections: cephalothorax, abdomen
    2. Covered with hair, bumps, and spines of skin
  B. Eyes
    1. On top and front of head
    2. Most have eight eyes
  C. Mouth
    1. Below eyes
    2. Uses straw-like appendage to drink the prey's body fluids

  D. Chelicerae
    1. Appendages between eyes and mouth with fangs at the ends
    2. Used to grab and kill prey
  E. Pedipalpi
    1. Appendages like small legs on sides of mouth
    2. For crushing food and male reproductive organ
  F. Legs
    1. Four pairs with seven segments each, ending with 2-3 claws
    2. Bend using muscles, extend using blood pressure
  G. Spinnerets
    1. At rear of abdomen
    2. Used for spinning silk
II. Food sources
  Grasshoppers, locusts, flies, mosquitoes, tadpoles, frogs, fish, mice, other spiders
III. Usefulness of spiders
  Eat insects that destroy crops and carry diseases
IV. Spider silk
  A. Made of protein in three types of glands
  B. Used for nest, catching prey, egg sacs
V. Types of spiders
  A. Tarantula
  B. Black widow
  C. Tangled-web weavers
VI. Enemies
  Wasps, snakes, lizards, frogs, toads, fish, insect-eating animals

Page 29

Hercules Quiz Card

1. Hercules showed that he had great strength by killing two serpents who were about to attack him.
2. Hercules had a terrible temper.
3. Hercules was banished from Thebes.
4. Hercules had 12 tasks to complete.
5. The hydra had several heads which could grow back if they were cut off.
6. Hercules had to use two rivers to clean the king's stables.
7. Hercules had to capture the bull that belonged to King Minos.
8. The horses Hercules stole from King Diomedes were dangerous because they ate people.
9. The tasks that made Hercules immortal were taking cattle away from the monster called Geryon, stealing Golden Apples from the Tree of Life, and catching a three-headed watchdog named Cerberus.
10. Answers will vary.

Atalanta Quiz Card

1. Atalanta's father abandoned her on the mountain because he wanted a son.
2. Atalanta was raised by a female bear.
3. Meleager was a prince who came to hunt on the mountain where Atalanta lived.
4. Meleager's family interfered in his life by refusing to let him marry Atalanta.
5. Meleager's mother caused him to die rather than let him marry Atalanta.
6. When Atalanta left the mountain, she went to Arcadia and was reunited with her father.
7. Hippomenes was afraid of losing his life and his love, Atalanta.
8. Hippomenes was able to win the race because he distracted Atalanta by throwing three golden apples in front of her feet.
9. Answers will vary.
10. Answers will vary.

Alexander the Great Quiz Card

1. Alexander was born in 356 B.C. in Pella, Macedonia, which was located in the northern part of ancient Greece.
2. As a boy, Alexander learned about military tactics from his father and about Greek culture from his tutor, Aristotle.
3. Alexander become king at a young age because his father was murdered in 336 B.C.
4. Alexander left his home in Greece to fulfill his father's dream of conquering the Persian Empire.
5. Alexander was considered a military genius because he was able to conquer an enemy's army even when his troops were greatly outnumbered.
6. Alexander chose the locations for his new cities based on water supplies.
7. Alexander immersed conquered peoples in the Greek culture and language.
8. Alexander's empire extended to the east past the Indus River in India.
9. Alexander become known as Alexander the Great because he spread Greek culture throughout his vast empire.
10. Suggested answer: After Alexander's death, his kingdom was broken up.

Helen of Troy Quiz Card

1. Stories about Helen's beauty were told throughout the land.
2. Paris kidnapped Helen and took her back to Troy with him.

3. Answers will vary.
4. Menelaus asked the Greek warriors to help him go to war against Troy and retrieve his wife.
5. Answers will vary.
6. The Greeks were never able to penetrate the walls around Troy.
7. The Greeks and Trojans fought for ten years.
8. Odysseus secretly built a large wooden horse inside of which fifty soldiers could hide.
9. The Trojans were curious about the large wooden horse.
10. Answer will vary.

Page 30

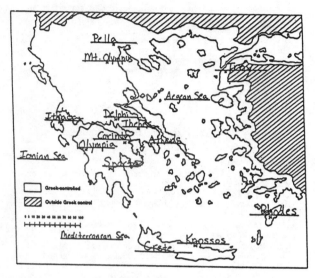

Page 32

Answers may vary. Suggested answers:

Athens: On the southern end of Attica, a peninsula in the Aegean Sea; Named after Athena, the Greek goddess; Became the world's first democracy; Democracy was set up after the tyrant Hippias was forced out of Athens; 500 citizens formed a council that suggested new laws; All citizens voted on the laws; Citizens served as jurors in courts of law; Citizenship was only given to men over age 18; Metics, foreigners who worked in Athens, could not vote or be public officials; Slaves had no rights and were assigned jobs; Had a farming economy; Used a barter system; Gold and silver coins were used later; Baby boys were preferred, so some baby girls were abandoned at the city gates where they were sometimes picked up and raised by people who passed by; Private tutors taught wealthy boys until age 7; At age 7, wealthy boys went to school for physical, cultural, and military training; Mothers taught their daughters crafts and poetry; At age 18, men served for two years in the army and then could become part of the army reserve; Men took care of the farms.

Sparta: Capital of Laconia; On the bank of the Eurotas River; Monarchy changed to an oligarchy with 30 senators, 5 of whom were ephors, or leaders; Citizens were males over age 30 who owned land; Citizens elected senators who had to be at least 60 years old; Citizens could only vote to approve or disapprove of a law; Citizens were given land and slaves for farming; Economic emphasis was on having a strong army; All men were soldiers; Unhealthy babies are left in caves to die; At age 7, boys moved into barracks and were given physical and military training; At age 7, girls were given physical training; At ages 18-30, men joined the army to complete their military training and became full citizens; Held religious festivals with chorus and dance contests.

Both: Greek city-states; Largest city-states in Greece; Governments started as monarchies; About age 15, girls married and cared for the home and children; Joined forces to fight the Persian army, their common enemy.

Page 45

King Arthur Quiz Card

1. King Uther Pendragon was said to be Arthur's father.
2. Merlin, the Celtic magician, raised Arthur.
3. Arthur pulled Excalibur from the stone, and that could only be done by the person who should be the king.
4. Arthur married Princess Guinevere.
5. Camelot was Arthur's favorite castle.
6. The knights greatly respected Arthur and wanted to serve him. They wanted to be knights of the Round Table.

7. Arthur felt that this was the best way to prevent his knights from arguing.
8. Arthur is said to have conquered most of western Europe by defeating the Roman Empire.
9. While Arthur was away, his nephew Mordred took over his kingdom.
10. Answers will vary.

Robin Hood Quiz Card

1. Robin Hood's adventures were usually described in stories and ballads beginning sometime during the 1300's.
2. Guy of Gisborne, Robin Hood and the Potter, and Lytyll Geste of Robin Hode.
3. Answers will vary.
4. Robin Hood meets the outlaws when he is rescued by them.
5. The outlaws live in Sherwood Forest in Nottinghamshire.
6. Maid Marian is the love of Robin Hood's life.
7. Friar Tuck is a rather portly and good-hearted priest.
8. Little John is a seven-foot giant of a man who is a marksman with a bow and arrow
9. The sheriff of Nottingham was one of the corrupt officials Robin Hood treated with contempt.
10. Robin Hood treated them with respect, and he stole from the rich and gave to the poor.

Joan of Arc Quiz Card

1. Joan herded sheep and cattle and helped with the crops.
2. Joan believed she was having visions of the saints.
3. Joan was told by the saints to take the king to be crowned and to get the English off of French soil.
4. Joan passed through enemy lines dressed as a soldier.
5. King Charles asked Joan to go to Orleans.
6. The French were losing against the English.
7. King Charles was crowned.
8. Joan was captured by the soldiers in Burgundy and handed over to the English.
9. Joan was found guilty of heresy and sorcery and burned at the stake.
10. Joan was about 19 years old at the time of her death.

Vassilissa Quiz Card

1. Staver was invited to a feast in Kiev given by the Grand Duke Vladimir.
2. Staver said that his wife was his most valuable possession and that she could beat any man.
3. Vladimir became angry, threw Staver in the dungeon, and sent his soldiers to get Vassilissa.
4. Pavel warned Vassilissa.
5. Vassilissa wanted the Duke's soldiers to think that she was the messenger from Kahn.
6. Vassilissa, as the messenger, told them that she had already escaped their capture.
7. The Duke had prepared a feast.
8. The Duke asked the messenger to fight three strong men.
9. The Duke proposed an archery contest.
10. Vassilissa played a game of chess and won a musician, who was her husband.

Page 46

1. During medieval times, the land that is now Spain was called the Kingdom of León, the Kingdom of Castile, the Kingdom of Navarre, the Kingdom of Aragon, and Barcelona.
2. During medieval times, the land that is now Portugal was called the Kingdom of León and the Muslim Territory.
3. During medieval times, the land that is now Great Britian was called the Kingdom of Scotland, Wales, and the Kingdom of England.
4. During medieval times, the land that is now Netherlands was called Friesland.
5. During medieval times, the land that is now Italy was called Lombardy, the Territory of Verona, the Papal States, Tuscany, and Spoleto.
6. During medieval times, the land that is now Sweden was called the Kingdom of Sweden.

Page 61

Sacajawea Quiz Card

1. Answers will vary. Possible answer: No records were made of births.
2. Sacajawea means Bird Woman.
3. She was captured by another tribe and sold to him.
4. Her husband was hired as a guide and interpreter.
5. Meriwether Lewis and William Clark led the expedition.
6. The purpose of the expedition was to explore the Northwest.
7. They met a band of Shoshone Indians.
8. She convinced the Indians not to harm them.
9. She got some horses and supplies from the Indians.
10. There is a famous statue of Sacajawea in Portland, Oregon.

Answer Key (cont.)

Wild Bill Hickok Quiz Card
1. Wild Bill Hickok's real name was James Butler Hickok.
2. He was born in Troy Grove, Illinois, in 1837.
3. He moved to Kansas.
4. It was active in the antislavery movement.
5. He was attacked by a bear and had to recover.
6. He took charge of a wagon train that took supplies from Fort Leavenworth to Sedalia.
7. He became the marshal in Hays City, Kansas.
8. He brought law and order to these wild frontier towns.
9. Hickock went with Buffalo Bill's Wild West Show.
10. He was shot in the back by Jack McCall during a poker game.

Bill Pickett Quiz Card
1. He was born near Liberty Hill, Texas, which is located on the South San Gabriel River.
2. Answers will vary. Possible answer: He needed a job to earn money.
3. He was a range rider and helped tame wild horses and mules.
4. Pickett grabbed the steer's horns, turned its head, bit it on the lip, and wrestled it down to the ground.
5. He started using it as a rodeo stunt.
6. Pickett started working for the Miller brothers in their Wild West Show.
7. He performed for about 30 years.
8. He purchased land in Oklahoma near Chandler.
9. He was stomped by a wild horse and died from his injuries.
10. Bill Pickett was honored as the first African American cowboy by the Rodeo Hall of the National Cowboy Hall of Fame in 1972.

Annie Oakley Quiz Card
1. Annie's name at birth was Phoebe Ann Moses.
2. Annie first learned to shoot at age 8.
3. Annie met Frank when she beat him in a shooting match.
4. Annie joined Buffalo Bill's Wild West Show.
5. Annie's husband assisted her during the performances.
6. The card was thrown up in the air and Annie shot a hole through it.
7. Sitting Bull's nickname for Annie was Little Sure Shot.
8. She stopped doing performances in 1901 because she was hurt in a train accident.
9. Annie joined a theatrical group in 1902.
10. During World War I, Annie worked with American soldiers to show them how to shoot.

Page 62

Page 77

Crispus Attucks Quiz Card
1. Attucks was a slave, but he ran away.
2. Answers will vary.
3. They were unhappy about conditions that were forced upon them by England.

4. He went to the town square.
5. A group of unarmed colonists went with Attucks.
6. A soldier knocked down a child.
7. Attucks grabbed the soldier's bayonet and knocked him down.
8. The soldiers opened fire on the colonists.
9. He was killed by the British soldiers.
10. This incident is recognized as the beginning of the American Revolution. It is called the Boston Massacre.

Andrea Castanon Ramirez Candalaria Quiz Card
1. Candalaria was born in Mexico.
2. Candalaria moved to Laredo, Texas.
3. She moved to San Antonio when she was 25 years old.
4. The Alamo was built by the Spanish in 1718.
5. It lasted for 12 days.
6. Candalaria was the nurse inside the Alamo.
7. He was the second in command at the Alamo.
8. Bowie died from an illness.
9. She asked them to bury rather than burn Bowie's body.
10. Thirteen women and children survived the battle.

Harriet Tubman Quiz Card
1. Harriet Tubman was a slave.
2. Her master threw an iron weight to get her to move, and the weight hit her in the head.
3. Tubman learned that her master planned to send her further south, where she knew life would be even worse.
4. It was a network of roads, underground tunnels, and homes that were used to take slaves to freedom.
5. The Underground Railroad was run by abolitionists, or people who believed that slavery was wrong.
6. Tubman was finally free when she got to Philadelphia, Pennsylvania.
7. Tubman got a job as a maid so she could help her brothers and sisters escape to freedom.
8. She joined the abolitionists in their work to free the slaves.
9. She helped 300 slaves escape to freedom.
10. Her heroic efforts led to the rescue of 756 slaves and the destruction of enemy property, the value of which totaled millions of dollars.

Audie Murphy Quiz Card
1. Murphy was born in 1924, in Kingston, Texas.
2. The Japanese bombed Pearl Harbor, and the U.S. entered World War II.
3. He was appointed to second lieutenant.
4. Murphy stood on a burning tank destroyer and killed 50 Germans with his machine gun.
5. Murphy earned the Medal of Honor.
6. Murphy was the most decorated American soldier during World War II.
7. Murphy won a total of 28 medals.
8. He was discharged in 1945.
9. He became an actor.
10. He died in a plane crash.

Page 78

World War I
European Allied Powers: Belgium, British Empire, France, Greece, Italy, Montenegro, Portugal, Romania, Russia, Serbia
European Central Powers: Austria-Hungary, Bulgaria, Germany

World War II
European Allied Powers: Belgium, Czechoslovakia, Denmark, France, Great Britain, Greece, Luxembourg, Netherlands, Norway, Poland, Russia, Yugoslavia
European Axis Powers: Albania, Bulgaria, Finland, Germany, Hungary, Italy, Romania

Page 93

Jim Thorpe Quiz Card
1. Jim Thorpe was born May 28, 1888, in Prague, Oklahoma.
2. People began to realize Thorpe's talents when he played football at the Indian Industrial School in Carlisle, Pennsylvania.
3. He gained national recognition by winning all-American honors.
4. He participated in the pentathlon and the decathlon.
5. The Amateur Athletic Union said that Thorpe had not been eligible to participate in the games because he was a professional athlete.
6. They decided to put his name back on the list of Olympic champions for 1912 and to give his gold medals to his family.
7. He started playing professional baseball.
8. He began to play professional football in 1915.
9. He became the first president of the American Professional Football Association, which today is called the National Football League.
10. He became one of the first athletes to be chosen as a member of the National Football Foundations' Hall of Fame.

Wilma Rudolph Quiz Card

1. Rudolph had double pneumonia and scarlet fever as an infant.
2. She had polio which left one of her legs crippled.
3. The doctors told her mother to massage the crippled leg and to bring Rudolph to Nashville every week for a unique water and heat therapy.
4. She wore a brace for six years.
5. Ed Temple asked Rudolph to participate in the Tennessee State College summer athletic program, and he helped her train for the 1956 and 1960 Olympics.
6. She went to Nashville to run track for the Tennessee State College in a summer athletic program.
7. She won a bronze medal.
8. She competed in the 100-meter race, the 200-meter race, and the 400-meter relay.
9. She was the first American woman to win three gold medals.
10. They gave her the Athlete of the Year award.

Orel Hershiser Quiz Card

1. Hershiser played racquetball, tennis, golf, hockey, and baseball.
2. The contest was held at Yankee Stadium in New York.
3. He needed to improve his grades and his playing ability.
4. He improved his grades and increased the speed of his pitch by five miles per hour.
5. Hershiser started playing professional baseball for the Los Angeles Dodgers' minor-league team.
6. In 1984 he pitched four shutout games.
7. In total, Hershiser pitched 532 innings in 1987 and 1988.
8. He pitched 59 innings without allowing any home runs to be scored.
9. They beat the Oakland A's.
10. Hershiser earned the Cy Young Award and was voted the Most Valuable Player of the World Series.

Kristi Yamaguchi Quiz Card

1. Kristi Yamaguchi was born with a clubfoot.
2. Before Yamaguchi was ten, Christy Kjarsgaard Ness became her coach.
3. Rudi Galindo was Yamaguchi's partner.
4. Yamaguchi won the national junior pairs championships in 1985.
5. Yamaguchi was the junior singles and pairs world champion in 1988.
6. Yamaguchi won sixth place in the singles skating.
7. Yamaguchi had more time to spend on her singles training because she discontinued her pairs training with Galindo.
8. She won both world championships in figure skating in 1991 and 1992.
9. She went to Albertville, France.
10. Yamaguchi won a gold medal in singles skating. It had been 16 years since an American woman had won a gold medal in the singles event.

Page 109

George Washington Carver Quiz Card

1. The Civil War was being fought when Carver was born.
2. His father was killed in an accident, and his mother was abducted by night raiders.
3. Carver learned to read and write from his adoptive parents.
4. The first school Carver attended was in Neosho.
5. Carver received his degrees in agriculture from Iowa State Agricultural College.
6. Carver became a faculty member at Tuskegee Institute.
7. He educated farmers by writing articles, giving lectures and demonstrations, and by taking exhibits from place to place.
8. In 1914, Carver was the head of the research department at Tuskegee.
9. Peanuts became an important cash crop because Carver discovered more than 300 ways to use peanut plants.
10. The George Washington Carver National Monument is located on part of the farm where Carver had been born.

Madame C.J. Walker Quiz Card

1. Madame C.J. Walker's name at birth was Sarah Breedlove.
2. Walker and her parents were sharecroppers, and they worked in the cotton fields.
3. She moved to Mississippi after her parents died.
4. She married Moses McWilliams to get away from her abusive brother-in-law.
5. Answers will vary.
6. Walker's husband had been murdered and she needed help raising her two year old daughter.
7. Walker realized that she, like other African-American women, was experiencing hair loss due to the tightly wrapped hairstyle that was popular at that time.
8. Walker's sister-in-law and nieces helped prepare her hair-care products.
9. She got her name from a newspaperman to whom she was married at one time.
10. Answers will vary.

Marie Curie Quiz Card

1. Marie Curie was born in 1867, in Warsaw, Poland.
2. Curie put her sister through school by working as a governess. Then Curie's sister worked to put her through school.
3. Curie earned her degree in physics at Sorbonne University.
4. He was a physicist and Marie Curie's husband.
5. They conducted their experiments on radioactivity in their shed.
6. She discovered uranium ore was extremely radioactive because it contained two elements that were previously unknown.
7. She named the elements radium and polonium.
8. She earned the 1903 Nobel Prize in physics and the 1911 Nobel Prize in chemistry.
9. She died from a disease that was the result of prolonged exposure to radiation.
10. She saw patients lives were saved when the diseases they were suffering from were treated using radiation therapy.

Albert Einstein Quiz Card

1. Einstein attended public school in Munich, Germany, and Aarau, Switzerland.
2. He graduated in 1900.
3. He worked as a patent examiner in Bern, Switzerland.
4. This theory stated that the faster you move the slower time passes.
5. Einstein used $E=mc^2$ to explain his theory of relativity.
6. Einstein described how electrons were released when photons of light energy collided with atoms in a metal.
7. This theory stated that any tiny particles suspended in a gas or liquid moved irregularly.
8. Einstein was awarded the Nobel Prize for his work in physics.
9. The Nazi government seized all of Einstein's property and refused to let him back into the country.
10. Answers will vary.

Page 110

Answers will vary.

Page 125

Benjamin Banneker Quiz Card

1. Benjamin Banneker's grandmother was from England and his grandfather was from Africa.
2. Banneker's grandmother taught him how to read and write.
3. Banneker used a pocket watch and a picture as models to make his clock.
4. Historians believe that Banneker's clock was the first mechanical clock in America.
5. Banneker taught himself about the stars using telescopes and books about astronomy.
6. Banneker published his astronomical observations in an almanac.
7. Banneker made predictions about eclipses and patterns of weather using information he had obtained by observing the sun, moon, and stars.
8. President George Washington asked Banneker to work for the federal government.
9. Banneker was a surveyor and astronomer for the federal government.
10. Answers will vary.

Neil Armstrong Quiz Card

1. Neil Armstrong was born in 1930, in Wapakoneta, Ohio.
2. The Korean War was taking place when Armstrong was a Navy pilot.
3. He went to Purdue University after being in the Navy.
4. He worked for the National Advisory Committee for Aeronautics, which today is called the National Aeronautics and Space Administration (NASA).
5. He tested the X-15 rocket airplane.
6. Armstrong took his first flight into space on *Gemini 8*.
7. After docking their spacecraft with an unmanned spacecraft, they began to roll violently.
8. He went in July, 1969.
9. He was the first person to walk on the moon.
10. He was asked to help investigate the *Challenger* space shuttle disaster.

Christa McAuliffe Quiz Card

1. Christa McAuliffe was born in Boston, Massachusetts, in 1948.
2. She earned her bachelor's degree from Framingham State College.
3. McAuliffe earned her master's degree from Bowie State College.
4. McAuliffe was a social studies teacher in Concord, New Hampshire.
5. More than 11,000 teachers applied.
6. She was going to keep a diary.
7. Answers will vary.
8. McAuliffe's mission on the *Challenger* began on January 28, 1986.
9. Shortly after take-off the *Challenger* exploded, and all seven crew members on board were killed.
10. Scholarships have been established in her name, and libraries and schools have been named after her.

Mae C. Jemison Quiz Card

1. Jemison's parents encouraged her to pursue the things that interested her.
2. She had a National Achievement Scholarship to go to Stanford University.
3. She earned her bachelor's degrees in chemical engineering and Afro-American studies.
4. She went to study health conditions in Kenya.
5. She went to Cornell University.
6. She was a medical officer in the Peace Corps.
7. She worked for an HMO.
8. She trained to be a mission specialist.
9. She was the first African-American woman in space.
10. They performed experiments related to life science, materials processing, and the effects of gravity.

Page 126

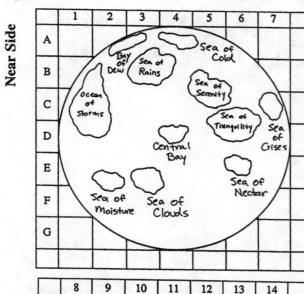

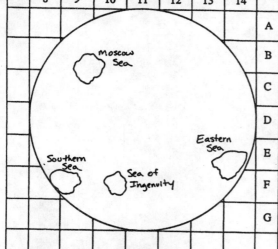

Page 131

Answers may vary. Suggested answers:

Mercury -Atlas
height - just over 95 feet (29.1 m); used in the Mercury program; U.S. astronauts orbited the Earth; 1.5 stages

Titan 2
developed from Titan missile; height - 109 feet (33.2 m); used in the Gemini program; 2 stages

Saturn 5
height - 363 feet (110.6 m); used in the Apollo program took astronauts to the moon; 3 stages

Space Shuttle
184 feet (56.1 m); uses an external tank and two solid rocket boosters to launch an orbiter; reusable orbiter; orbiter lands on a runway; holds seven crew members; 3 stages

Page 141

Henry Ingersoll Bowditch Quiz Card

1. His father was a famous mathematician named Nathaniel Bowditch.
2. He graduated from Harvard College in 1828.
3. During his internship at Massachusetts General Hospital, Bowditch discovered that he really enjoyed the field of medicine.
4. He did not feel that the English were as advanced in the field of medicine as the French.
5. He started a medical practice.
6. He helped many slaves escape to the North and spoke out against fugitive slave laws.
7. He was a doctor for the Union soldiers.
8. He wanted an army ambulance corps so that wounded soldiers could be taken off the battlefield.
9. He spoke out on public health issues.
10. Answers will vary.

Florence Nightingale Quiz Card

1. Florence Nightingale was a nurse during the Crimean War.
2. The hospital was located in Scutari, Turkey.
3. The outside of the hospital was surrounded by mud and trash.
4. Everything in the hospital was dirty and falling apart. Rats moved about freely. There were not enough beds to go around, so many other soldiers were on the floor. The hospital had few or no supplies. The soldiers often went without food and medicine. There were not enough clothing, blankets, or equipment.
5. They did not welcome the nurses and felt the nurses would be too much trouble. They would not allow the nurses to help the soldiers.
6. She went to Constantinople for supplies.
7. She had everything cleaned and scrubbed, had the patients' clothes washed regularly, obtained money for additional supplies, and spent countless hours caring for the sick and dying.
8. The doctors were inspired by her dedication, and the soldiers felt that she was an angel of mercy.
9. She was honored as a hero.
10. She worked to improve army and civilian hospitals.

Daniel Hale Williams Quiz Card

1. He was a barber and an abolitionist.
2. He learned how to sew.
3. He became ill.
4. He became an apprentice for Dr. Henry Palmer.
5. He went to Chicago Medical College.
6. He was particularly interested in surgery.
7. He had his own medical office, was a doctor for an orphanage, and was a surgeon for a couple of different companies.
8. It accepted patients of all races and never turned anyone away.
9. During a fight, Cornish had been stabbed in the chest with a knife and his heart had been cut.
10. He had to perform heart surgery and sew up the cut in Cornish's heart.

Jane Cooke Wright Quiz Card

1. Jane Cooke Wright was born on November 20, 1919, in New York City.
2. Her grandfather, step-grandfather, and father were all doctors.
3. She earned her bachelor's degree from Smith College.
4. She attended New York Medical College.
5. She was an intern and completed her assistant residency at Bellevue Hospital in 1945 and 1946.
6. She did her residency in internal medicine at Harlem Hospital.
7. She was a physician at a school and at Harlem Hospital.
8. She performed experiments to see how drugs affected tumors.
9. Her research helped advance chemotherapy treatment for cancer patients.
10. She created a research program to study cancer, heart disease, and stroke.

NO LONGER THE PROPERTY
OF THE
UNIVERSITY OF R.I. LIBRARY

UNIVERSITY OF RHODE ISLAND

3 1222 01036 023 1

Answer Key (cont.)

Page 142

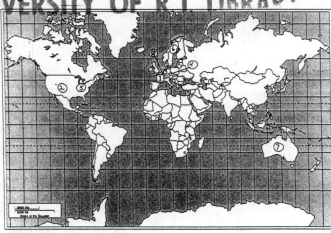

Page 157

Mother Teresa Quiz Card

1. She studied to be a nun in Dublin, Ireland, and Darjeeling, India.
2. She became the principal of a Catholic high school in Calcutta.
3. In 1948, Mother Teresa was given permission to learn how to be a nurse so she could begin a ministry for the poor and sick in India.
4. It is a group of Roman Catholic women who dedicate their lives to helping the poor.
5. Answers will vary.
6. "Pure Heart" was for people who were penniless and dying.
7. The colony was called "Town of Peace."
8. They started working to help people in more countries.
9. The government in India gave her an award called the Padmashri.
10. In 1971, she was given the first Pope John XXIII Peace Prize, and in 1979 she won the Nobel Peace Prize.

Cesar Chavez Quiz Card

1. Cesar Chavez was born on a farm near Yuma, Arizona, in 1927.
2. Chavez's parents became migrant farm workers in California.
3. Answers will vary but may include the following: They worked long hours under miserable conditions, they earned very little money, they didn't have a home, they didn't have much clothing or food, and the children never got to stay in one school for very long.
4. Answers will vary.
5. Chavez worked for an agency in California called the Community Service Organization.
6. Chavez created the National Farm Workers Association.
7. The union helped farmers use nonviolent methods, such as strikes and protests, to improve their working conditions and pay.
8. He wanted the grape growers to lose money and be forced to work with the union.
9. The majority of the grape growers began to work with the union.
10. The UFWOC changed its name to the United Farm Workers of America (UFW).

Martin Luther King, Jr., Quiz Card

1. Martin Luther King, Jr., was born in Atlanta, Georgia, on January 15, 1929.
2. King was only 15 years old.
3. He earned his Ph.D. from Boston University.
4. He told African Americans to boycott the buses.
5. He told them to use nonviolent protest.
6. He led the March on Washington.
7. Some people did not agree with his views.
8. President John F. Kennedy supported King's cause.
9. He won the Nobel Peace Prize in 1964.
10. King was assassinated.

Corazon Aquino Quiz Card

1. She went to school in Manila as well as parochial school in the United States.
2. She attended Mount St. Vincent College.
3. She attended Far Eastern University in Manila.
4. This party opposed the actions of President Ferdinand Marcos.
5. She spoke out against the Marcos government and ran for president.
6. In the 1984 election, one-third of the legislature was from the Liberal party.
7. The military and the people of the Philippines rebelled and declared Aquino as their president.
8. She gave the country a new constitution and held elections for the legislature in 1987.
9. In 1989 some of those who were opposed to Aquino tried to take over the government, but they failed.
10. Answers will vary.

Page 158

Poor: AK, ID, NV, AZ, WY, ND, SD, NM, TX, OK, KS, MO, AR, LA, MS, AL, TN, KY, WV, SC
Fair: WA, MT, UT, CO, NE, IL, IN, OH, PA, GA
Good: MN, IA, MI, VA, MD, DE, NJ, RI, VT, NH, ME
Excellent: OR, CA, WI, FL, NC, CT, MA, NY, HI

CML Text LT3410 H21 T291
1994
Burke, Betty
Heroes

University of Rhode Island Library

Y0-EFQ-112

Dinosauring
Contents

Jumanji

Study the picture carefully.
Then use the words in the box
to answer the questions.

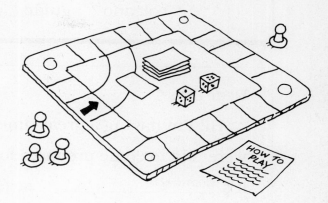

select	dice
board game	
shortcut	instructions

1. What does the picture show? <u>board game</u>

2. What do you read to find out how to play? <u>instructions</u>

3. What do you do before starting the game? Before
   starting the game, you <u>select</u> a playing
   piece.

4. What can you roll to see how many spaces to move? <u>dice</u>

5. What can you do if you land on the space with an
   arrow? You can take a <u>shortcut</u> across the
   board.

   Now write about a board game you enjoy playing with
   your friends. <u>(Answers will vary.)</u>

   _____

   _____

   _____

   _____

   _____

Copyright © Houghton Mifflin Company. All rights reserved.

Use the words in the box to complete the letter.

tsetse flies   monsoon   stampede   jungle
volcano   guide   python

Dear Jill,

Hi! I'm having a great time on Danger Island. We were told to come prepared for wet weather, because it's __monsoon__ season here. So far, though, we've had a lot of sunshine. The day we arrived, we heard — and felt — a __volcano__ rumble, but it did not erupt.

Today a __guide__ led us into the __jungle__ to see the animals. We saw a giant __python__ wrapped around a tree branch, waiting for its dinner to come by. Then we almost got caught in a __stampede__ of wart hogs. Luckily, we got out of the way just in time. We were warned about being bitten by __tsetse flies__, but I don't think we saw any.

I'm getting sleepy right now, so I'll close this letter. I'll try to write again soon.

Your friend,

Tony

Copyright © Houghton Mifflin Company. All rights reserved.

Jumanji

Below are five events from the story *Jumanji*. Write why each event is important.   (Sample answers)

1. Peter and Judy find the game JUMANJI in the park.

    They don't know it yet, but the game is soon to bring them more excitement

    and adventure than they could have imagined.

2. Judy reads aloud the last instruction: "ONCE A GAME OF JUMANJI IS STARTED IT WILL NOT BE OVER UNTIL ONE PLAYER REACHES THE GOLDEN CITY."

    Peter and Judy have to continue the game until the end regardless of

    what happens.

3. Peter lands on the space that says, "Lion attacks, move back two spaces."

    When a lion appears, Peter begins to take the game seriously.

4. Judy reaches the Golden City on the game board and quickly yells, "Jumanji!"

    Judy ends the game, saving them from the snake, lion, and other dangers.

5. Peter and Judy watch as Danny and Walter Budwing run through the park with a long thin box.

    Peter and Judy know that the same frightening events will probably happen

    to the two boys.

Copyright © Houghton Mifflin Company. All rights reserved.

The Mysterious Girl in the Garden

Write a sentence that means the opposite of each of the sentences below. Change the underlined words. The first one has been done for you. **(Sample answers)**

1. The newspaper printed the scandal about the mayor.
The newspaper printed a story that praised the mayor.

2. That's a pathetic-looking dog.
That's a very healthy-looking dog.

3. Usually Melanie is a very obnoxious person.
Usually Melanie is a very sweet, nice person.

4. Kenny told his friends gossip about his brother.
Kenny told his friends good things about his brother.

5. It's impossible to finish this in time.
It's possible to finish this in time.

6. Christina is very impatient when she has to wait.
Christina is very patient when she has to wait.

7. I'm going to ignore you.
I'm going to pay attention to you.

8. Bill acts uppity around other people.
Bill acts very humble around other people.

9. I detest Brussels sprouts.
I love Brussels sprouts.

Copyright © Houghton Mifflin Company. All rights reserved.

The Mysterious Girl in the Garden

Think about the story *The Mysterious Girl in the Garden*. Complete the sentences below. (Sample answers)

1. Terrie was upset about spending the summer in England because _she had no one to play with and she wanted to spend the summer with her grandmother._

2. Tuesday turned out to be a special day for Terrie because _she met Charlotte and her dog, Lioni, at Kew Botanic Gardens._

3. Terrie felt that she was like Charlotte in several ways because they both _had no one to play with and both were told what to do by their families._

4. Terrie was shocked when she saw the museum portrait of the princess and her dog because _they looked exactly like the girl and the dog she had met the day before._

5. Terrie stared at the portrait for a long, long time because _she wasn't sure if Charlotte was playing a trick on her or if Charlotte really was a princess from long ago._

Terrie thought Charlotte was both pathetic and obnoxious. Answer these questions about Charlotte.

What made Charlotte seem pathetic? _She was lonely and sad because her parents were fighting over her._

How was Charlotte obnoxious? _She was rude and uppity and ordered Terrie around._

Copyright © Houghton Mifflin Company. All rights reserved.

Making Inferences

As you read this story beginning, think about which events are realistic, which are fantastic, and what the rules for this fantasy are. Then follow the directions after the story.

Fantastaplex

"**A**re *you* the kind of kid who likes to build things and take things apart?" asked a very friendly voice from the TV set.

"Yep," said Randy, without looking up. In fact, at that moment he was taking apart an old telephone his mother had given to him. At the same time he was watching — or at least listening to — his favorite Saturday morning cartoon.

"Do you just *love* wheels, gears, motors, and electric switches?" continued the friendly voice.

"Sure," answered Randy. The commercial interested him, but he couldn't look up because he was trying to unscrew the last tiny screw that held on the telephone's plastic shell. Then he'd be able to lift it off and look inside.

"If this sounds like *you*," said the voice, "then you'll have *fantastic fun* with FANTASTAPLEX — the toy that lets *you* be the builder!"

Oh — Fantastaplex, thought Randy. Big deal. He had hoped that the commercial was for a toy he had never heard of. He had played with a Fantastaplex set at Eric's house. There was nothing fantastic about it. All the parts (the ones that Eric hadn't lost) were cheaply made, and the moonwalker they had put together fell to pieces before it had taken two steps.

The voice was still talking about the wonders of Fantastaplex. Randy glanced up. A space-age car was zooming across someone's living room while the boy and the girl working the controls looked as if they were having the greatest time of their lives.

"Yeah, right!" said Randy. "Good luck making a car like that with dumb old Fantastaplex." He was feeling

Copyright © Houghton Mifflin Company. All rights reserved.

grumpy because he couldn't get the shell off the telephone.

Then something odd happened. As soon as the words "dumb old Fantastaplex" came out of Randy's mouth, the two children on the screen suddenly dropped the controls of their space-age car. The looks on their faces changed from delight to disbelief. "What does he mean, 'dumb old Fantastaplex'?" the girl asked the boy.

Then a man in jeans and a T-shirt rushed into view. He turned out to be the owner of the friendly voice, but now he didn't sound very friendly.

"Just who do you think you are, young man?" he demanded, pointing his finger into the TV camera. "If you think you can get away with calling Fantastaplex 'dumb,' you've got another think coming!"

The man and the children, all three, glared out of the TV — straight at Randy!

(Sample answers)

1. Which events in the story are realistic?

   Randy is watching cartoons and is taking apart an old telephone. The

   cartoon has been interrupted by a toy commercial.

2. At what point did you know for sure that this story is a fantasy?

   The children in the commercial stop playing with the car, and the girl asks,

   What does he mean? in response to something Randy says.

3. Think about the rules the author has set for this fantasy. Then finish these sentences:

   One rule is that TV characters can see Randy and speak to him.

   Another rule is that Randy can talk to the people in TV commercials.

4. Based on the rules for this fantasy, what do you think might happen next?

   (Answers will vary, but students' responses should be based on the rules

   above.)

Copyright © Houghton Mifflin Company. All rights reserved.

The Shrinking of Treehorn

Read each question, paying attention to the underlined words. Then write your answer on the lines. (Sample answers)

1. If you dropped your mother's favorite vase <u>on purpose</u>, what <u>privileges</u> might you lose?

   You might not be able to watch television or have dessert.

2. Why would it be <u>strange</u> for an elephant to <u>disappear</u>?

   An elephant is so large that it would be unusual if

   one disappeared.

3. What would your teacher say if you <u>shirked</u> your homework?

   He or she might tell you to stay after school.

4. What could you do if you wanted to <u>pretend</u> that you were <u>shrinking</u>?

   You could get on your knees or wear extra large clothing.

5. What could you do to stop your shoes from <u>shuffling</u>?

   You could stuff newspaper in them or else buy smaller shoes.

Copyright © Houghton Mifflin Company. All rights reserved.

The Shrinking of Treehorn

Think about *The Shrinking of Treehorn.* From the box, choose the name of the character who made each statement below, and write the name on the blank. Then tell why the person made the statement. The first one has been done for you.

Moshie	Principal	Father	Teacher
	Bus Driver	Treehorn	

1. **Father** "Do sit up, Treehorn. I can hardly see your head." (Page 57) **Treehorn was getting small, but his father thought he wasn't sitting up straight.**

2. Moshie "How come you can't mail it yourself, stupid?" (Page 62) **He could not figure out why Treehorn could not reach the mailbox.**

3. Bus Driver "First time I ever heard of a family naming two boys the same name." (Page 64) **Treehorn was so small that the bus driver thought he must be Treehorn's younger brother.**

4. Teacher "We don't shrink in this class." (Page 64) **She did not want any disturbances in her classroom.**

5. Principal "We can't have any shirkers here, you know." (Page 66) **He thought Treehorn had written "shirking" instead of "shrinking."**

6. Treehorn "If I don't say anything, they won't notice." (Page 71) **Treehorn noticed that he was green but thought his parents wouldn't notice it if he didn't mention it.**

Copyright © Houghton Mifflin Company. All rights reserved.

BOOK 2

Tyrannosaurus

Read each group of words below. Draw a line through the word that does not belong in the group. Then write why the other three words belong together. The first one has been done for you. **(Sample answers)**

1. tracks   footprints   trail   ~~hoof~~

   All except *hoof* are signs left behind by a creature that has moved through an area.

2. catastrophe   ~~health~~   disease   disaster

   All except *health* name something harmful.

3. armor   weapons   shield   ~~feathers~~

   All except *feathers* name something used for fighting or in battle.

4. ~~hunter~~   prey   food   victim

   All except *hunter* name something that could be hunted and eaten.

5. suddenly   quickly   ~~gradually~~   swiftly

   All except *gradually* mean "fast."

6. mighty   strong   ~~weak~~   powerful

   All except *weak* describe something that has great strength.

7. ~~slept~~   roamed   wandered   traveled

   All except *slept* relate to movement across an area.

8. cow   pig   ~~dinosaur~~   sheep

   All except *dinosaur* are animals that are still alive today.

Copyright © Houghton Mifflin Company. All rights reserved.

Tyrannosaurus

Think about the selection *Tyrannosaurus*. Then answer each question.   (Sample answers)

1. What were some of the ways that dinosaurs protected themselves? Some ran from trouble. Some moved together to form a wall. Some had armor on their bodies and horns on their heads.

2. How was the body of the Tyrannosaurus "designed for hunting"? It had strong back legs for chasing its prey, three sharp claws on each foot, and six-inch teeth with sharp edges.

3. What strange problem did the Tyrannosaurus's small, weak arms create for it? If it lay down, it probably had a hard time getting back up again.

4. What do tracks and other evidence suggest to scientists about the family life of the Tyrannosaurus? It probably traveled alone or in pairs. It probably laid eggs.

5. What other questions do scientists still hope to answer about the Tyrannosaurus? How did Tyrannosaurus mothers care for their young? What caused it and other dinosaurs to die out 65 million years ago?

Copyright © Houghton Mifflin Company. All rights reserved.

Identifying Main Idea and Supporting Details

Read the article below. Think about the main idea, the most important idea the author presents. Also look for details that support this main idea. Then follow the directions on the next page.

The Mangrove Trees of South Florida

Imagine that you are flying in a plane over southern Florida. As you fly over the part nearest the sea, you see thousands of tiny islands that look like green puzzle pieces scattered on a shiny mirror. These are mangrove islands.

Mangrove islands are formed by mangrove trees. Mangroves are very unusual and useful trees. Unlike most trees, they can live in seawater, which is salty. Their long roots act like nets in the water and trap dirt and rocks. Over time, the dirt and rocks build up on the roots, forming islands around the trees.

Mangrove trees are useful to the many kinds of animals that live on the mangrove islands. Tiny worms and crabs eat the leaves of mangrove trees. In turn, the worms and crabs provide food for raccoons, snakes, and other larger animals that hunt among the roots of the mangroves. Birds build their nests in the high branches of mangrove trees. Underwater, the mangrove roots make good homes for shrimp and other marine life.

Mangrove trees also help protect the land. During storms, mangrove trees act as a barrier between the sea and the land. The sea hits the mangroves hard, but the mangroves break the power of the waves, keeping the land behind and around them from being washed away.

Copyright © Houghton Mifflin Company. All rights reserved.

1. Read the sentences below. Decide which sentence best tells the main idea of "The Mangrove Trees of South Florida." Then write the sentence on the lines.

  A. Mangrove roots make good homes for marine life.
  B. Mangroves are very unusual and useful trees.
  C. Mangrove trees act as a barrier between the sea and the land.

Mangroves are very unusual and useful trees.

2. Write three details that support the main idea.   (Sample answers)

  A. Unlike most other trees, mangrove trees can live in salt water.

  B. The leaves of mangrove trees provide food for tiny worms and crabs.

  C. During storms, mangrove trees protect the nearby land from high waves.

Now use the main idea and supporting details you wrote to write a brief summary of the article.

(Answers will vary.)

Copyright © Houghton Mifflin Company. All rights reserved.

Wild and Woolly Mammoths

Read each sentence. Find a word in the box that means almost the same as the underlined word or words. Write the word on the line.

trunk	tusks	ruins	mammoths
extinct	enemies	climate	

1. Thousands of years ago woolly <u>animals that looked like elephants</u> lived on the earth.

   mammoths _____

2. On the sides of its face, this animal had two <u>long teeth</u> that it used for digging.

   tusks _____

3. It had a <u>long nose</u> that it used to breathe and smell with and to carry food and water to its mouth.

   trunk _____

4. This animal's long, hairy coat was good protection against the very cold <u>weather of the area</u> where it lived.

   climate _____

5. These animals had few <u>creatures that wanted to cause them harm</u> — except for saber-toothed tigers and Stone Age people.

   enemies _____

6. Scientists have found clay figures and bone carvings of these animals among the <u>remains of buildings</u> where Stone Age people once lived.

   ruins _____

7. Today this animal is <u>no longer living on the earth</u>, but it lives on in books, museums, and our imaginations.

   extinct _____

Copyright © Houghton Mifflin Company. All rights reserved.

Wild and Woolly Mammoths

Think about the selection *Wild and Woolly Mammoths*. Decide whether each statement below is true or false, and circle that answer. Then write a reason for your answer. The first one has been done for you.

(Sample answers)

1. Woolly mammoths looked like cows. True (False)

   They looked like furry elephants with two curved tusks, a long hairy trunk, and a heavy coat.

2. Scientists can only guess about the habits of woolly mammoths because none of these creatures have ever been found. True (False)

   Scientists have found frozen mammoths, including one that still had food in its stomach.

3. Woolly mammoths were reptiles like dinosaurs. True (False)

   They were mammals. They were warm-blooded, had hair, and nursed their young.

4. Archaeologists have learned a great deal about how Stone Age people lived. (True) False

   By studying villages, caves, and carvings, scientists know much about these people.

5. Stone Age hunters figured out skillful ways to trap and kill woolly mammoths. (True) False

   They used fire to scare mammoths down steep cliffs. They covered deep pits with branches.

6. Stone Age people hunted woolly mammoths only for their meat. True (False)

   They also used mammoth bones and tusks for tent frames, jewelry, fuel, and musical instruments.

Copyright © Houghton Mifflin Company. All rights reserved.

Identifying Main Ideas Across Texts

Read passage 1. Then read passage 2.
Ask yourself what topic both passages share.

1. The Everglades in southern Florida is home to some of the most beautiful and unusual creatures in the world. The graceful egret and the great white heron are among the many birds that can be seen in the skies. White-tailed deer, bobcats, and the rarely seen Florida panther live in the woods.

In the warm, swampy waters of the Everglades, crocodiles, alligators, giant turtles, and snakes can be found. Another creature that makes its home in the water is the manatee, or sea cow. These large mammals can eat more than one hundred pounds of water plants in one day!

2. Many of the creatures in the Everglades were once in danger of becoming extinct. The manatees — large, slow-moving mammals that live underwater — were almost wiped out by speeding motor boats and people who hunted them for their flesh, hide, and oil. Certain kinds of turtles were hunted for their shells or killed for food. At one time, nearly all the egrets in the Everglades were killed for their valuable feathers.

In recent times, successful efforts have been made to save endangered wildlife in the Everglades. Manatees are now protected in parts of the Everglades set aside for their safety. Turtles now live unharmed in turtle preserves. And many once-endangered birds such as the egret are now protected by law. Once again, the Everglades has become a place where many kinds of wildlife can live safely.

Copyright © Houghton Mifflin Company. All rights reserved.

Now follow the directions below. **(Sample answers)**

What topic do both of these passages tell about? creatures that live in the Everglades

Fill out the chart below. Write a sentence that tells the main idea in each passage. Then write two details that support each main idea.

Passage 1

Main Idea: Some of the most beautiful and unusual creatures in the world live in the Everglades.

Details:

1. Deer, bobcats, and panthers live in the woods of the Everglades.

2. Alligators, snakes, and manatees can be found in the warm, swampy waters of the Everglades.

Passage 2

Main Idea: Many creatures of the Everglades that were once in danger of becoming extinct are now protected by law.

Details:

1. Manatees are now protected in some parts of the Everglades.

2. Egrets and other once-endangered birds are now protected by law.

Use what you wrote on the chart above to write a paragraph that sums up the information from both passages.

Many beautiful and unusual creatures live in the Everglades. Egrets, bobcats, panthers, and white-tailed deer live there. Manatees, alligators, and giant turtles can be found in the warm waters. Many of these creatures, which were once in danger of becoming extinct, are now protected by law.

Copyright © Houghton Mifflin Company. All rights reserved.

Strange Creatures That Really Lived

Read each question below. Write your answers on the lines. (Sample answers)

1. Why do scientists go on **expeditions**?
   They go to do research. They go to find
   answers to questions about the past.

2. What do you think a **tar pit** looks, smells, and feels like? A tar pit might look black and
   bubbly, smell like tar, and feel very sticky.

3. Why might a **tar pit** be a good place for an
   expedition? Animals of long ago might have become stuck in a tar pit.
   A scientist might be able to find their remains there.

4. A **lizard** is one kind of **reptile**. What are some other
   reptiles? Alligators, turtles, snakes

5. Some reptiles, such as lizards, have **scaly** skin. What
   do you think scaly skin feels like? Dry, hard, rough

6. When an animal dies, its flesh **decays**. What happens
   to flesh when it **decays**? It rots and falls away from the bone.

   Now imagine that you are a scientist about to go on
   an expedition. Where are you going and what are you
   looking for?

Copyright © Houghton Mifflin Company. All rights reserved.

Strange Creatures That Really Lived

Look back at *Strange Creatures That Really Lived.*
Write two or more details from the selection to explain
why each creature below seems strange.   (Sample answers)

1. **pteranodon:** It looked like a huge bat. It had leathery wings and a long, pointed bill.

2. **archelon:** It was a twelve-foot-long sea turtle. It weighed 6,000 pounds. It once swam in an inland sea that covered what is now South Dakota.

3. **archaeopteryx:** It looked like a small dinosaur with feathers. It had a tail and rounded wings.

4. **uintatherium:** It had six horns on its head. It had sharp teeth even though it was a plant-eater.

5. **baluchitherium:** It looked like a rhinoceros but had no horns. It was the size of a small house. It could stretch out its long neck like a giraffe.

6. **dodo:** It was the size of a turkey. It waddled like a duck. It had wings but could not fly.

Copyright © Houghton Mifflin Company. All rights reserved.

BOOK 3

The Boy of the Three-Year Nap

Read each group of words below. Draw a line through the word that does not belong in the group. Then write why the other three words belong together.   (Sample answers)

1. samurai warrior   patron   guard   ~~merchant~~
   All except *merchant* can provide protection.

2. ~~gentle~~   fierce   violent   wild
   All except *gentle* could describe an angry person.

3. frown   sneer   ~~smile~~   scowl
   All except *smile* are angry facial expressions.

4. church   ~~storehouse~~   temple   shrine
   All except *storehouse* are buildings where someone might worship.

5. a command   an order   ~~a request~~   a demand
   All except *a request* are orders to do something.

6. debate   bargain   ~~listen~~   convince
   All except *listen* involve arguing or discussing.

7. decreed   ordered   demanded   ~~pleaded~~
   All except *pleaded* mean "told to do something."

8. ~~refuse~~   allow   consent   agree
   All except *refuse* mean "to give permission."

Copyright © Houghton Mifflin Company. All rights reserved.

The Boy of the Three-Year Nap

Think about the folktale *The Boy of the Three-Year Nap.* Then answer the questions below. (Sample answers)

1. Why was Taro known as "The Boy of the Three-Year Nap"? <u>He was so lazy that the villagers said he could sleep for three years at a time.</u>

2. Why was Taro so impressed with his new neighbors? <u>They lived in a large mansion with a lovely garden, pond, and teahouse. They wore fine clothes.</u>

3. How did Taro prepare to put his plan into action? <u>He dressed himself in a black kimono and priest's hat. He painted scowl lines on his face. He waited by the shrine for the merchant.</u>

4. How did Taro fool the merchant? <u>He pretended to be the ujigami and convinced the merchant that Taro must wed his daughter.</u>

5. How did Taro's mother fool the merchant? <u>She would not let Taro marry the man's daughter until the house had been fixed up so his daughter could live in comfort.</u>

6. How did Taro's mother outsmart Taro? <u>She made the merchant promise to give Taro a job so Taro would have to work to get what he wanted.</u>

Copyright © Houghton Mifflin Company. All rights reserved.

Farmer Schulz's Ducks

Use the words in the box to complete the article.

accelerated	concussion
wreckage	frustration
impatience	semitrailer
swerve	contented

CRASH KEEPS SCHOOL COOL

A freak accident occurred yesterday when a
__semitrailer__ loaded with ice cream was chugging
up Route 99. A sports car came speeding up from behind,
the driver honking his horn with __impatience__.
He __accelerated__ to pass the truck, but had to
__swerve__ to avoid an oncoming car. Both the
truck and the sports car ended up in a ditch.

The ice cream landed in front of nearby Happy
Valley School. Children ran from class, attacking the
ice cream with plastic spoons. Both drivers sat near
the __wreckage__ of their vehicles, eating
butterscotch ice cream. Asked if he felt any
__frustration__ over the accident, the truck driver
said, "Nope! These kids have the right idea!"

The sports car driver complained of a headache
and was treated for a mild __concussion__.
The __contented__ children returned to class.

Copyright © Houghton Mifflin Company. All rights reserved.

Farmer Schulz's Ducks

Think about *Farmer Schulz's Ducks*.
Then read each problem below and explain
how the problem was solved. (Sample answers)

PROBLEM

1. Farmer Schulz's ducks liked to swim on the Onkaparinga River, but after dark, the river became too dangerous for them to stay.

2. As the city grew, more and more drivers began to race back and forth on the road. Sometimes they did not stop for the ducks.

3. Not all cars stopped for Farmer Schulz's "Ducks Crossing" sign. Finally, a car crashed into the ducks.

4. A semitrailer hit the duck bridge, destroying it. Several ducks were hurt or killed.

5. Farmer Schulz wanted to avoid any trouble with the government about building a duck pipe.

6. Farmer Schulz needed to teach his ducks how to use the duck pipe.

SOLUTION

1. Each night the ducks returned to Farmer Schulz's yard, where it was safer for them.

2. Farmer Schulz nailed up a sign that read "Ducks Crossing" where the drivers could see it.

3. Farmer Schulz built a bridge over the road with safety fences and ramps for the ducks to use.

4. Farmer Schulz decided to put in a pipe so the ducks could travel underneath the road.

5. He wrote a letter to the government, asking for official permission to build a pipe.

6. He built mesh flaps to guide the ducks into the tunnel. His family shooed the ducks into the tunnel.

Copyright © Houghton Mifflin Company. All rights reserved.

Comparing Solutions

Read both stories. As you read, think about the problem that has to be solved in each story. Also think about how the characters solve their problems.

The Fishers and the Greedy Duke

There once was a selfish Duke who seized a fishing boat that was the home of a clever old couple.

The next day the old couple appeared at the Duke's castle. "We have no place to live and no way to make a living," they told the keeper of the castle. "So we have come here to work." They were hired at once.

The Duke was afraid of being robbed, so he had guards at the castle gate to search everyone going out. At mid-morning the old couple was stopped at the gate. They were leading four of the Duke's mules with forty bags strapped to their backs out of the castle.

"What's in those bags?" asked the guards.

"Twigs to make the Duke's brooms," the couple replied.

The guards emptied every bag but found no stolen gold, so they let the couple go.

At noon, the couple came to the gate again with forty bags on four more mules. They told the guards, "We're carrying straw to make the Duke's bricks."

The guards searched every bag but found no stolen gold, so they let the couple go.

At mid-afternoon, the couple came to the gate again with forty bags on four more mules. They said, "We're carrying only feathers to make the Duke's pillows."

The guards took every feather out of every bag but found no stolen gold, so they let the couple go.

At the end of the day, the guards looked for the old couple, but they never came back. They had sold the Duke's twelve fine mules, bought a new fishing boat, and sailed far away.

Copyright © Houghton Mifflin Company. All rights reserved.

Yours, Mine, and His

The three Choy boys usually got along well, but sometimes they quarreled.

"Hey, that's my sweat shirt you have on," said ten-year-old John.

"No, it's mine," said his twin, James. "You left yours at school."

Or twelve-year-old Matthew would snap, "You ran off with my notebook this morning."

One day after such a quarrel, their father made a suggestion. "Why don't you put your names on your things?"

"Oh, Dad," they groaned, "only *little* kids have their names on everything."

"Well then," Mr. Choy said, "I'll count on you boys to come up with your own solution."

The next day Matthew came home carrying a bag. He called his brothers together and emptied the bag. Out came three markers — blue, red, and yellow.

"Pick a color," he said to the twins. We can mark the labels of our things with these colors. That way we'll always know whose things are whose."

And that is what they did.

Answer these questions about the two stories. **(Sample answers)**

1. What is the problem in "The Fishers and the Greedy Duke"? <u>The selfish Duke took the old couple's fishing boat where they lived and worked.</u>

2. How was the problem solved? <u>The old couple tricked the Duke by leading twelve of his mules out of the castle. Then they sold the mules and bought a new boat.</u>

3. What is the problem in "Yours, Mine, and His"? <u>The three Choy brothers argued about their clothes and other belongings.</u>

4. How was the problem solved? <u>Each boy chose a different color to mark his things.</u>

With a partner, compare the ways in which the characters in the two stories solved their problems. Which characters used a clever trick? Which used common sense?

Copyright © Houghton Mifflin Company. All rights reserved.

The Sign in Mendel's Window

Read the story below, paying attention to the underlined words.

In the village of Rivka, there lived a ¹poor ²tenant named Grinkov who decided to run for mayor. He gave speeches in the marketplace, telling everyone what he would do if elected. Although Grinkov was a very ³awkward speaker, the villagers were not ⁴disappointed by what he had to say. Everyone who knew Grinkov said he was a ⁵humble man. He was also regarded throughout the village as ⁶an honest person. The people of Rivka believed these qualities would make Grinkov a good mayor, and so they voted for him.

Below is the same story, with blanks in place of the underlined words. On each blank, write a word from the box that means nearly the opposite of the word with the same number in the first story. The first one has been done for you.

In the village of Rivka, there lived a

¹ **prosperous** ² landlord named Grinkov who decided to run for mayor. He gave speeches in the marketplace, telling everyone what he would do if elected. Although Grinkov was a very ³ eloquent speaker, the villagers were not ⁴ impressed by what he had to say. Everyone who knew Grinkov said he was a ⁵ braggart . He was also regarded throughout the village as a ⁶ scoundrel . The people of Rivka believed these qualities would *not* make Grinkov a good mayor, so they did not vote for him.

> scoundrel
> landlord
> impressed
> prosperous
> eloquent
> braggart

Copyright © Houghton Mifflin Company. All rights reserved.

The Sign in Mendel's Window

Think about *The Sign in Mendel's Window.* Then complete each sentence below. (Sample answers)

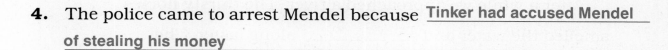

1. Mendel and Molly's neighbors were worried about the FOR RENT sign in the butcher shop window because <u>they were afraid that Mendel and Molly were sick or leaving town</u>.

2. At first Mendel was impressed by Tinker because <u>Tinker was eloquent, well-dressed, and humble</u>.

3. Tinker encouraged Mendel to count the shop's earnings aloud because <u>Tinker wanted to know exactly how much money Mendel had</u>.

4. The police came to arrest Mendel because <u>Tinker had accused Mendel of stealing his money</u>.

5. Simka proved that Tinker was lying because <u>everyone in town knew how much money was in the box</u>.

6. Molly dumped the coins into a pot of boiling water because <u>she wanted to show that they were covered with fat, which proved they belonged to a butcher</u>.

7. Indeed, Tinker's biggest mistake was in coming to Kosnov because <u>the neighbors were very close and always knew what was going on in town</u>.

Copyright © Houghton Mifflin Company. All rights reserved.

BOOK 4

Little House on the Prairie

Use the words in the box to complete the diary entry below. Write one word on each line.

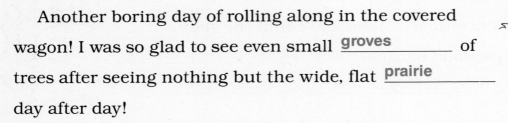

groves	ford	cliffs	prairie
bluffs	trotted	lurched	

August 29, 1880

Dear Diary,

Another boring day of rolling along in the covered wagon! I was so glad to see even small <u>groves</u> of trees after seeing nothing but the wide, flat <u>prairie</u> day after day!

After a while we approached a river. The thirsty horses smelled the water and <u>trotted</u> along faster. The wagon <u>lurched</u> from side to side on the uneven ground. Soon we came to a <u>ford</u> where the river was not deep and we could cross in safety.

On one side of the river, tall, steep <u>cliffs</u> rose up from the flat land. Beyond that were smaller, sloping <u>bluffs</u>. Father said that is where our new home will be. The long journey is almost over!

Now write a few sentences telling what you know about the *prairie*.

(Answers will vary.) _____

_____

_____

Copyright © Houghton Mifflin Company. All rights reserved.

Little House on the Prairie

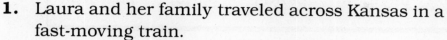

Think about the story *Little House on the Prairie*. Decide whether each statement below is true or false, and circle that answer. Then explain your answer.

1. Laura and her family traveled across Kansas in a fast-moving train.

   True   (False)

   They traveled in a covered wagon that moved very slowly.

   _____

2. The Ingalls family had no trouble crossing the creek.

   True   (False)

   The water was very deep, and Pa had to help the horses cross. The family

   lost Jack during the crossing.

3. At the end of the day, the Ingalls family was too tired to prepare and eat supper.

   True   (False)

   They made coffee, cornmeal cakes, and salt pork. Then they ate in front of

   the fire.

4. The wolf Laura thought she saw turned out to be their dog, Jack.

   (True)   False

   Jack had made his way to their camp. When Laura saw his green eyes

   shining in the dark, she thought he was a wolf.

   Write at least one way Laura Ingalls' life was different from yours and one way her life was similar to yours.

   Different: **(Answers will vary.)** _____

   _____

   Similar: _____

   _____

Copyright © Houghton Mifflin Company. All rights reserved.

Farmer Boy

Study the picture carefully. Write each word from the box by the place or thing in the picture that it names.

| buggy | colt | haymow | pantry | parlor | pasture |

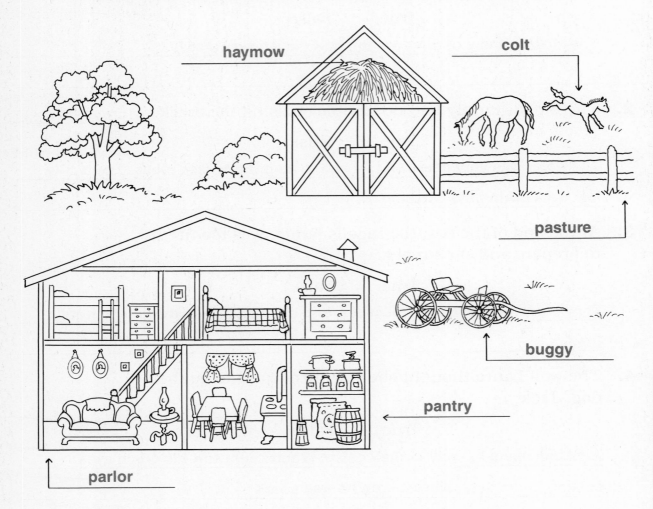

Now write a few sentences telling what might happen if the *colt* got out of the *pasture*.

(Answers will vary.)

_____

_____

_____

Copyright © Houghton Mifflin Company. All rights reserved.

Read each sentence. Find the meaning of the underlined word in the list of meanings below. Write the word on the line before its meaning.

1. Luke's big sister was always trying to be the <u>boss</u> and tell him what to do.

2. He found this very <u>aggravating</u> and he sometimes got angry with her.

3. One day she told him to <u>churn</u> the butter, even though that was really her chore.

4. "I don't have to <u>obey</u> you!" he shouted. "You're not my mother."

5. "If you don't," she said, "I'll tell Father to give you a <u>licking</u> you won't forget!"

6. Luke did not feel <u>anxious</u> because he knew his father wouldn't do that.

7. Still, the milk would be <u>ruined</u> if they let it sit in the churn while they argued.

8. Luke <u>hesitated</u> just a bit, and then he began to do the churning.

licking	a beating or whipping
ruined	spoiled
boss	a person who controls or manages
anxious	worried; concerned
aggravating	annoying; irritating
hesitated	paused or stopped for a short while
obey	follow the orders of
churn	to beat milk or cream to make butter

Now write about something you have found *aggravating*.

(Answers will vary.)

_____

_____

Copyright © Houghton Mifflin Company. All rights reserved.

Farmer Boy

Below are some incomplete sentences about the story *Farmer Boy*. Fill in the blanks with the name of the character who performed each action. Then answer the questions that follow.

The Wilders:
Eliza Jane
Royal
Almanzo
Alice

1. __Royal__ scolded Almanzo for bothering the colts in the pasture. Why? __Father Wilder had told the children not to bother the colts.__

2. __Almanzo__ fed molasses candy to Lucy the pig. What happened to poor Lucy? __Lucy's teeth became stuck together, and she could not eat, drink, or squeal.__

3. __Almanzo__ threw the blacking brush at the wall-paper. What happened next? __He hid in the haymow and later felt so sick that he couldn't eat.__

4. __Alice__ admitted to Mother that they had eaten almost all the sugar. What was Mother's response? __She said that she wouldn't scold because the children had been so good.__

5. __Eliza Jane__ patched over the splotch on the parlor wall-paper. Why? __She was sorry that she had been so aggravating to Almanzo, so she wanted to help him.__

Copyright © Houghton Mifflin Company. All rights reserved.

Identifying Characteristics of Historical Fiction

Read the story. Think about which details are based on historical fact and which are probably from the author's imagination. Then follow the directions after the story.

The Pinto

It was a clear morning in 1842 when Monterey was still the capital of California, and California still belonged to Mexico. The excitement of the upcoming rodeo stirred the air as groups of cowhands gathered at the Customs House. They joked and boasted about their horses, tied in a long line.

The cowhands wore shiny leather boots or deerskin shoes embroidered with silver. They were dressed in velvet pants with gold braid and silver buttons and wore their wide, flat-topped hats. These people lived in the saddle. They roped cattle at full gallop. It was easy for them to pick up a coin, a handkerchief, or a trailing lasso from their galloping horses.

As Hernando, a cowhand, stepped out of the Customs House, he nearly bumped into his younger brother Antonio.

"Azul is gone!" Antonio cried. Anger and pain mixed in his voice.

Hernando circled his brother's shoulders with one arm. "I'm sorry, Antonio," he said, "but horses are easy to come by. You know that."

"Azul was special!" Antonio insisted.

Antonio loved the large brown spots on his pony's shiny white coat. He loved the flecks of blue in the pony's eyes. That was why he called his pony Azul — the Spanish word for blue.

"Without Azul, I can't ride in the rodeo," Antonio said. "I must find him!"

"I see," Hernando said, "but he might have joined a wild herd. He will not be easy to find. The herd may be in the valley by now, and that's a day's journey."

Copyright © Houghton Mifflin Company. All rights reserved.

Antonio had not thought of this. He was not thinking clearly.

"There will be other ponies and other rodeos," Hernando said, trying to comfort Antonio.

"There is no pony like Azul!" Antonio said. "With Azul, I was ready for the rodeo. I have worked with him all year. We were partners. We *are* partners!"

Suddenly Antonio had an idea. "Will you help me track Azul, Hernando?" he asked.

Hernando gave his younger brother a long look. He had watched Antonio and Azul practice turns and roping day after day. For a year now, hardly a day had passed without Antonio riding out into the pasture to work on his roping.

"All right, Antonio," Hernando sighed. "We will look for this little pinto of yours. Tomorrow morning we will leave before sunrise. Now I have work to do."

1. Look back at the story. Find details that are probably based on historical fact, and write them on the lines below. Hints: Where and when does the story take place? What did the cowhands wear? **(Sample answers)**

   In 1842, Monterey was still the capital of California, and California still

   belonged to Mexico.

   The cowhands wore shiny leather boots or deerskin shoes embroidered with

   silver.

   _____

2. Look back at the story again. Find details that are probably from the author's imagination, and write them below. Hints: What do the characters say to each other? What happened to Antonio's pony? How does Antonio feel? **(Sample answers)**

   "Azul is gone!" Antonio cried. Anger and pain mixed in his voice.

   "There will be other ponies and other rodeos," Hernando said, trying to

   comfort Antonio.

   _____

   _____

Copyright © Houghton Mifflin Company. All rights reserved.

On the Banks of Plum Creek

Use the words in the box to complete the story below.
Write one word on each line.

blizzard	whirling	swiftly	suddenly	bitter
swirled	hauled	stagger	frantically	

Amy and her little sister were walking home from
school when, without warning, a winter storm
__suddenly__ hit. The air became so __bitter__
cold that Amy's nose hurt. At first, the snowflakes
__swirled__ in circles in the air. Then the wind blew
in a __whirling__ blast against their faces. Amy
gripped her sister's hand and fought her way against the
heavy snow and strong wind. She knew that this storm
was a real __blizzard__!

The girls ran for home as __swiftly__ as they
could. The wind made them __stagger__ and almost
fall. When they reached home, snow was piled against the
door. Amy tugged __frantically__ at the door until it
finally opened. She fell inside and __hauled__ her
sister in after her.

Now describe a *blizzard* or other storm you have been in.
(Answers will vary.)

_____

_____

_____

_____

_____

Copyright © Houghton Mifflin Company. All rights reserved.

On the Banks of Plum Creek

Think about what happened in the story *On the Banks of Plum Creek*. Then fill out the story map below. **(Sample answers)**

Setting

Time: __winter, late 1800s__

Place: __near Walnut Grove,__
__Minnesota__

Characters:

__Pa and Ma Ingalls, Mary,__

__Laura, and Carrie__

Problem:

__While Ma and Pa are away, a sudden blizzard hits.__

Action / Events:

__Ma and Pa go to town for the day, leaving the girls alone at home.__

__A blizzard unexpectedly hits. Mary and Laura, afraid of freezing to__

__death, bring all the wood from the woodpile into the house.__

Resolution / Ending:

__Ma and Pa return home safely and laugh at the sight of all the wood__

__in the house.__

Copyright © Houghton Mifflin Company. All rights reserved.

Meg Mackintosh and the Case of the Missing Babe Ruth Baseball

Read each group of words below. Draw a line through the word that does not belong in the group. Then write why the other three words belong together.

1. fake   false   ~~authentic~~   untrue

   All except *authentic* mean "not real."
   _____

2. investigate   detect   examine   ~~ignore~~

   All except *ignore* are part of a detective's job.
   _____

3. ~~difference~~   resemblance   similarity   likeness

   All except *difference* mean "ways in which things are alike."
   _____

4. deduction   ~~confusion~~   conclusion   solution

   All except *confusion* are answers to a problem or mystery.
   _____

Read the story below. Find a word in the box that completes the meaning of each sentence. Write the word in the blank.

> solved
> proof
> decode
> deduce
> telltale

Detective Snoop examined the note carefully for clues to help him __deduce__ who had left it — and why. Snoop was convinced that it was a secret spy note, although he had no __proof__ that spies were involved.

"This __telltale__ reddish stain on the note makes me think that whoever wrote it was in a struggle with another spy," Snoop said to himself. "And this unusual green scribbling could be a secret code. I must __decode__ it!"

Just then, Baby Buster came into the room holding a hot dog with ketchup in one hand and a green crayon in the other. The case of the mysterious note was __solved__.

Copyright © Houghton Mifflin Company. All rights reserved.

Meg Mackintosh and the Case of the Missing Babe Ruth Baseball

This is your Detective's Note Pad. Use it to help you solve the "Case of the Missing Babe Ruth Baseball."

Words You Should Know   Be on the lookout for these words as you read this mystery:

decipher	deduction
resemblance	telltale

You can figure out what the words mean by looking for familiar word parts and by thinking about what meanings make sense in the sentence. If you need more help, look up these words in the Glossary.

Before You Read   Think about the prediction you wrote on Journal page 121. Keep your prediction in mind as you read this mystery.

Read from page 275 to the end of page 278.   Find out what Meg does to unravel the first clue. Then answer the questions below.

What was Clue One? <u>Not a father / Not a gander / Take a look / In her book</u>

_____

Which book did Meg reach for, and why? <u>She reached for *Mother Goose*</u>
<u>because its title fit the clue: a mother is not a father, and a goose is not</u>
<u>a gander.</u>

Read from page 279 to the end of page 288.   Then answer the following questions.

What was Clue Two? <u>Little Boy Blue with the cows in the corn / Whatever</u>
<u>you do / Don't blow this ___?___</u>

Copyright © Houghton Mifflin Company. All rights reserved.

What horn did Alice mean? an old powder horn on the mantle

When Clue Three was unscrambled, what did it say?
little bo peep lost her ___?___

Where did this clue lead Meg? to an old painting of sheep

What was Clue Four? rub a dub/three men in a ___?___

Where did this clue lead Meg? to an old washtub in Gramps's toolshed

Read to the end of the selection. Then fill in the rest of this note pad. See if you can solve the mystery before Meg does!

How did Meg know that the next clue was a fake? It looked different from the other clues and was numbered Clue #4, even though Meg had already found the fourth clue. Also, it had nothing to do with Mother Goose rhymes.

What was the next **real** clue? The little dog laughed

Where did Meg discover the hidden baseball? inside an old stuffed dog

After You Read Answer these questions to help you piece together the parts of the puzzle.

What did all the clues have in common? They all had to do with Mother Goose rhymes and were hidden in Gramps's house. They were written on unlined paper in Alice's handwriting. Also, all of the clues were found in old things.

How was Meg able to solve the mystery? by paying attention to small details and figuring out the meaning of each clue; by thinking logically and making a list of deductions; by being patient and observant

Copyright © Houghton Mifflin Company. All rights reserved.

Meg Mackintosh and the Case of the Missing Babe Ruth Baseball

Think about *Meg Mackintosh and the Case of the Missing Babe Ruth Baseball*. Read each clue below. Write how Meg used the clue to figure out where to look for the next clue.   (Sample answers)

CLUE

1. Not a father
Not a gander
Take a look
In her book

2. Little Boy Blue
with the cows in
the corn
Whatever you do
Don't blow this   ?

3. ucle reeth
tillet ob epep
stol reh   ?

4. rub a dub
three men in a   ?

HOW MEG FIGURED IT OUT

1. Not a father is a mother. Not a gander is a goose. Meg decided to look for the next clue in the Mother Goose book.

2. Meg figured out that the answer was *horn.* At first she looked in the bugle. Then she looked for a clue in the old powder horn.

3. When unscrambled, clue three said "little bo peep lost her ____?____ ." *Sheep* was the missing word. Meg looked behind a painting of sheep.

4. Meg decided that the missing word was *tub.* She found the next clue scratched into the bottom of the old metal bathtub.

Copyright © Houghton Mifflin Company. All rights reserved.

Noting Details About Clues in a Mystery

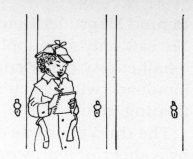

Read this story. See if you can figure out who the thief is. Then answer the questions on page 42.

The Mystery of the Missing Matsuko

"I'm so glad you came quickly, Detective Yee," Mr. Daley sighed miserably. "My prize Matsuko painting has vanished. It's worth thousands of dollars!"

Detective Yee took out her notebook. "Suppose you tell me what happened."

"Well, the painting was here an hour ago, just before I went out," Mr. Daley said. "I usually bring my lunch and eat in the back room, but today it's so hot that I decided to eat by the pond in the park. I carefully locked up the gallery, as I always do. Then five minutes ago I came back — and the painting was gone."

Detective Yee was exploring the small gallery. "It doesn't look as if anyone broke in. Does anyone else have a key?"

"Yes," said Mr. Daley. "I rent three small rooms upstairs to three artists. Each artist has a key. They've all been here since about nine."

"Hmmmm," said Detective Yee thoughtfully. "It is quite possible that one of them came through here on an errand, saw that you were gone, and stole the painting. I'd better find out what they've all been doing in the last hour."

Detective Yee went upstairs and knocked on the first door. It was opened by a woman with bushy white hair. She put down her half-eaten sandwich and gave her name as Jennie Mahoney. In the room, Officer Yee could see an unfinished oil painting of a vase of flowers. On a paint-stained table were a crumpled lunch bag and an orange. Jennie Mahoney said that she had not been out of her room since ten.

The second door had the name Dwight Magruder on it. It was opened by a thin young man with a stringy beard. In answer to Detective Yee's questions, he pointed to a nearly finished drawing. "I was so wrapped up in my work that I haven't been out of this room since I got here at nine."

Copyright © Houghton Mifflin Company. All rights reserved.

Behind Magruder Detective Yee saw only art supplies and a half-empty paper cup of lemonade with ice cubes still floating in it.

The third door was opened by a cheerful man wearing a green apron smeared with clay. He told Detective Yee that his name was Andy Gooden, and he showed her a statue of a fox he'd been working on all morning. He'd gone out once at around eleven to talk to Mr. Daley, but he hadn't been out since. Detective Yee didn't see any signs of lunch in the room and asked whether he had gone out to eat. "Oh, I always go out late — at around three — to get a bite," he told her.

Detective Yee went back into the hallway and nodded to herself. She was sure now that she knew who the thief was. Then she knocked again on one of the doors. When it opened, she said, "Since you clearly didn't tell the truth, you'd better come down to the station with me. I have a lot more questions for you now, Mr. Magruder."

(Sample answers)

1. What was the most important thing that Detective Yee tried to find out from each of the artists?

whether they had gone out in the last hour

2. What two things did Detective Yee especially notice in the room of Dwight Magruder?

A. his art supplies

B. a cup half-full of lemonade and ice

3. What did Detective Yee see in Mr. Magruder's room that told her that he must have gone out on an errand?

the ice in the cup

4. How did Detective Yee know that Mr. Magruder had not brought this item in with him at nine o'clock?

It was hot, and by noon the ice would have melted.

5. What do you know from real life that helped you figure out the mystery?

Ice melts quickly on a hot day.

Copyright © Houghton Mifflin Company. All rights reserved.

Paddington Turns Detective

Dogstar Detective Agency

Imagine that you are interviewing for a job with the Dogstar Detective Agency. Read the questions below, paying attention to the underlined words. Then answer the questions. Use the underlined words in your response. The first one has been done for you. **(Sample answers)**

1. "Your application looks strong, but I have a few questions. First, what special characteristics do you think a detective needs to <u>solve</u> a mystery?"

   "To solve a mystery, a detective needs to have a good eye for details and a good mind to understand clues."

2. "Good! What signs make someone look <u>suspicious</u>?"

   "Someone looks suspicious if that person seems to be in a hurry or gets very nervous when I ask questions."

3. "Excellent! How would you <u>track</u> down a criminal?"

   "I would carefully follow the clues left behind by the criminal until I had tracked the criminal to his or her hideout."

4. "Very good! What could you do to <u>recognize</u> criminals who often <u>disguise</u> themselves?"

   "To recognize criminals who disguise themselves, I'd look for things that may not change, such as voice, height, and weight."

5. "Perfect. Now, what would you do before you <u>accused</u> someone of a crime?"

   "Before I accused anyone, I would be sure that I had enough proof."

6. "Hmmmmm. Finally, what would you use to <u>secure</u> a criminal to make sure he or she doesn't escape?"

   "I would secure a criminal with this special rope I always carry with me."

   "I am impressed. When can you start working?"

Copyright © Houghton Mifflin Company. All rights reserved.

Paddington Turns Detective

Think about *Paddington Turns Detective*. Decide whether each statement below is true or false, and circle that answer. Then write a reason for your answer. **(Sample answers)**

1. Mr. Brown's prize squash was missing.   (True)   False

It had disappeared sometime Wednesday night. Mr. Brown thought that

someone had stolen it.

2. Paddington did not think that the flashing light in the garden was connected to the missing squash.   True   (False)

He saw the light the same night the squash had disappeared, so he thought

the person with the light must be the thief.

3. Paddington wanted to catch the thief.   (True)   False

He disguised himself with a beard. He got rope and batteries for his

flashlight. He hid in the greenhouse that night.

4. Mr. Curry was amused by Paddington's claims that he was a burglar.   True   (False)

He said that Paddington would be sorry for accusing him. He demanded that

the bear be punished and that Mr. Curry be paid damages.

5. Mrs. Brown cooked the prize squash by mistake.   (True)   False

She hadn't realized it was the prize one and had served it for dinner.

6. Paddington was unhappy about the trouble he had caused.   (True)   False

He slipped away, packed his bags, and decided to return to darkest Peru.

Copyright © Houghton Mifflin Company. All rights reserved.

The Case of the Missing Roller Skates

Read the news brief below.
Then answer the questions.

"We interrupt this program to bring you a special report: A valuable statue of the founder of Chocodonuts has disappeared from the lawn of City Hall. We go to Carmen Perez, reporting live. Carmen?"

"Thank you, Douglas. With me here at City Hall is Detective Jones. Detective Jones, I understand that you became aware of this theft when the lawn sprinkler system at City Hall went off unexpectedly. Do you think that whoever set off the sprinklers also stole the statue?"

"Carmen, I can't say. We have no leads, except some doughnut crumbs by the spot where the statue had stood. Perhaps the thief wasn't working alone. The statue would be too heavy for anyone except a weightlifter to lift."

"Thank you, Detective. Citizens of Centerville, please contact City Police if you have any clues."

1. Where was the **scene of the crime**? <u>the lawn of City Hall</u>

2. What was Detective Jones able to report with **certainty**? <u>He could report that the statue was gone, that the sprinkler system had gone off unexpectedly, that there were doughnut crumbs on the spot where the statue had once stood, and that the statue was too heavy for one person.</u>

3. How did the detective **reason** that the thief might have had a **partner**? <u>Detective Jones said that the statue was too heavy for one person to carry, unless that person was a weightlifter.</u>

4. What clues might the police use to **trip** up a **suspect**? <u>The doughnut crumbs; the fact that only a weightlifter could lift the statue.</u>

Copyright © Houghton Mifflin Company. All rights reserved.

The Case of the Missing Roller Skates

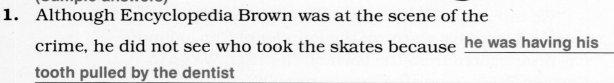

Think about *The Case of the Missing Roller Skates.* Complete each sentence below.

(Sample answers)

1. Although Encyclopedia Brown was at the scene of the crime, he did not see who took the skates because <u>he was having his tooth pulled by the dentist</u>.

2. Encyclopedia reasoned that he should not look for a grown-up thief because <u>a grown-up was not likely to steal an old pair of skates. A grown-up would be too hard to catch in the busy medical building</u>.

3. Encyclopedia checked *every* office in the building to see if a boy or girl had been there that morning because <u>he assumed that a child had taken the skates. He wanted to gather all the information he could about any suspects</u>.

4. Billy Haggerty became Encyclopedia's number one suspect because <u>Billy had been the only other child in the building that morning</u>.

5. When Billy was asked about Dr. Wilson, he gave himself away because <u>he referred to the doctor as *he*, which meant that Billy must have seen the doctor before or had been to his office</u>.

6. When Billy said, "I had a sprained wrist, not a toothache," he made another mistake because <u>this meant that Billy knew Dr. Wilson was a dentist</u>.

Copyright © Houghton Mifflin Company. All rights reserved.

BOOK 6

Walt Disney: Master of Make-Believe

Read each group of words below. Draw a line through the word that does not belong in the group. Then write why the other three words belong together.

1. animator ~~author~~ cartoonist artist

All except *author* are people who draw.

2. cartooning tracing ~~typing~~ painting

All except *typing* are part of an animator's job.

3. ~~scissors~~ celluloid airbrush colored inks

All except *scissors* are tools or materials an animator uses.

4. competitors opponents rivals ~~friends~~

All except *friends* are people who are against one another.

5. series ~~single~~ several multiple

All except *single* mean "more than one."

Use the words in the box to complete the story below.

At last *Mavis Meets the Swamp Monster* was completed. The filmmakers had spent months on the <u>production</u> of the film. They were sure they would make a huge <u>profit</u> on the movie.

> profit
> projected
> production
> contract

Opening night arrived. The filmmakers had signed a <u>contract</u> to show their film at the Capitol Theater. From the moment the first scene was <u>projected</u> on the screen, the audience started laughing. Unfortunately, the movie wasn't supposed to be a comedy.

Copyright © Houghton Mifflin Company. All rights reserved.

Walt Disney: Master of Make-Believe

Think about the biography of Walt Disney. Write an answer to each question below. **(Sample answers)**

1. How did Walt Disney become interested in cartoon animation? <u>He got a job at the Kansas City Film Ad Company making</u> <u>cartoon ads. He liked the job so much that he learned as much about</u> <u>animation as he could.</u>

2. In what ways was Walt a good salesman? <u>He talked people into lending</u> <u>him money for his business or into buying his work.</u>

3. How did Walt improve his animated cartoons? <u>Instead of photographing</u> <u>cutout figures, he photographed a series of drawings to create more lifelike</u> <u>figures. Later he added sound to his cartoons and used storyboards.</u>

4. Why was Walt usually so short of money in the years before he created Mickey Mouse? <u>Starting a new business was expensive.</u> <u>Walt was always using any profits he made to improve his cartoons.</u>

5. What lesson did the Oswald Rabbit series teach Walt? <u>After Mintz had</u> <u>copyrighted Oswald in his own name, Walt vowed to never again work for</u> <u>anyone else.</u>

6. How did Walt get the idea for Mickey Mouse? <u>He sketched a mouse</u> <u>based on his old pet mouse, Mortimer, but his wife suggested that he change</u> <u>the name to Mickey.</u>

Copyright © Houghton Mifflin Company. All rights reserved.

Marian Anderson

Read the advertisement below, paying attention to the underlined words. Then find the meaning of each underlined word in the list of meanings. Write the word on the line next to its meaning.

Are you looking for a <u>career</u> in music? Do you have musical <u>talent</u>, the desire to be a <u>success</u>, and, most important, a <u>spirit</u> of cooperation and hard work?

The Bay City Orchestra and Chorus is looking for you. The first <u>concert</u> of the season is scheduled for late October. This group of <u>professional</u> musicians, which has received many <u>honors</u> from critics across the nation, has openings for the following positions:

▶ An assistant <u>conductor</u> to lead the orchestra rehearsals
▶ An <u>accompanist</u> to play the piano with guest singers
▶ A qualified tenor and soprano to sing <u>duets</u>
▶ Singers with experience in performing <u>spirituals</u>

MEANINGS

1. religious songs
2. person who plays an instrument as the singers sing
3. ability
4. person who directs an orchestra
5. signs of respect or high regard
6. someone who has done well
7. songs sung by two singers
8. paid and trained
9. a musical performance
10. way of earning a living
11. one's nature or character

WORDS

spirituals

accompanist

talent

conductor

honors

success

duets

professional

concert

career

spirit

Copyright © Houghton Mifflin Company. All rights reserved.

Marian Anderson

Think about *Marian Anderson.* Use details from the biography to complete each sentence below.   (Sample answers)

1. Even as a child in the church choir, Marian's voice
    stood out because **it was rich and velvety and she could sing any part of a song** .

2. Marian was able to begin taking private music lessons
    because **the people of the Union Baptist Church believed in her talent and held a concert to raise money for her** .

3. Marian decided to go to Europe to study and perform
    because **her career was standing still. She was rarely asked to perform in important theaters at home** .

4. Although they could not always understand English,
    people the world over loved Marian's singing because
    she poured her heart and soul into her music. They loved her voice and they loved her .

5. Marian gave an outdoor concert at the Lincoln
    Memorial on Easter Sunday because **she had not been allowed to sing in Constitution Hall. She wanted to do whatever she could to gain justice for her people** .

6. When Marian sang with the Metropolitan Opera
    Company, she "opened a door for her own people"
    because **she was the first black person to sing such an important part in an opera. She sang the difficult part successfully** .

Copyright © Houghton Mifflin Company. All rights reserved.

Understanding Influences on People's Lives

Read this biographical article. Think about the influences that made José Clemente Orozco a great artist. Then answer the questions that follow.

Clemente Becomes an Artist

When José Clemente Orozco was a young boy, his family moved to Mexico City. Across the street from their apartment was a printing shop.

Clemente watched for hours at a time as an artist and several helpers made beautiful pictures. He was fascinated by what he saw.

The artist first drew a picture on a metal plate, using a sharp tool instead of a pencil or paintbrush. Next, the artist used the plate to print copies of the picture he had drawn. When they came off the printing press, the pictures were black and white. Then the helpers went to work, coloring in the pictures. Plain prints became colorful works of art.

"This was my awakening to the world of painting," Clemente would later write.

Clemente decided then and there that he would become an artist. He begged his mother to let him study drawing. Finally she agreed. She took him to meet the director of an art school.

"Why, this little child is hardly old enough to be in school!" the director exclaimed. But when he saw some of Clemente's pictures, he let the boy visit a drawing class.

Clemente soon showed the teachers at the school that he had real artistic talent. The director called to tell Clemente's parents that their son was a better drawer than any of the older students in his class. Clemente was then allowed to become a regular student at the art school. He was certain he could become an artist.

When he finished school, Clemente was given an award of money to study further. But the award wasn't given to study art — it was to study farming! Clemente's father was happy. After all, his family was

Copyright © Houghton Mifflin Company. All rights reserved.

poor. If Clemente learned how to help farmers, he would soon be able to earn money.

Clemente was not happy. He wanted to be an artist, but he did go on to study farming. The only part he liked, however, was drawing maps of farms.

Soon after that, an event happened that would change Clemente's life. One day Clemente and a friend were trying to make fireworks. Suddenly there was a huge explosion! Clemente's left hand was so badly burned that a doctor had to operate and remove it. Clemente's eyes were injured too. He would wear thick glasses for the rest of his life.

But Clemente did not let the accident ruin his life. In fact, it made him more determined than ever to pursue his dream of being an artist. He began taking art classes at night and taking odd jobs as an artist.

At art school Clemente's favorite teacher was Dr. Atl. Dr. Atl suggested that Clemente paint some pictures showing important events in Mexico's history. Clemente took Dr. Atl's advice. When the paintings were shown, people loved them. This was only the beginning of José Clemente Orozco's fame as one of the great Mexican painters of the twentieth century.

Think about these actions. What does each one show about Clemente? Write your answer in the second column. (Sample answers)

Action	What It Shows About Clemente
1. He spent hours watching the printers make beautiful pictures at the print shop across the street.	1. He was curious and had a lot of patience. He loved art.
2. He asked his mother if he could go to art school.	2. He knew at a young age that he wanted to be an artist. He knew he needed to work at his talent.
3. After his terrible accident, Clemente went back to art school.	3. He didn't allow the accident to ruin his life. He was determined to become an artist.

Copyright © Houghton Mifflin Company. All rights reserved.

Roberto Clemente

Use the words in the box from the selection *Roberto Clemente* to complete this biography about a baseball player named Lou Gehrig.

Even as a young man, Lou Gehrig was a powerful hitter. Many professional baseball teams in the <u>major leagues</u> wanted him to play for them. When Lou's father needed money for an operation, it was Lou's greatest <u>desire</u> to help. So he signed to play with the New York Yankees.

Lou didn't get to play right away, but he was <u>patient</u>. After two years, he got to bat in the ninth <u>inning</u> of a game. He hit the ball far into the <u>outfield</u>, but it was caught. However, after that he never missed playing in another game.

Lou became one of the all-time great hitters, once hitting four home runs in one game. With Lou, the Yankees won many <u>championships</u>, including the World Series seven times. He was also known as a gentleman who <u>treated</u> others with respect and as <u>equals</u>.

Sadly, Lou found out that he had a disease, which forced him to retire. The Yankees set aside a game to honor him. The <u>stadium</u> was packed with fans. As Lou stood in the infield one last time, he told the crowd, "Today I consider myself the luckiest man on the face of the earth." Two years later, he died.

Today, Lou Gehrig lives on at the Baseball Hall of Fame and in the hearts of all who knew him.

stadium
championships
inning
equals
outfield
major leagues
desire
treated
patient

Copyright © Houghton Mifflin Company. All rights reserved.

Roberto Clemente

Think about *Roberto Clemente.* Write two or more details from the biography to support each statement below.   (Sample answers)

1. As a boy, Roberto loved to play baseball.

    He and his friends made their own baseballs out of string and played

    baseball after school. He ran track and threw the javelin in high

    school to improve his baseball skills.

2. Roberto's efforts to become a good player soon paid off.

    He was picked to play for a team in Santurce before he finished high school.

    He played on the Brooklyn Dodgers' farm team when he was nineteen.

3. Clemente played outstanding baseball for the Pittsburgh Pirates.

    He was a tremendous fielder. He got a hit in every game of the 1960 and 1971

    World Series. He won many batting titles. He was a member of the All-Star

    team many times. He made 3,000 hits.

4. Clemente was not always happy in the United States.

    He felt that he and other Spanish-speaking players were not always treated

    fairly. He was often sick or injured. After each baseball season, he returned

    to Puerto Rico.

5. Although Clemente died in 1972, he is still honored today.

    He was elected to the Hall of Fame. A sign was placed on the door of the

    room where he had lived. His dream of a sports center for Puerto Rican

    children became a reality.

Copyright © Houghton Mifflin Company. All rights reserved.

BOOK 7

Teacher's Pet

Read each statement below, paying attention to the underlined words. Then answer the question that follows the statement.   (Sample answers)

1. It is the first day of school, and Mrs. Bartles's students want to <u>enhance</u> the blank bulletin board in their classroom. What can they do to enhance it?

   They could put up posters or paint a mural on it.

2. Stanley hopes to <u>impress</u> Mrs. Bartles on the first day. What can he do to impress her?

   He might raise his hand if he has a question. He might be in his seat when the bell rings.

3. Mrs. Bartles does not have a very good <u>memory</u> and cannot remember the names of all her students. What can she do to help her memory?

   She could make a seating chart or have the students wear name tags.

4. Claudia has always been the best student in science, but now that Matthew has joined the class, she has finally met her <u>match</u>. How do you think she feels?

   She might be determined to study harder or to do work for extra credit.

5. José is trying to <u>convince</u> his classmates to vote for him for class president. How can he convince them?

   He might tell them how honest and hardworking he is.

6. Shirley put much <u>effort</u> into writing a report, but her puppy ate it. How do you think she felt afterward?

   She was probably angry that she had to start all over again after spending so much time on the first report.

Copyright © Houghton Mifflin Company. All rights reserved.

Teacher's Pet

Think about the story *Teacher's Pet*. Read each event below, and choose the word from the box that best tells how Cricket felt. Write the word on the line. Then write a reason for your choice. **(Sample answers)**

> stunned   eager   strange
> foolish   proud

Beverly Cleary

How Did Cricket Feel When . . .

1. . . . she realized that Zoe was as good a student as she was? <u>strange</u>

   Cricket felt strange not being the best student in class, but at the same time, the competition made her learn more.

2. . . . Mrs. Schraalenburgh said that everyone had to write a book report once a month? <u>eager</u>

   Cricket liked writing book reports and hoped to prove to the teacher that she was the best student.

3. . . . she completed her book report? <u>proud</u>

   She had copied it over neatly and had made a special cover for it. She thought the book report would impress her teacher.

4. . . . she saw a B− written at the top of her book report? <u>stunned</u>

   Cricket was certain she had done A+ work.

5. . . . Mrs. Schraalenburgh wrote Beverly Cleary's name on the chalk board? <u>foolish</u>

   Cricket realized she should have taken more care in writing her book report, instead of wasting time making a fancy cover.

Copyright © Houghton Mifflin Company. All rights reserved.

Making Room for Uncle Joe

Use the words in the box to complete the two journal entries below.

responsible   routine   embarrassing
appreciates   nuisance   encouraged

Dear Journal,

My friend Gil went on vacation and left his dog, Mayonnaise, with me. That dog is always causing trouble — he's a real __nuisance__. Yesterday I went to the park to play ball, and Mayonnaise followed me. I petted him and __encouraged__ him to behave himself, but every time someone hit the ball, that crazy mutt chased it and ran off with it. Finally we had to stop the game. The guys actually thought that dog was mine! It was really __embarrassing__. I sure hope Gil __appreciates__ what I'm doing for him.

Dear Journal,

Sorry I haven't written in a while, but I've been busy taking care of you-know-who. I'm __responsible__ for feeding him in the morning and walking him three times a day. That's been our __routine__ all week. At night he sleeps beside my bed. I think I'm going to miss that old Mayonnaise when Gil comes home. I'm sure glad they live next door.

Copyright © Houghton Mifflin Company. All rights reserved.

Making Room for Uncle Joe

Think about the story *Making Room for Uncle Joe.*
Complete the chart below by explaining why the family
members felt as they did at different points in the story.
(Sample answers)

WHEN UNCLE JOE FIRST CAME

1. Beth was upset because she was embarrassed to have Uncle Joe around the house. She didn't want any of her friends to come over with Joe there.

2. Amy was excited because she thought she could help Uncle Joe and be his friend.

3. Dan was worried because he thought Uncle Joe might be a nuisance. His friend Ben had made fun of retarded people.

4. Uncle Joe felt out of place because he missed his old friends. He tried to be helpful around the house but didn't always succeed.

AFTER THEY GOT TO KNOW ONE ANOTHER

1. Beth felt happy because she gave Uncle Joe piano lessons. She enjoyed being a teacher.

2. Amy was thrilled because she had found a friend who listened to her read and tell stories.

3. Dan felt relieved because he and his friends learned to enjoy being with Joe. They had fun bowling, playing, and working together.

4. Uncle Joe felt that he belonged because he found ways to be helpful and he got along with everyone.

Copyright © Houghton Mifflin Company. All rights reserved.

Making Inferences About Characters

Read this story. Try to understand what Marty is like by paying attention to what he says, thinks, and does.

First Day

Marty's classmates were listing the products of Texas while he was listing his good points to himself: "I'm nice. People say I have a good sense of humor. I'm a good shortstop ... and I'm pretty smart." He stopped. Marty wasn't sure whether being smart would be okay with all the students at his new school.

"Jason!" said Mrs. Thornsby sharply. "You seem to have lots to say. Perhaps you can tell me: What is Texas's leading crop?"

Marty already knew which of his new classmates was Jason. He was the one who came into class that morning wearing his baseball cap backwards, clowning around.

But at this moment Jason's face was a blank wall. "Corn?" he responded loudly.

Mrs. Thornsby shook her head. "Marty, can you answer the question, please?" she said.

Marty had been slouching in his chair, trying to look invisible. But now he sat up and looked around the room.

"Ummmm . . . cotton?" he said in a quiet voice.

"Very good," Mrs. Thornsby said.

Marty hunched over his open book and blushed.

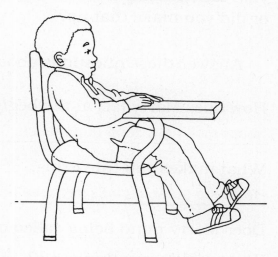

Just before noon, Mrs. Thornsby said to the class, "I introduced Marty Chapman to you this morning. We have a few minutes before lunch. Marty, would you tell us a little about yourself?"

Marty stood up slowly, then said, "I'm from Virginia." He glanced around the room.

"Where in Virginia?" asked Mrs. Thornsby.

"Just outside Norfolk. There's a huge base there and my father just retired from

Copyright © Houghton Mifflin Company. All rights reserved.

the Navy, so we lived there until last year —"

There was much chatter at this remark. Had he said something wrong? To Marty's relief, the noon bell rang.

Marty tried to slip past Jason and the rest of his classmates without being noticed. Then, to his horror, Marty heard his name called in a loud voice, and then: "Was your father really in the Navy, or did you make that up?"

Marty froze. He recognized that clowning voice behind him. He turned around. "Yes, it's true," he replied carefully.

"Wow!" Jason exclaimed. "Have you ever been on a battleship?"

Marty let out a sigh. "Yeah, my dad was an officer and one time our whole family got to sail on . . ." he began as they walked together toward the lunchroom. He had passed the first test of the new school year.

Answer these questions about the story.   (Sample answers)

1. How does Marty feel at the beginning of the story? scared, nervous about making a good impression

What makes you think this? He lists what he thinks are his good points. He keeps quiet in class because he doesn't want to seem like a showoff.

2. Does Marty mind being called on by Mrs. Thornsby? yes
What makes you think this? Marty is slouching in his chair to avoid attention. He hunches over and blushes after he has answered and is praised.

3. Why does Marty freeze when he hears Jason call his name? He isn't sure whether Jason is being friendly or mean. He's nervous about talking to Jason for the first time.

4. How does Marty feel after he hears Jason's question about being on a battleship? relieved, at ease

How do you know this? He lets out a sigh and starts chatting with Jason.

Copyright © Houghton Mifflin Company. All rights reserved.

Justin and the Best Biscuits in the World

Read each group of words below. Draw a line through the word that does not belong in the group. Then write why the other three words belong together.

1. festival   party   carnival   ~~ordeal~~

   All except *ordeal* are kinds of celebrations.

2. fairgrounds   pavilion   ~~ranch house~~   competitions

   All except *ranch house* are part of a festival.

3. entry rules   categories   prizes   ~~ingredients~~

   All except *ingredients* are part of a contest.

4. ~~buried~~   displayed   showed   exhibited

   All except *buried* mean "set out for viewing."

5. rolls   ~~pumpkins~~   buns   biscuits

   All except *pumpkins* are types of bread.

6. determine   ~~hesitate~~   conclude   decide

   All except *hesitate* mean "to make up one's mind."

7. eagerness   ~~boredom~~   enthusiasm   excitement

   All except *boredom* mean "great interest in something."

8. declare   announce   proclaim   ~~conceal~~

   All except *conceal* mean "to make known."

Copyright © Houghton Mifflin Company. All rights reserved.

Justin and the Best Biscuits in the World

Think about *Justin and the Best Biscuits in the World.* Write two or more sentences to support each statement below, using details from the story.
(Sample answers)

1. Justin was excited about going to the festival.

   He jumped out of bed that morning. He put on his clothes quickly and joined Grandpa in the kitchen.

2. Grandpa took great care to keep the biscuits hot.

   He planned to arrive just before the contest deadline. He wrapped the hot skillet of biscuits in towels. Once at the festival, he covered the plate of biscuits with a napkin.

3. Justin was a good sport about losing the pie-eating contest.

   He praised the winner. He was glad he hadn't eaten any more.

4. Grandpa took great care to get ready to return to the festival that night.

   He took a long time to shower and get dressed. He wore a sharp-looking suede vest with fringe. He put on a nice fragrance.

5. By the time the judges were ready to announce the winner for the best biscuits, Justin was worried.

   He wondered why the announcer didn't hurry up. His stomach felt weak, and his hands were cold.

6. Grandpa was thrilled about winning first prize in the biscuit-baking competition.

   He smiled and rushed up to receive his prize. He celebrated later by dancing with all the ladies.

Copyright © Houghton Mifflin Company. All rights reserved.

Chasing After Annie

Read the story below, paying attention to the underlined words. Then find the meaning of each underlined word in the list of meanings. Write the word on the line next to its meaning.

The scrawny kitten was meowing in its cage. Its previous owner had abandoned it. Luckily, someone had found the little ball of fur in an alley and brought it to Joan's animal shelter.

Joan Steiner, director of the shelter, had seen lots of animals that had been abandoned, but it was always a shock when it happened. Joan was a true animal lover. Everyone who knew her said she wasn't a phony who ran the shelter only to make money.

Joan liked to brag that she could immediately tell someone's personality just by the way he or she acted toward animals. "You can't pretend with me," she liked to say. She made sure her animals were placed only with people who had a genuine love of animals.

MEANINGS	WORDS
a person's nature	personality
fake	phony
act in a false way	pretend
a great surprise	shock
real	genuine
boast	brag
a place for stray animals	animal shelter
earlier	previous

Copyright © Houghton Mifflin Company. All rights reserved.

Chasing After Annie

Think about the story *Chasing After Annie*.
Answer each question below.   (Sample answers)

1. Why didn't Annie like Richie at first?

    He bragged all the time about everything he did.

2. Why did Richie *think* Annie liked him?

    Richie thought Annie was impressed by his muscles, his good grades, and

    his fish scrapbook. He also thought she liked him because he could play

    chess, spell *microgroove,* **and high dive.**

3. What did Annie and Richie do to try to find
    Annie's dog?

    Richie and Annie looked all over the neighborhood for Fritz. Richie drew

    a picture of Fritz and put it up at school. He also went to the animal shelter

    to look for Fritz.

4. What made Richie give the dog from the animal
    shelter to Annie?

    He thought she needed any Fritz she could get. He wanted to make a good

    impression on her.

5. How did Annie feel toward Richie when he gave
    her the dog?

    She began to like Richie more. When she thought of Richie, she no longer

    thought of bugs and itches and liver. She smiled at him in school, and she

    bought him a book about high diving.

Copyright © Houghton Mifflin Company. All rights reserved.

6. Why did the new Fritz seem strange to Annie?

He smelled funny, had to be trained again, had two different-colored eyes,

and had a funny bump on his leg.

7. What made Richie feel like a phony?

He had played a dirty trick on Annie by pretending to find Fritz. Now Annie

was so grateful that she wanted to give him a present, which he knew he

didn't deserve.

8. Why did Richie suddenly run from Annie's door just
as he was about to tell her the truth about the dog?

He saw the real Fritz returning and was embarrassed that he had been

caught in a lie.

9. How did Annie feel toward Richie when she found
out the truth about the two dogs?

She was mad that he had tricked her. She hated Richie more than bugs,

itches, and liver.

10. What made Annie finally decide that there were
worse people in the world than Richie Carr?

She saw how he treated Duchess and realized he was a dog person

like herself.

Copyright © Houghton Mifflin Company. All rights reserved.

Unfamiliar Word Meanings

Read the paragraphs below, paying attention to the underlined words. Write what you think each underlined word means. Then write any clues that helped you understand the word.

Frank was so hungry that he <u>consumed</u> two helpings of meat loaf and mashed potatoes for dinner. His mother had to <u>restrain</u> him from eating the cherry pie afterward, because she was saving it for company later. Frank didn't want to wait, but his mother promised to give him a big piece if he was patient.   **(Sample answers)**

1. meaning of <u>consumed</u>: ate

   clues: so hungry, meat loaf and mashed potatoes

2. meaning of <u>restrain</u>: hold back

   clues: saving it for later, didn't want to wait

At first Luisa was <u>hesitant</u> about writing to a pen pal, but later she was glad she had decided to do it. Luisa found that she and her pen pal had many things in common. They enjoyed reading each other's letters so much that they <u>corresponded</u> at least once a week.

3. meaning of <u>hesitant</u>: not certain

   clues: at first, but later, glad she had decided

4. meaning of <u>corresponded</u>: wrote

   clues: reading each other's letters

Now use a dictionary to check the meanings that you wrote.

Copyright © Houghton Mifflin Company. All rights reserved.

Parts of a Book

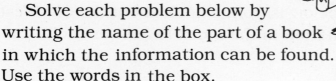

Solve each problem below by writing the name of the part of a book in which the information can be found. Use the words in the box.

title page	copyright page	table of contents	glossary

1. Becky has six books about space, and she wants to read the one with the most up-to-date facts. Which book part will tell her when each book was published?

   copyright page

2. Rick wants to know if his book titled *Great Baseball Players* has a chapter on Babe Ruth. Where can he look?

   table of contents

3. Carlos is writing a book report on the book he just read. He wants to list the title, the author, and the publisher in his report. Where can he find this information?

   title page

4. Brenda came across the word *fuse* in her science textbook and wants to find out what it means. What part of the book can she use to find the meaning?

   glossary

5. Gaby wants to know how many stories there are in her new book of folktales. Where should she look?

   table of contents

Now use a textbook of your own to find the date the textbook was published, the name of the publishing company, and the title of the first chapter or section.

Copyright © Houghton Mifflin Company. All rights reserved.

Using an Index

The index below is from a book about the Old West. Use the information in the index to answer each question.

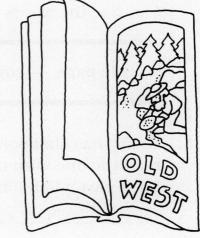

Games: indoor, 21; outdoor, 22
Gold: discovery of, 28–29; gold rush,
 34–35; mining of, 40
Goodnight, Molly, 51, 53

Hickok, Wild Bill, 46–48, 50
Hispanic settlers, 4, 17–19
Homes: building of, 8, 10, 15–16;
 furnishings for, 13–14; types of, 11–12
Homesteaders, 7, 14, 27

1. How many pages tell about Wild Bill Hickok? _four_

2. Which pages might you look at to find out who the homesteaders were? _7, 14, 27_

3. What are the subtopics listed under the main topic **Games**? _indoor, outdoor_

4. Under which main topic can you find out about how gold was mined? _Gold_

5. Which pages give information about Hispanic settlers? _4, 17–19_

6. How many pages give information about Molly Goodnight? _two_

7. On which pages would you expect to find information about log cabins, sod houses, or other types of homes? _11–12_

Use the index of a social studies book to find the main topic **Indians** or **Native Americans**. On a separate sheet of paper, list a few of the subtopics found under that topic.

Copyright © Houghton Mifflin Company. All rights reserved.

Following Directions

Read the directions for making homemade clay. Then answer the questions that follow.

You can enjoy hours of fun modeling with clay. It's even more fun when you make the clay yourself! First, you will need to gather the following: a large mixing bowl, 2 cups of flour, 1/2 cup of salt, 1 cup of water, 1 tablespoon of oil, and 1 tablespoon of hand lotion.

Mix the flour and the salt together in the mixing bowl. Next, add the oil and water. Then work the mixture with your hands until it is doughlike. If the clay is too stiff, add more water. If it is too wet, add more flour. When the clay is a thickness that you like, knead in the hand lotion.

After you have made the clay, you can store it in the refrigerator or make something with it right away!

1. What is the first thing you do after gathering the items needed? <u>Mix the flour and salt in the mixing bowl.</u>

2. What key word tells you when to add the oil and water? <u>next</u>

3. What do you do if the clay is too stiff? <u>Add more water.</u>

4. When might you need to add more flour to the mix? <u>if the clay is too wet</u>

5. When do you knead in the hand lotion? <u>when the clay is a thickness that you like</u>

6. What two things can you do with the clay after you have made it? <u>Put the clay in the refrigerator or make something with it right away.</u>

Copyright © Houghton Mifflin Company. All rights reserved.

Card Catalog

There are three kinds of cards in the card catalog. Look at the sample card catalog cards below. Then use what you know about the card catalog to answer each question.

```
598.61   Patent, Dorothy Hinshaw
Pa         Wild turkey, tame turkey, by
             Dorothy Hinshaw Patent. Photos
```
Author card

```
598.61   Wild turkey, tame turkey
Pa         Patent, Dorothy Hinshaw
             Wild turkey, tame turkey, by
```
Title card

```
           TURKEYS
598.61   Patent, Dorothy Hinshaw
Pa            Wild turkey, tame turkey, by
             Dorothy Hinshaw Patent. Photos
             by William Muñoz.
             New York, Clarion Books, 1989
             52 p. illus.
                Relates the history of the native
             North American turkey and compares
             that proud bird with its farmyard cousin.
```
Subject card

1. Which kind of card would you use to find out what books the library has by Patricia McKissack? __author__

2. Which kind of card would you use to find out if the library has any books on hockey? __subject__

3. Which kind of card would you use to find out if the library has the book *Stone Fox*? __title__

4. What letter would the title card for *The Hundred Dresses* be listed under? __H__ Why? __because the first important word in the title is *hundred*__

5. What letter would the author cards for books written by Daniel Pinkwater be listed under? __P__

The next time you go to the library, use the card catalog to find the title of one book about hockey, the title of one book by Daniel Pinkwater, and the author of *Stone Fox*. Write your answers on a separate sheet of paper.

Copyright © Houghton Mifflin Company. All rights reserved.

Using the Library

The top part of four card catalog cards are shown below. Study each card and decide in which section of the library — **Fiction, Nonfiction,** or **Biography** — you would look to find the book. Write the name of the section. Then write where in that section you would look to find the book. **(Sample answers)**

362.42   Bergman, Thomas
Be   Finding a common
     language: children
     living with deafness,
     by Thomas Bergman
	Hurwitz, Johanna
	
	Hurray for Ali Baba Bernstein,
	by Johanna Hurwitz; illustrated
	by Gail Owens

1. Section: <u>Nonfiction</u>

2. Where to Find Book: <u>The</u> <u>call number tells me this book</u> <u>would be on the 300's shelf.</u>

5. Section: <u>Fiction</u>

6. Where to Find Book: <u>It</u> <u>would be on the Fiction</u> <u>shelves under H for Hurwitz.</u>

B Wilbur & Orville Wright
W Rowland-Entwistle, Theodore
  Wilbur & Orville Wright, by
  Theodore Rowland-Entwistle;
  illustrated by W. Francis
  Phillipps
	ELECTRICITY — EXPERIMENTS
	
	537.07 Markle, Sandra
	Ma Power up: experiments,
	    puzzles, and games
	    exploring electricity, by
	    Sandra Markle

3. Section: <u>Biography</u>

4. Where to Find Book: <u>The</u> <u>book would be under W for</u> <u>Wright on the Biography</u> <u>shelves.</u>

7. Section: <u>Nonfiction</u>

8. Where to Find Book: <u>It has</u> <u>a call number and would be</u> <u>on the 500's shelf.</u>

Copyright © Houghton Mifflin Company. All rights reserved.

Using an Encyclopedia

Look at the picture of the set of encyclopedias. Then read each topic listed below. Write the key word or words you would use to find information about the topic and the volume number in which you could find it. The first one has been done for you.

	Topic	Key Word or Words	Volume
1.	Explorer Thor Heyerdahl's journeys	**Heyerdahl, Thor**	**9**
2.	The history of the United Nations	United Nations	20
3.	The crops grown in North Dakota	North Dakota	14
4.	How motion pictures are made	motion pictures	13
5.	The habits of koalas	koalas	11
6.	The parts of the solar system	solar system	18
7.	Rachel Carson's work for wildlife	Carson, Rachel	3
8.	Why Yorktown, Virginia, is famous	Yorktown	21

Now answer these questions about guide words.

9. Would information about koalas be on, before, or after the pages with the guide words *Knoxville* and *Korea*? on

10. Would information about North Dakota be on, before, or after the pages with the guide words *North America* and *North Carolina*? after

Now use an encyclopedia to find out some facts about one of the above topics. Write the facts on a separate sheet of paper.

Copyright © Houghton Mifflin Company. All rights reserved.

Reading a Street Map

Study the street map of Fairy Tale Village. Use the information on the map to answer the questions that follow.

1. In the legend, what does ☐ stand for? <u>Building</u>

2. How many parks or forests are there in Fairy Tale Village? <u>two</u>

3. If you wanted to go from Elves' Workshop to Gingerbread House, in which direction would you travel on Candy Cane Lane? <u>north</u>

4. What intersection is near the Fairy Godmother's Cottage? <u>Rumpelstiltskin Road and Beanstalk Street</u>

5. How would you go from Magic Mirror Mansion to Cinderella's Castle? <u>Go north on Beanstalk Street, turn west on</u> <u>Snow White Boulevard, and cross over the footbridge.</u>

6. How would you go from Toadstool Park to Fairyland Forest? <u>Go east on Rumpelstiltskin Road, turn north on Beanstalk</u> <u>Street, and turn east on Pirate Alley.</u>

Copyright © Houghton Mifflin Company. All rights reserved.

Reading Diagrams

Read the paragraph below and study the diagram.
Then answer each question.

The Plains Indians lived in tepees. The word *tepee*
means "used to dwell in." Tepees were not just simple
tents. The tepee was made of a frame of tall wooden poles.
First, the frame poles were arranged in a cone shape.
Then the framework was covered with a cover made of
buffalo hides. The cover was fastened together in front
with lacing pins and attached to the ground with pegs.
Openings were left at the top and near the base. The flaps
at the top could be opened to let out the smoke from
cooking fires. Two poles set behind the tepee held the
smoke flaps open.

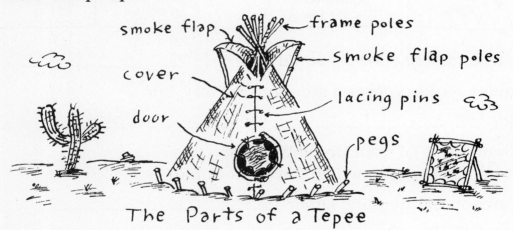

The Parts of a Tepee

1. What does the diagram above show? <u>the parts of a tepee</u>

2. How was the cover fastened together in front? <u>with lacing pins</u>

3. Why was an opening left at the top of the tepee? <u>so smoke from</u>
   <u>cooking fires could be let out</u>

4. How many poles held the smoke flaps open? <u>two</u>

5. What were used to attach the cover to the ground? <u>pegs</u>

6. If you wanted to make a model of a tepee, how might
   this diagram help you? (Sample answer) <u>It shows what parts are needed</u>
   <u>and how they fit together.</u>

Copyright © Houghton Mifflin Company. All rights reserved.

Bar Graphs and Line Graphs

Study the bar graph and the line graph. Use the graphs to answer the questions below.

Student Use of Computers in 4 Schools

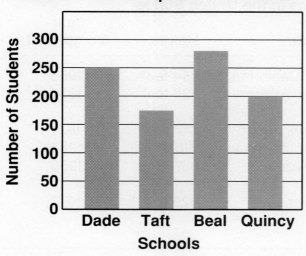

Use of Computers — Grade 4, Beal School

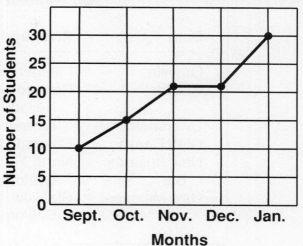

1. In which school do the most students use the computer? __Beal__

2. How many students at the Dade School use computers? __250__

3. In which school is the student use of computers greater, Taft or Quincy? __Quincy__

4. How many more students use the computer at Dade than use the computer at Quincy? __50__

5. In what month did the most fourth grade students at Beal use computers? __January__

6. How many Beal fourth graders used computers in October? __15__

7. How did the number of fourth graders who used the computer change from September to October? __It went up by 5.__

8. During what two months did the number of fourth graders using computers stay the same? __November and December__

Copyright © Houghton Mifflin Company. All rights reserved.

Tables

Study the table below. Use the information on the table to answer the questions.

Six Highest Dams in the United States			
Dam	River and State	Height	Year Completed
Oroville	Feather River, California	754 feet	1968
Hoover	Colorado River, Arizona/ Nevada	726 feet	1936
Dworshak	Clearwater River, Idaho	717 feet	1974
Glen Canyon	Colorado River, Arizona	710 feet	1964
New Bullards Bar	North Yuba River, California	637 feet	1968
New Melones	Stanislaus River, California	625 feet	1978

1. Which U.S. dam is the highest? Oroville Dam

2. Which of the six dams is the newest? New Melones Dam

3. Which of the six dams is the oldest? Hoover Dam

4. Where is Dworshak Dam located? on the Clearwater River in Idaho

5. Which of the dams listed are located on the Colorado River? Hoover Dam, Glen Canyon Dam

6. Which of the dams listed are located in California? Oroville Dam, New Bullards Bar Dam, New Melones Dam

7. Which one of the two dams completed in the 1970's is higher? Dworshak Dam

8. How many of these dams are over 700 feet high? four

Copyright © Houghton Mifflin Company. All rights reserved.

Locating Information Quickly

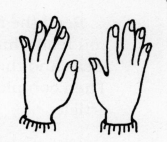

Skim the article by reading the title, headings, and first paragraph. Try to get an idea of what the article is about in general. Then answer the questions that follow.

Fingernail Factories

How do fingernails grow? Not by accident! They are designed like factories to make nail growth possible.

How Fingernails Grow

The main part of your fingernail is the nail plate, which protects the nail bed underneath. The nail plate is not like skin. No blood flows into the plate.

Look at your thumbnail. Can you see the half-moon at the base? The half-moon, or *lunula,* is the "nail-plate factory." It helps make new nail. When new nail is added to the old nail plate, the whole nail is pushed up and out. That is how nails grow.

How Fast Nails Grow

How fast nails grow depends on several things — your age, the time of year, your health and eating habits, and which hand you use the most. Nails grow more slowly as you get older. For an adult, a nail grows about one-eighth of an inch a month. Nails grow more slowly in winter than in summer. Being ill or not eating the right foods may slow nail growth. The nails on the hand you use most usually grow faster than those on your other hand.

1. What is the article about in general? <u>how fingernails grow</u>

2. What helped you figure this out? <u>the opening paragraph and the two</u> <u>subtitles</u>

Now scan the article to answer the following questions.

3. What part of the nail is the "nail-plate factory"? <u>half-moon or lunula</u>

4. What things affect how fast your nails grow? <u>your age, the time of year,</u> <u>your health and eating habits, which hand you use the most</u>

Copyright © Houghton Mifflin Company. All rights reserved.

Outlines

Read the following article. As you read, think about the main ideas and the important details. Then complete the outline of the article.

President's Day

President's Day is a national holiday that falls on the third Monday in February. This holiday celebrates the birthdays of two important United States presidents — George Washington and Abraham Lincoln.

The holiday has changed over the years. People first celebrated the holiday in the late 1700's in honor of George Washington's birthday on February 22. Later, people decided to also honor Abraham Lincoln, whose birthday was on February 12. Finally, the two holidays were combined into one day to honor these great men.

On President's Day many places are closed, just as they are on other national holidays. In most states, government and business offices are closed on this day. There is no mail delivery because post offices are closed, and schools and banks are closed, too.

Title: President's Day

I. What President's Day celebrates

    A. George Washington's birthday

    B. Abraham Lincoln's birthday

II. How the holiday has changed

    A. Used to be for Washington's birthday only

    B. Lincoln's birthday was added later

III. Which places are closed on President's Day

    A. Government and business offices

    B. Post offices, schools, and banks

Copyright © Houghton Mifflin Company. All rights reserved.

Summarizing Information Graphically

Read the article about camels. Then summarize the information graphically by completing the chart.

Camels

Why Camels Are Useful

Camels are best known for carrying heavy loads across the deserts of Asia and Africa. On long trips, a large camel can carry four hundred pounds on its back. Also, the hair, meat, and milk of camels are important to desert people. The camel's soft hair is woven into cloth, while its milk and meat are used as food.

The Camel's Body

A camel's body is well suited for desert travel. Its feet are broad and padded. Its hoof is only at the tip of the toes, which helps the camel to walk on loose sand. Fat is stored in its hump. When there is not much food, the camel's body draws on the fat. Besides the water stored in the fat, water may be stored in the camel's stomach. Camels can go three days without water.

Complaints About Camels

Camels are considered bad tempered, ungraceful, and ugly. No matter how well they are treated, they never seem to even notice their masters. Also, it is costly to keep camels. They can find some grasses for themselves, but they still must be fed hay and grain.

(Sample answers)

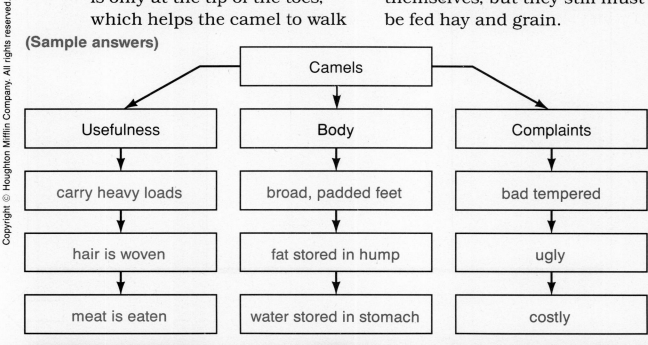

Copyright © Houghton Mifflin Company. All rights reserved.

K-W-L

Use the K-W-L chart to help you read the article on the next page. First, look at the article and identify what the topic is. Write the topic on the chart.

Next, write in the "Know" column what you already know about this topic. In the second column, write what you want to know about this topic.

Then read the article. When you finish reading, return to the chart and write in the third column what you learned.

Topic: Paul Revere's Many Skills

What I Know	What I Want to Find Out	What I Learned
(Answers will vary.)	(Students' notes will vary but will probably indicate that they want to learn what skills Paul Revere had.)	(Sample answer) Paul Revere was a famous silversmith. He also made false teeth. He was a leader of the Boston Tea Party.

Copyright © Houghton Mifflin Company. All rights reserved.

Paul Revere: A Man of Many Skills

For many people, the name Paul Revere brings to mind the image of a man on a galloping horse on his way to warn everyone that the British were coming. Revere's famous midnight ride has become a legend and the subject of poetry and art. Although he is best known today for his ride, the people of Revere's day knew him for many other reasons.

Paul Revere's Trade

Paul Revere was an outstanding silversmith who learned the trade from his father. When the senior Revere died, Paul worked as a silversmith to support the rest of the family. He made a wide range of items, from silver trays and teapots to more unusual things, such as a silver dog collar and a baby rattle. He was considered to be the best silversmith in Boston.

Revere's Other Occupations

When hard times came to Boston and people had less money to spend on items made from silver, Revere switched to other activities to earn a living. He made prints of political cartoons from engraved copper plates. These prints are collectors' items now, although Revere was not thought to be a great artist. Revere also worked for a while putting false teeth in place for people and fixing them with wires.

Revere the Patriot

Paul Revere was active in the colonial efforts against the British. He was a leader of the Boston Tea Party, and after the cases of tea had been dumped into Boston Harbor, Revere rode to New York and Philadelphia to spread the news. During this trip, Revere covered 800 miles in eleven days. He often went on long rides to carry important messages to other parts of the colonies. He did carry out his famous midnight warning ride, but it was only one of his many contributions to the American Revolution.

Copyright © Houghton Mifflin Company. All rights reserved.

SQRRR

Use the SQRRR study method to help you read the
article on the next page. Follow the directions below.
(Sample answers)

S **1.** Survey the text. Look at the title, headings, picture,
and caption to get an idea of what the text is about.
Write what you think the text is about.

what giant pandas look like, where they live, what they eat, and why

they are lucky

Q **2.** Read the first heading and turn it into a question.
Write your question below.

Heading 1: **What do giant pandas look like?**

R **3.** Read to answer your question. Write the answer to
your question below.

Pandas are partly black and partly white. They are very large.

R **4.** Now recite in your own words the answer to your
question.

Repeat steps 2 – 4 for Headings 2, 3, and 4. Write the
question and answer it.

Heading 2: **Where do pandas live?**

Answer: **They live in bamboo forests in China.**

Heading 3: **What are the panda's eating habits?**

Answer: **It picks bamboo shoots, then sits down to eat them slowly.**

Heading 4: **Why are pandas lucky?**

Answer: **They are thought of as ''treasures,'' are protected, and get**

special attention.

R **5.** Review the headings. Try to answer each question
from memory.

Copyright © Houghton Mifflin Company. All rights reserved.

Pandas

What animal is black and white, fat and furry, cute and comical? You guessed it — the panda! Pandas have always lived in the far-off forests of western China. Nowadays, a few pandas also live in zoos.

What Giant Pandas Look Like

The Chinese name for the panda is *beishung,* a word that means "white bear." However, giant pandas are white *and* black. They have black ears and eye patches. They look as if they are wearing a short jacket with a black collar and black sleeves, and high black socks. Giant pandas are very large. An adult panda can weigh up to 350 pounds!

Where Pandas Live

Pandas living in the wild in China almost never leave their forest home. They move about in the thick jungle of bamboo trees, far from people. Most adult pandas live on their own. In bad weather, they may go inside caves or hollow tree trunks. Most of the time, though, they spend the day eating, sleeping, and playing.

The Panda's Eating Habits

Because pandas are so large, they need a lot of food. Usually the only kind of food they eat is the leafy shoots, or stems, of bamboo trees. The panda stands on its hind legs and takes the bamboo shoot in its front paw. The panda's paw is the perfect "tool" for this job. Below its five claw pads is a thumblike pad, designed to grasp the bamboo shoot and pull it down. The panda gets several shoots and sits down to eat. It uses its strong jaws to chew the tough bamboo.

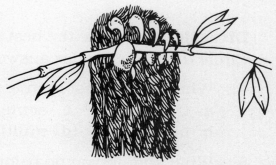

A panda's "thumb" allows it to grasp and pull down its food.

Why Pandas Are Lucky

Pandas might be called "lucky." These animals are rare, but efforts are being made to save them from dying out. The Chinese government has said that pandas are a "national treasure," so they are protected by law. The pandas that live in zoos are considered "treasures," too. These lovable animals get lots of special care and attention.

Copyright © Houghton Mifflin Company. All rights reserved.

Taking Tests

Complete this page as if you were taking a test. Pretend that you have fifteen minutes. Look quickly through the entire test before you begin.

Directions: Complete each sentence by writing the correct answer in the blank.

1. You should look over the entire test **before** you answer the questions.

2. If there's a question you can't answer, you should **skip it** and go on to the next one.

3. When you finish the test, you should **check** your answers.

Directions: Choose the best answer to each question. Circle the letter of your answer.

4. What kind of test item is this question an example of?
   a. true–false   **c.** sentence completion
   b. matching   **(d.)** multiple choice

5. What should you do before you write the answer for this kind of test item?
   a. go on to the next question   **c.** time yourself
   (b.) read all the answer choices   **d.** ask for help

Directions: Write **T** in the blank before the statement if the statement is true. Write **F** if it is false.

___F___ **6.** This kind of test item is an example of a multiple-choice question.

___F___ **7.** It is not important to read the directions for a test carefully.

___T___ **8.** Before you begin a test, you should find out how much time you have to answer all the questions.

Copyright © Houghton Mifflin Company. All rights reserved.

Different kinds of sentences have different jobs. A sentence that tells something is a **statement**. A statement ends with a **period** (.). A sentence that asks something is a **question**. A question ends with a **question mark** (?).

A sentence always begins with a capital letter.

Statements	**Questions**
The airport was crowded.	Was the airport crowded?
Her plane landed on time.	When did her plane land?
Carlos bought a ticket.	Did Carlos buy a ticket?

GUIDED PRACTICE You will need to guide students through the Guided Practice activity, providing support as necessary.

Is each sentence a statement or a question? What end mark should follow each sentence?

Example: The flight attendant welcomed all the passengers
statement   period

1. I pushed my small brown bag under the seat <u>S .</u>

2. Have you fastened your seat belts <u>Q ?</u>

3. The takeoff was very smooth <u>S .</u>

4. Can you see out the window <u>Q ?</u>

5. How high will the plane climb <u>Q ?</u>

6. We will land in about an hour <u>S .</u>

7. Is this your first flight <u>Q ?</u>

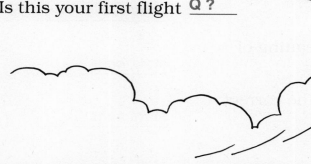
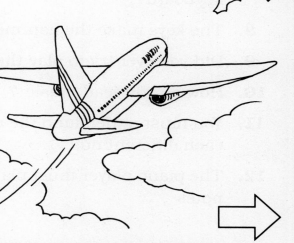

Copyright © Houghton Mifflin Company. All rights reserved.

REMINDER

▸ A **statement** tells something. It ends with a **period** *(.)*.

▸ A **question** asks something. It ends with a **question mark** *(?)*.

Statements	Questions
The concert is today.	**W**hen is the concert**?**
I know that tune**.**	**D**o you know that tune**?**

INDEPENDENT PRACTICE

Circle the end mark for each sentence. Write *statement* if the sentence tells something. Write *question* if the sentence asks something.

Example: The music is wonderful(.)   <u>**statement**</u>

1. What instrument is being played(?)   <u>question</u>

2. It sounds like a piano(.)   <u>statement</u>

3. A piano has eighty-eight keys(.)   <u>statement</u>

4. How does the piano make sounds (?)   <u>question</u>

5. There are wires inside the piano(.)   <u>statement</u>

6. Felt-covered hammers hit the wires (.)   <u>statement</u>

7. The piano player strikes the keys on the keyboard (.)   <u>statement</u>

8. The keys make the hammers work (.)   <u>statement</u>

9. Did you ever try to play the piano (?)   <u>question</u>

10. How do you read music (?)   <u>question</u>

11. You must understand the meaning of each different note(.)   <u>statement</u>

12. The piano player must play the correct notes (.)   <u>statement</u>

Copyright © Houghton Mifflin Company. All rights reserved.

You have learned about two kinds of sentences called statements and questions. Now you will learn about two other kinds of sentences.

A sentence that tells someone to do something is a **command**. A command ends with a period. A sentence that shows strong feeling such as surprise, excitement, or fear is an **exclamation**. It ends with an **exclamation point (!)**.

Remember to begin every sentence with a capital letter.

Commands	Exclamations
Please wait at the bus stop.	**T**he bus finally arrived!
Meet me at Page's Bookstore.	**W**hat a great store it is!
Take the subway home.	**H**ow fast the train travels!

GUIDED PRACTICE

Is each sentence a command or an exclamation? What end mark should be put at the end of each sentence?

Example: Planning a trip is so exciting   *exclamation*   !

1. Apply for your passport   C .
2. Please answer all questions carefully   C .
3. Have your picture taken   C .
4. We're leaving at last   E !
5. My dream is coming true   E !

Copyright © Houghton Mifflin Company. All rights reserved.

> ▶ A **command** tells someone to do something. It ends with a **period** (.).
>
> ▶ An **exclamation** shows surprise, excitement, or fear. It ends with an **exclamation point** (!).
>
> **Commands**
> **P**lease bake some bread.
> **F**ind a wooden spoon.
>
> **Exclamations**
> **W**hat a terrific idea!
> **H**ow easy this is!

INDEPENDENT PRACTICE

Circle the end mark for each sentence. Label each sentence *command* or *exclamation*.

Example: Get all the ingredients ready(.) **command**

1. Look in the refrigerator for butter and eggs(.) command
2. What large eggs these are (!) exclamation
3. Place all the ingredients on the table (.) command
4. Take out a large mixing bowl (.) command
5. How carefully you crack the eggs (!) exclamation
6. Finally we can add the yeast to the batter (!) exclamation
7. Stir the mixture in the bowl (.) command
8. Knead the dough for five minutes (.) command
9. This is so much fun (!) exclamation
10. Ask Charles to turn on the oven (.) command
11. How hot the oven gets (!) exclamation
12. Put the loaf pans on the middle rack(.) command
13. I can't wait to taste the bread (!) exclamation
14. The bread is finally done (!) exclamation
15. How delicious this wheat bread is (!) exclamation

Copyright © Houghton Mifflin Company. All rights reserved.

Complete Subjects and Complete Predicates

A sentence must have two parts to tell a complete thought. The **subject** tells *whom* or *what* the sentence is about. The **predicate** tells what the subject *does* or *is*.

All the words in the subject make up the **complete subject**. All the words in the predicate make up the **complete predicate**. A complete subject or a complete predicate may be one word.

Complete Subjects	Complete Predicates
Angela Kelly	is the captain of the boat.
We	waited at the dock.
The red ferryboat	stops.
Passengers	get off the boat.

You can find the subject of a sentence by asking *whom* or *what* the sentence is about. You can find the predicate by asking what the subject *does* or *is*.

GUIDED PRACTICE

What are the complete subject and the complete predicate of each sentence?   **Subj. underlined once; pred., twice.**

Example: The ocean was calm today.
   subject: The ocean   **predicate:** *was calm today*

1. Several sea gulls flew overhead.
2. They landed on the water.
3. John Day fished from the wharf.
4. He cast his line into the sea.
5. Fish swam below.
6. A large fish tugged on John's line.
7. The excited boy pulled in his catch.

Copyright © Houghton Mifflin Company. All rights reserved.

> ▸ The **complete subject** includes all the words that tell *whom* or *what* the sentence is about.
>
> ▸ The **complete predicate** includes all the words that tell what the subject *does* or *is*.
>
> | **Complete Subjects** | **Complete Predicates** |
> |---|---|
> | Many children | like cartoons. |
> | Cartoons | are exciting for people of all ages. |

INDEPENDENT PRACTICE

Tell what is underlined in each sentence. Write *CS* for the complete subject or *CP* for the complete predicate.

Example: Many people <u>listen to the radio</u>. **CP**

1. People <u>enjoy different kinds of shows</u>. **CP**
2. <u>Television</u> offers many kinds of programs. **CS**
3. <u>Many adults</u> like evening comedy shows. **CS**
4. Movies <u>are very popular</u>. **CP**
5. <u>Walt Disney</u> made many fine films. **CS**
6. <u>Children of all ages</u> enjoy his adventure films. **CS**
7. My family <u>attends concerts</u>. **CP**
8. <u>The sound of violins</u> is beautiful. **CS**
9. <u>Grandmother</u> goes to many plays in the city. **CS**
10. *My Fair Lady* <u>is her favorite musical</u>. **CP**
11. The circus <u>is made up of many acts</u>. **CP**
12. A happy audience <u>cheers</u>. **CP**
13. <u>Other people</u> attend operas. **CS**
14. <u>They</u> listen to the trained voices of the singers. **CS**
15. Good shows <u>are an important part of life</u>. **CP**

Copyright © Houghton Mifflin Company. All rights reserved.

You have learned that the complete subject includes all the words that tell whom or what the sentence is about. In every complete subject, there is one main word. Sometimes this main word is a name. This main word or name tells exactly whom or what the sentence is about. It is called the **simple subject**. Sometimes the complete subject and the simple subject are the same. The simple subjects below are in bold type.

Complete Subjects	Complete Predicates
Many **people**	watch ball games at the park.
Martin Johnson	slides into third base.
He	pitched five innings.
The **palm** of his glove	is torn.

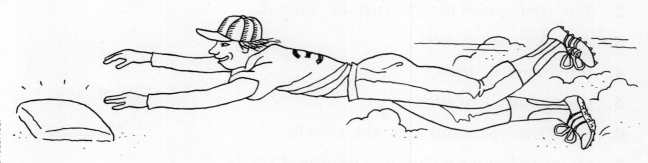

GUIDED PRACTICE The complete subject of each sentence is underlined. What is the simple subject?

Example: James Naismith invented basketball in 1891.
James Naismith

1. He was a teacher in Springfield, Massachusetts.
2. The head of the school wanted an indoor winter game.
3. Naismith tacked peach baskets to the walls of the gym.
4. The first players used soccer balls.
5. Each team had nine players.

Copyright © Houghton Mifflin Company. All rights reserved.

REMINDER

> ▶ The **simple subject** is the main word or words in the complete subject. Sometimes the complete subject and the simple subject are the same.
>
> **Subjects**
> Beautiful **seashells**
> **Mr. Roe**
>
> **Predicates**
> come from the ocean.
> collects all kinds of shells.

INDEPENDENT PRACTICE

The complete subject of each sentence is underlined. Write the simple subject.

Example: Most creatures with shells live in or near the water.

creatures

1. Animals with soft bodies live in shells.

   Animals

2. The shell grows bigger with the animal.

   shell

3. A snail grows a shell.

   snail

4. It lives on the land.

   It

5. Clams have two shells.

   Clams

6. They can open and close their shells.

   They

7. Many artists have painted pictures of shells.

   artists

8. People collect shells as a hobby.

   People

9. Ms. Roe strings shells to make necklaces.

   Ms. Roe

10. She finds very few unbroken shells.

    She

11. The tide brings the shells up onto the beach.

    tide

12. Sunlight can change the color of shells.

    Sunlight

13. The force of the ocean breaks many shells.

    force

14. The broken pieces stay on the sand.

    pieces

15. These treasures from the ocean are beautiful.

    treasures

Copyright © Houghton Mifflin Company. All rights reserved.

Simple Predicates

You know that the complete predicate includes all the words that tell what the subject does or is. In every complete predicate, there is one main word. This main word tells exactly what the subject does or is. It is called the **simple predicate**.

In each sentence below, the simple predicate is in a box.

Complete Subjects	Complete Predicates
Some students	go to space camp.
The camp	is in Alabama.
Campers	build rockets.
They	wear real space suits.

GUIDED PRACTICE The complete predicate of each sentence is underlined. What is the simple predicate?

Example: Students come from all over the country.
come

1. Campers are astronauts for a week.
2. They work in teams of ten.
3. The members name their teams after planets.
4. Some of the teams launch rockets into the air.
5. Other teams take a make-believe space flight.

Copyright © Houghton Mifflin Company. All rights reserved.

REMINDER

▶ The **simple predicate** is the main word in the predicate.

Subjects	Predicates
Most dogs	**make** great pets.
They	**are** good friends for children.

INDEPENDENT PRACTICE

The complete predicate of each sentence is underlined. Write the simple predicate.

Example: People <u>teach dogs different kinds of tricks</u>.   teach

1. Puppies <u>catch newspapers in their mouths</u>.   catch
2. Other dogs <u>beg for food</u>.   beg
3. Many dogs <u>play quietly inside the house</u>.   play
4. Some pets <u>do important jobs</u>.   do
5. Guide dogs <u>help blind people</u>.   help
6. Watchdogs <u>guard people's homes</u>.   guard
7. These dogs <u>bark at strangers</u>.   bark
8. Dogs <u>depend on their owners for daily care</u>.   depend
9. These animals <u>need exercise every day</u>.   need
10. Meat and chicken <u>are good foods for them</u>.   are
11. Some children <u>feed vitamins to their dogs</u>.   feed
12. Some owners <u>enter their dogs in shows</u>.   enter
13. Judges <u>vote for the best dogs</u>.   vote
14. The most obedient dog <u>wins a blue ribbon</u>.   wins
15. The prettiest dog <u>gets a prize at some shows</u>.   gets
16. Dogs <u>make good pets indeed</u>!   make

Copyright © Houghton Mifflin Company. All rights reserved.

There are ways to combine sentences to make your writing more interesting. Sometimes you can combine two sentences that have different subjects but the same predicate. Join the subjects with the connecting word *and* to make one **compound subject**.

Kim watched.
Ben watched. > Kim and Ben watched.

Sometimes you can combine two sentences that have different predicates but the same subject. Join the predicates with *and* to make one **compound predicate**.

They smiled.
They reported the news. > They smiled and reported the news.

GUIDED PRACTICE

How would you combine each pair of sentences into one sentence with a compound subject or a compound predicate?

Example: Carl visited Hollywood. Ann visited Hollywood.   (subject)
Carl and Ann visited Hollywood.

1. Movies are filmed in Hollywood. TV shows are filmed in Hollywood.
   (subject) <u>**Movies and TV shows are filmed in Hollywood.**</u>

2. Ann visited a movie studio. Ann toured the sets. (predicate)
   <u>**Ann visited a movie studio and toured the sets.**</u>

3. She liked the special effects. Her mother liked the special effects.
   (subject) <u>**She and her mother liked the special effects.**</u>

4. Carl went to a TV studio. Carl saw a show. (predicate)
   <u>**Carl went to a TV studio and saw a show.**</u>

Copyright © Houghton Mifflin Company. All rights reserved.

> ► You can combine two sentences with the same predicate. Join the subjects with *and* to make a **compound subject**.
>
>   **Russ** liked to fish.   compound subject
>   **Cindy** liked to fish.   **Russ** *and* **Cindy** liked to fish.
>
> ► You can combine two sentences with the same subject. Join the predicates with *and* to make a **compound predicate**.
>
>   compound predicate
>   They **walked** to the lake.   They **walked** to the lake *and*
>   They **rowed** to an island.   **rowed** to an island.

INDEPENDENT PRACTICE

Write each pair of sentences as one sentence with a compound subject or a compound predicate. Join the underlined words with the connecting word *and.*

Example: My family went fishing. I went fishing.

          My family and I went fishing.

1. We took out our gear. We baited our hooks. **We took out our gear and baited our hooks.**

2. Russ needed help with the line. Cindy needed help with the line. **Russ and Cindy needed help with the line.**

3. Dad caught some small fish. My sister caught some small fish. **Dad and my sister caught some small fish.**

4. Russ got the food basket. Russ passed out some fruit. **Russ got the food basket and passed out some fruit.**

5. Mom had a great time. Cindy had a great time. **Mom and Cindy had a great time.**

6. They caught the most fish. They pulled in the biggest trout. **They caught the most fish and pulled in the biggest trout.**

Copyright © Houghton Mifflin Company. All rights reserved.

Correcting Run-on Sentences

When two sentences run into each other, they make a **run-on sentence**. Do not use run-on sentences in your writing.

A run-on sentence can be corrected by writing each complete thought as a separate sentence. Remember to use capital letters and end marks correctly.

Incorrect:	Our class visited a museum we saw whaling ships.
Correct:	Our class visited a museum. We saw whaling ships.

GUIDED PRACTICE

Which of the following sentences are run-on sentences? Which sentences are correct? What are the two complete thoughts in each run-on sentence?

Example: Many cities have history museums there are many different kinds.　　*run-on*
Many cities have history museums.
There are many different kinds.

1. History museums are fun they teach about the past.

2. A whole village can sometimes be a museum.

3. People dress in costumes people can ask them questions.

History museums are fun. They teach about the past.

People dress in costumes. Visitors can ask them questions.

Copyright © Houghton Mifflin Company. All rights reserved.

REMINDER

▸ A **run-on sentence** has two complete thoughts that run into each other. Correct a run-on sentence by writing each complete thought as a separate sentence.

Incorrect: They went on a trip the three of them took the train.

Correct: They went on a trip. The three of them took the train.

INDEPENDENT PRACTICE

Correct each run-on sentence by writing it as two separate sentences.

Example: Cora and Theo visited Seaside Farm Mr. Li went with them.

Cora and Theo visited Seaside Farm.

Mr. Li went with them.

1. Seaside Farm is very old it's the oldest farm in the state.
Seaside Farm is very old. It's the oldest farm in the state.

2. Seaside is two hundred years old it is a very large farm.
Seaside is two hundred years old. It is a very large farm.

3. There are seventy chickens there they lay sixty eggs a day.
There are seventy chickens there. They lay sixty eggs a day.

4. On some days there are hay rides many visitors enjoy them.
On some days there are hay rides. Many visitors enjoy them.

5. People ride in a wagon full of hay everybody brings picnic lunches.
People ride in a wagon full of hay. Everybody brings picnic lunches.

6. The owner lets visitors milk the cows this job isn't for everyone.
The owner lets visitors milk the cows. This job isn't for everyone.

7. Farmers wake up early it takes all day to get the chores done.
Farmers wake up early. It takes all day to get the chores done.

Copyright © Houghton Mifflin Company. All rights reserved.

There are two kinds of nouns. A noun that names any person, place, or thing is called a **common noun**. A noun that names a particular person, place, or thing is called a **proper noun**.

	Common Nouns	Proper Nouns
Persons	girl uncle queen	**M**arie **U**ncle **G**eorge **Q**ueen **E**lizabeth
Places	state country bay park	**K**ansas **C**anada **B**ay of **F**undy **G**lacier **N**ational **P**ark
Things	pet day holiday	**P**atches **S**aturday **F**ourth of **J**uly

When you write a proper noun, always begin it with a capital letter. If a proper noun is more than one word, capitalize the first letter of each important word.

GUIDED PRACTICE

Find the common noun and the proper noun in each sentence. Which nouns should begin with capital letters? **CN underlined once; PN twice. PN should be cap.**

Example: tanya is an explorer.
   common: *explorer*   ***proper:*** *(cap.) Tanya*

1. Her kitten magellan is too!
2. Their trips to florida are always exciting.
3. Do the alligators in the everglades national park look scary?
4. The guides at cape canaveral are helpful.
5. Is there lost treasure in the gulf of mexico?

Copyright © Houghton Mifflin Company. All rights reserved.

▶ A **common noun** names any person, place, or thing.

▶ A **proper noun** names a particular person, place, or thing.

▶ Capitalize each important word in a proper noun.

proper noun	common noun	common noun

The **Sahara Desert** is the largest **desert** in the **world**.

INDEPENDENT PRACTICE

Write *C* for each underlined common noun and *P* for each underlined proper noun. Then write the proper nouns correctly.

Example: At its longest, the *sahara* is 3200 miles.   **P — Sahara**

1. This desert is located in northern <u>africa</u>.   P—Africa

2. It stretches from the Atlantic Ocean to the <u>red sea</u>.   P—Red Sea

3. Only about four inches of <u>rain</u> fall there each year.   C

4. Very few <u>people</u> live there.   C

5. Most of the <u>sahara</u> is made up of rock, not sand.   P—Sahara

6. Some of the sand dunes rise over two hundred <u>feet</u>.   C

7. The <u>namib desert</u> is in southeastern Africa.   P—Namib Desert

8. It is along the <u>atlantic ocean</u>.   P—Atlantic Ocean

9. The <u>orange river</u> is south of the desert.   P—Orange River

10. Two more large <u>rivers</u> lie north of the desert.   C

11. The <u>cape of good hope</u> is also in Africa.   P—Cape of Good Hope

12. It is located at the southern <u>tip</u> of Africa.   C

13. An <u>explorer</u> first sailed around the Cape in 1487.   C

14. His name was <u>dias</u>.   P—Dias

Copyright © Houghton Mifflin Company. All rights reserved.

A noun can name one or more than one. A noun that names only one person, place, or thing is called a **singular noun**. A noun that names more than one is called a **plural noun**.

Singular Nouns	Plural Nouns
One **goat** is in the **barn**.	Many **goats** are in those **barns**.
This **hen** laid one **egg**.	These **hens** laid a dozen **eggs**.

HOW TO FORM PLURALS

Rules	Singular	Plural
Add *s* to most singular nouns.	one boy one puddle a rose	two boy**s** both puddle**s** ten rose**s**
Add *es* to a singular noun that ends with *s, x, ch,* or *sh*.	one bus this box one bunch a wish	three bus**es** some box**es** six bunch**es** many wish**es**

GUIDED PRACTICE

What is the plural form of each of the following singular nouns?

Example: peach   *peaches*

1. brush <u>es</u>
2. gift <u>s</u>
3. class <u>es</u>
4. patch <u>es</u>
5. prize <u>s</u>
6. circus <u>es</u>
7. inch <u>es</u>
8. fox <u>es</u>

Copyright © Houghton Mifflin Company. All rights reserved.

▸ A **singular noun** names one person, place, or thing.

▸ A **plural noun** names more than one person, place, or thing.

▸ To form plural nouns, add *s* to most singular nouns.

▸ Add *es* to singular nouns that end with *s, x, ch,* or *sh.*

Singular: toy   store   glass   fo*x*   lun*ch*   di*sh*
Plural: toy**s**   store**s**   glass**es**   fox**es**   lunch**es**   dish**es**

INDEPENDENT PRACTICE

Underline each singular noun. Write each plural noun.

Example: I have worked on my
project for weeks.   **weeks**

1. One girl is building a house from tiny boxes.   **boxes**

2. A boy will hang balloons from the ceiling.   **balloons**

3. That picture was made with patches of cloth.   **patches**

4. One student is busy with paints and brushes.   **paints, brushes**

5. His picture is full of bright colors.   **colors**

6. Our teacher is making roses from paper.   **roses**

7. Bunches of flowers are on the table.   **Bunches, flowers**

8. Chairs will be placed in a circle on the floor.   **Chairs**

9. Each parent will bring snacks or drinks.   **snacks, drinks**

10. Sandwiches will be served on a large tray.   **Sandwiches**

11. My mother will bring glasses.   **glasses**

12. Invitations were sent to other classes.   **Invitations, classes**

13. Three teachers and their students are coming.   **teachers, students**

14. Some mothers and fathers will come too.   **mothers, fathers**

15. All the guests will enjoy our show.   **guests**

Copyright © Houghton Mifflin Company. All rights reserved.

Nouns Ending with y

You have already learned some rules for making nouns plural. Here are two special rules for making the plural forms of nouns that end with *y*.

HOW TO FORM PLURALS

Rules	Singular	Plural
If the noun ends with a vowel and *y*, add *s*.	one toy a monkey	many toy**s** five monkey**s**
If the noun ends with a consonant and *y*, change the *y* to *i* and add *es*.	one family this city a baby	some famil**ies** six cit**ies** two bab**ies**

GUIDED PRACTICE

What is the plural form of each noun?

Example: pony   *ponies*

1. berry — berries
2. holiday — holidays
3. turkey — turkeys

4. boy — boys
5. blue jay — blue jays
6. party — parties

7. lady — ladies
8. donkey — donkeys
9. puppy — puppies

10. sky — skies
11. hobby — hobbies
12. key — keys

Copyright © Houghton Mifflin Company. All rights reserved.

REMINDER

▶ Some nouns end with a vowel and *y*. Add *s* to make these nouns plural.

▶ Some nouns end with a consonant and *y*. Change the *y* to *i* and add *es* to make these nouns plural.

Singular Nouns: one **valley**   one **country**
Plural Nouns: four **valleys**   two **countries**

INDEPENDENT PRACTICE

Write the plural form of each singular noun.

Example: penny   **pennies**

1.	city	cities	18.	toy	toys
2.	subway	subways	19.	puppy	puppies
3.	alley	alleys	20.	day	days
4.	factory	factories	21.	play	plays
5.	chimney	chimneys	22.	hobby	hobbies
6.	company	companies	23.	party	parties
7.	entry	entries	24.	boy	boys
8.	lobby	lobbies	25.	grocery	groceries
9.	story	stories	26.	key	keys
10.	sky	skies	27.	supply	supplies
11.	library	libraries	28.	way	ways
12.	display	displays	29.	monkey	monkeys
13.	highway	highways	30.	berry	berries
14.	journey	journeys	31.	lady	ladies
15.	family	families	32.	daisy	daisies
16.	holiday	holidays	33.	majesty	majesties
17.	birthday	birthdays	34.	bay	bays

Copyright © Houghton Mifflin Company. All rights reserved.

More Plural Nouns

You know that you add *s* or *es* to form the plurals of most nouns. There are some nouns, however, that have special plural forms. Since these words follow no spelling pattern, you must remember them.

Singular and Plural Nouns			
Singular	**Plural**	**Singular**	**Plural**
one child	two child**ren**	each tooth	five t**ee**th
a man	many m**e**n	one goose	both g**ee**se
this woman	three wom**e**n	an ox	nine ox**en**
that foot	these f**ee**t	a mouse	some m**ice**

Other nouns are the same in both singular and plural forms.

SINGULAR NOUNS
One **deer** nibbled the bark.
Did you see a **moose**?
I have a pet **sheep**.

PLURAL NOUNS
Several **deer** ate quietly.
Two **moose** crossed a stream.
These **sheep** have soft wool.

GUIDED PRACTICE

Complete each sentence with the plural form of the underlined noun.

Example: One child helped both smaller __children__ tie their sneakers.

1. That man sang while two other __men__ played guitars.
2. This sheep is my pet, and those __sheep__ belong to Fred.
3. Pat hopped on one foot and then jumped with both __feet__.
4. One goose flew by, and three __geese__ swam in the pond.
5. Rex had a loose tooth, but his other __teeth__ were fine.
6. Ana saw one moose in Maine and four __moose__ in Canada.

Copyright © Houghton Mifflin Company. All rights reserved.

> ▶ Some nouns have special plural forms.
> ▶ Some nouns have the same singular and plural forms.

Singular Nouns:	child	man	woman	foot	tooth	ox
Plural Nouns:	children	men	women	feet	teeth	oxen

Singular Nouns:	goose	mouse	deer	moose	sheep
Plural Nouns:	geese	mice	deer	moose	sheep

INDEPENDENT PRACTICE

Write each underlined noun. Label it *S* for singular or *P* for plural.

Example: The <u>children</u> saw an ox at the farm.   **children — P**

1. Some <u>men</u> hitched an ox to a wagon.   men — P
2. There were two more <u>oxen</u> in the barn.   oxen — P
3. Each ox had many strong white <u>teeth</u>.   teeth — P
4. A <u>woman</u> showed the children some baby sheep.   woman — S
5. Two men were cutting the wool from a big <u>sheep</u>.   sheep — S
6. One child saw some <u>mice</u> in the barn.   mice — P
7. A little <u>mouse</u> was near her foot.   mouse — S
8. She moved her <u>foot</u> out of the way.   foot — S
9. Several women were feeding some <u>geese</u>.   geese — P
10. A <u>goose</u> has feet like a duck's.   goose — S
11. A farmer saw some <u>deer</u> eating the corn.   deer — P
12. Can a moose eat as much as ten <u>sheep</u>?   sheep — P
13. Did you see three <u>moose</u> in the field?   moose — P
14. Each moose was even bigger than an <u>ox</u>.   ox — S
15. Every <u>child</u> had a good time at the farm.   child — S

Copyright © Houghton Mifflin Company. All rights reserved.

Action Verbs

You know that every sentence has a subject and a predicate. The main word in the predicate is the verb. A **verb** is a word that can show action. When a verb tells what people or things do, it is called an **action verb**.

Subjects	Predicates
Rita and Eric	dig slowly and carefully.
The students	helped the scientists.
Rita	uncovered some pottery.
The pieces of pottery	provide clues about the past.

GUIDED PRACTICE

What is the action verb in each of the following sentences?

Example: Rita cleaned the pieces of pottery.   *cleaned*

1. Eric found some old tools.
2. Raul made a map of the site.
3. Two students stand in the water.
4. They hold a tub with a screen in the bottom.
5. Water fills the tub.
6. Raul pours dirt into the tub.
7. Light objects float in the water.
8. Dirt goes through the screen.
9. The students take careful notes.
10. They attach labels to the objects.
11. The scientists take the objects to their lab.
12. They learn many things about early people.

Copyright © Houghton Mifflin Company. All rights reserved.

▶ An **action verb** is a word that tells what people or things do.

verb
The ship **sailed** away weeks ago.
predicate

verb
Bill **looks** for the ship every day.
predicate

INDEPENDENT PRACTICE

Write the action verb in each underlined predicate.

Example: Bill stood on the dock.   **stood**

1. Bill watched the workers on the dock.   **watched**
2. The workers loaded boxes onto a large ship.   **loaded**
3. Bill's father works on this ship.   **works**
4. Some people boarded the ship.   **boarded**
5. The crew checked their names on a list.   **checked**
6. The captain blew the whistle.   **blew**
7. Bill heard three loud blasts.   **heard**
8. Tugboats towed the ship into deep water.   **towed**
9. The ship left the harbor after that.   **left**
10. Bill watches it for a long time.   **watches**
11. He walks home slowly.   **walks**
12. He misses his father already.   **misses**
13. Bill's father sends letters from far away.   **sends**
14. Bill goes to the docks again.   **goes**
15. The big ship arrives home at last!   **arrives**

Copyright © Houghton Mifflin Company. All rights reserved.

Main Verbs and Helping Verbs

A verb may be more than one word. The **main verb** is the most important verb. The **helping verb** comes before it.

Some Common Helping Verbs

am	was	has
is	were	have
are	will	had

The main verbs below are in bold. Helping verbs are in italics.

> Alfredo *is* **training** for the Olympics.
> He *has* **run** five miles each day.
> His coach *will* **help** him next week.

Guided Practice

Find each helping verb and main verb.

Example: Sara had entered the summer Olympics.
helping verb: *had*   ***main verb:*** *entered*
HV is underlined once; MV, twice.

1. She was racing in a wheelchair race.
2. Sara had joined the Wheelchair Athlete Club.
3. The racers were using special racing wheelchairs.
4. They are training several times a week.
5. They have lifted weights too.
6. Sara has raced for several years.
7. She will race many more times.
8. She is practicing for next year's Olympics.

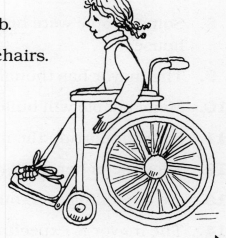

Copyright © Houghton Mifflin Company. All rights reserved.

REMINDER

> ► A verb may be more than one word.
> ► The **main verb** is the most important verb.
> ► The **helping verb** comes before the main verb.
>
> helping main   helping main
>   verb   verb   verb   verb
> I **am going** with my brother.   We **will walk** together.

INDEPENDENT PRACTICE

Look at each underlined verb. Write *helping* if it is the helping verb. Write *main* if it is the main verb.

Example: My brother Pablo <u>is</u> taking me to
the park.   helping

1. We <u>will</u> see an old tree house.   helping

2. Pablo was <u>telling</u> me about it yesterday.   main

3. Pablo has <u>seen</u> it many times.   main

4. We <u>were</u> reading about it in the newspaper.   helping

5. The tree house <u>has</u> stood for years.   helping

6. Last year the wind <u>had</u> blown off the roof.   helping

7. The rain has <u>hurt</u> the house too.   main

8. Some people were <u>hoping</u> to save the old tree
    house.   main

9. The mayor has <u>thought</u> of a plan.   main

10. Many people <u>will</u> build a new tree house together.   helping

11. I am <u>supporting</u> the mayor's plan.   main

12. I have <u>seen</u> her work in our parks.   main

13. We <u>are</u> telling everyone in town the news.   helping

14. The mayor <u>is</u> expecting success.   helping

15. She has <u>worked</u> hard.   main

Copyright © Houghton Mifflin Company. All rights reserved.

Present, Past, and Future

A verb tells when something happens. The **tense** of a verb lets you know whether something happens in the present, in the past, or in the future.

Present	**Past**	**Future**
hunt, hunts	hunted	will hunt
fly, flies	flew	will fly

Verb Tenses

A verb in the **present tense** shows action that is happening now.	Bats **hunt** at night. Now the bat **flies.**
A verb in the **past tense** shows action that has already happened. Many verbs in the past tense end with *-ed.*	It **hunted** last night. The bats **flew.**
A verb in the **future tense** shows action that will happen. Verbs in the future tense use the helping verb *will.*	They **will hunt** tonight. The bat **will fly.**

GUIDED PRACTICE What is the verb in each sentence? Is it in the present tense, the past tense, or the future tense?

Example: Sherry likes many kinds of animals. *likes — present*

1. We will go to the library tomorrow.   fut.
2. I finished a book about birds yesterday.   past
3. Sherry will look for a book about bats.   fut.
4. She collects facts about animals.   pres.
5. The librarian always helps us.   pres.

Copyright © Houghton Mifflin Company. All rights reserved.

REMINDER

▶ A **present tense** verb shows action that is happening now.

▶ A **past tense** verb shows action that has already happened.

▶ A **future tense** verb shows action that will happen.

Present Tense: The Kamals **live** here now.

Past Tense: The Kamals **lived** here last year.

Future Tense: The Kamals **will live** here for many years.

INDEPENDENT PRACTICE

Write *present, past,* or *future* for each underlined verb.

Example: The Kamals <u>will leave</u> early in the morning. **future**

1. Kate Kamal's family <u>moved</u> to Los Angeles. **past**

2. Mrs. Kamal <u>works</u> in Long Beach. **present**

3. She <u>rides</u> a long way to her job every day. **present**

4. Soon the Kamals <u>will move</u> to Long Beach. **future**

5. Then Mrs. Kamal <u>will travel</u> only a few miles to work. **future**

6. The Kamals <u>prepare</u> everything for the move. **present**

7. Last week Mr. Kamal <u>found</u> many empty boxes. **past**

8. He <u>saved</u> them for moving day. **past**

9. Now the Kamals <u>pack</u> books and records into boxes. **present**

10. The Kamals <u>will pack</u> the pots and pans next. **future**

11. Tonight they <u>will eat</u> dinner at a restaurant. **future**

12. Kate <u>gave</u> her new address to all her friends. **past**

13. She <u>will give</u> us her new phone number soon. **future**

14. Everyone <u>wished</u> Kate good luck. **past**

15. Now the Kamals <u>wave</u> good-by to us. **present**

Copyright © Houghton Mifflin Company. All rights reserved.

Making Subjects and Verbs Agree

A verb in the present tense must **agree** with the subject of the sentence. This means that the subject and the verb must work together. They must both be singular or both be plural.

	Subject-Verb Agreement
Singular subjects	When the subject is a singular noun or *he*, *she*, or *it*, add *s* to the verb. A <u>computer</u> **helps** people. <u>It</u> **solves** problems.
Plural subjects	When the subject is a plural noun or *I, we, you,* or *they,* do not add *s* to the verb. <u>Computers</u> **help** people. <u>They</u> **solve** problems.

GUIDED PRACTICE

Which verb correctly completes each sentence?

Example: Felita (own, owns) a small computer.
owns

1. She (use, <u>uses</u>) it to do her homework.
2. The computer (help, <u>helps</u>) her parents too.
3. Her brothers (<u>play</u>, plays) games on it.
4. Many companies also (<u>buy</u>, buys) computers.
5. Computers (<u>work</u>, works) very rapidly.
6. They (<u>store</u>, stores) a great deal of information.
7. I (<u>want</u>, wants) to learn more about computers.

Copyright © Houghton Mifflin Company. All rights reserved.

REMINDER

▶ A present tense verb must **agree** with the subject of the sentence.

▶ Add *s* to the verb when the subject is a singular noun or *he, she,* or *it*.

▶ Do not add *s* to the verb when the subject is a plural noun or *I, we, you,* or *they*.

The <u>cat</u> **plays**.	The <u>cats</u> **play**.
My <u>puppy</u> **barks**.	Both <u>puppies</u> **bark**.
Now <u>it</u> **hides**.	Now <u>they</u> **hide**.

INDEPENDENT PRACTICE

Write the verb that agrees with the underlined subject.

Example: My <u>dog</u> (follow, follows) me everywhere. **follows**

1. <u>Razz</u> (hide, hides) in the tall grass. **hides**
2. <u>We</u> (run, runs) together in the field. **run**
3. <u>Dogs</u> (need, needs) daily exercise. **need**
4. My <u>brother</u> (tell, tells) me about dog care. **tells**
5. <u>He</u> (find, finds) a box for Razz. **finds**
6. An old <u>towel</u> (keep, keeps) the box warm. **keeps**
7. <u>Razz</u> (curl, curls) up in the bed. **curls**
8. On cold nights, <u>Razz</u> (sleep, sleeps) on my bed. **sleeps**
9. <u>We</u> (clean, cleans) Razz's fur every morning. **clean**
10. <u>You</u> (comb, combs) a pet's fur regularly. **comb**
11. My <u>sisters</u> (enjoy, enjoys) cats more than dogs. **enjoy**
12. <u>They</u> (say, says) dogs are too noisy. **say**
13. <u>I</u> (like, likes) dogs the best anyway. **like**
14. <u>You</u> (care, cares) so much for your pet. **care**

Copyright © Houghton Mifflin Company. All rights reserved.

Irregular Verbs

Verbs that do not add -ed to show past action are called **irregular verbs**.

I **eat** now.   I **ate** earlier.   I **have eaten** already.

Because irregular verbs do not follow a regular pattern, you must remember their spellings.

IRREGULAR VERBS

Present	Past	Past with Helping Verb
begin	began	(has, have, had) begun
break	broke	(has, have, had) broken
bring	brought	(has, have, had) brought
come	came	(has, have, had) come
drive	drove	(has, have, had) driven
eat	ate	(has, have, had) eaten
give	gave	(has, have, had) given
grow	grew	(has, have, had) grown
know	knew	(has, have, had) known
say	said	(has, have, had) said
sing	sang	(has, have, had) sung
tell	told	(has, have, had) told
throw	threw	(has, have, had) thrown

GUIDED PRACTICE   What are the past tense and the past with a helping verb for each irregular verb below?

Example: sing   *sang*   *sung*

1. eat   ate, eaten
2. bring   brought, brought
3. give   gave, given

4. know   knew, known
5. come   came, come
6. break   broke, broken

Copyright © Houghton Mifflin Company. All rights reserved.

REMINDER

> ▶ Verbs that do not add *-ed* to show past action are called **irregular verbs**. You must remember their spellings.

Present	Past	Past with Helping Verbs
take	took	(has, have, had) taken
wear	wore	(has, have, had) worn
make	made	(has, have, had) made

INDEPENDENT PRACTICE

Write the correct form of the verb in ( ) to complete each sentence.

Example: I had __eaten__ a cherry. **(ate, eaten)**

1. The pit of the cherry had __broken__ two teeth. **(broke, broken)**

2. The dentist had __known__ what to do. **(knew, known)**

3. He had __taken__ a picture of the teeth. **(took, taken)**

4. Dr. Levy __said__ the teeth were fine. **(say, said)**

5. Then he __took__ a piece of warm clay from a bowl. **(took, taken)**

6. Dr. Levy __made__ a mold of the teeth out of clay. **(make, made)**

7. Since then he has __begun__ the work. **(began, begun)**

8. The dentist has __made__ two caps for my teeth. **(make, made)**

9. He __began__ by gluing them to my chipped teeth. **(began, begun)**

10. Then he __told__ me to look in the mirror. **(tell, told)**

11. I __gave__ him a big smile. **(gave, given)**

Copyright © Houghton Mifflin Company. All rights reserved.

The Special Verb be

The verb *be* has special forms for different subjects.

SUBJECTS	PRESENT	PAST
I	am	was
you	are	were
he, she, it	is	was
singular noun *(Lucia)*	is	was
we	are	were
they	are	were
plural noun *(stories)*	are	were

The verb *be* does not show action. It tells what someone or something is or is like.

I **am** a reporter.   You **are** a photographer.

That story **was** long.   Those cartoons **were** funny.

GUIDED PRACTICE

Which verb correctly completes each sentence? Is it in the present tense or the past tense?

Example: Lucia (is, are) a reporter.   *is — present*

1. I (<u>was</u>, were) a sportswriter last year.   <u>past</u>

2. Two stories (was, <u>were</u>) about basketball.   <u>past</u>

3. You (is, <u>are</u>) in one of my stories.   <u>pres.</u>

4. My best story (<u>is</u>, are) about bikes.   <u>pres.</u>

5. We (was, <u>were</u>) winners every time!   <u>past</u>

Copyright © Houghton Mifflin Company. All rights reserved.

REMINDER

▶ The special verb *be* does not show action. It tells what someone or something is or is like.

▶ Use the form of the verb *be* that agrees with the subject of the sentence.

Subject	Present	Past	Sentences
I	am	was	I **was** near the tree.
he, she, it	is	was	He **was** surprised.
singular noun	is	was	Silvio **is** here now.
we, you, they	are	were	We **are** good friends.
plural noun	are	were	Trees **were** around us.

INDEPENDENT PRACTICE

Write the verb in (   ) that agrees with each underlined subject.

Example: This tree _____is_____ a maple tree.
            (is, are)

1. The <u>branches</u> __are_____ close to the ground. **(is, are)**

2. <u>They</u> __are_____ thick and strong. **(is, are)**

3. <u>I</u> __am_____ up in the tree now. **(am, is)**

4. This <u>tree</u> __was_____ my sister's favorite. **(was, were)**

5. My <u>sister</u> __is_____ a good climber. **(is, are)**

6. <u>She</u> __is_____ away at school now. **(am, is)**

7. Many <u>trees</u> __were_____ here before the storm.
(was, were)

8. The <u>storm</u> __was_____ a very bad one. **(was, were)**

9. <u>It</u> __was_____ the worst storm in years. **(was, were)**

10. <u>I</u> __was_____ afraid of the strong winds. **(was, were)**

Copyright © Houghton Mifflin Company. All rights reserved.

You know that a noun is a word that names a person, a place, or a thing. In your writing, you may sometimes want to describe or give more information about a person, a place, or a thing. One way to do this is to use adjectives.

An **adjective** is a word that describes or gives more information about a noun. An adjective can tell you *what kind* or *how many*. It usually comes before the noun it describes.

What Kind

We have a large dog.

The dog has a curly coat.

How Many

Two dogs played in the yard.

Many dogs like children.

You can use more than one adjective to describe a noun.

We have a large, friendly dog.

The dog has five tiny puppies.

GUIDED PRACTICE

Find the adjectives that describe the underlined nouns. Does each adjective tell what kind, or does it tell how many? **Adjs. that tell what kind are underlined once; how many, twice.**

Example: Many dogs can learn to do useful work.
Many — how many   useful — what kind

1. Early people found that dogs made good hunters.
2. Strong sheepdogs help farmers with large herds of sheep.
3. One famous dog rescued forty lost people in the mountains.
4. Blind people use dogs to guide them through busy streets.
5. Some smart dogs learn to help deaf people.

Copyright © Houghton Mifflin Company. All rights reserved.

> ▶ An **adjective** is a word that describes a noun.
> ▶ An adjective can tell *what kind* or *how many*.
>
> **What Kind:** We wanted to make **hot** soup.
>
> We like soup on a **cold, rainy** day.
>
> **How Many:** We made **ten** bowls of soup.
>
> There are **many** people in my family.

INDEPENDENT PRACTICE

Write the adjective or adjectives that describe each underlined noun.

Example: Soup is a healthy <u>food</u>.

healthy

1. We cooked homemade <u>soup</u>.

   homemade

2. We had to buy several <u>things</u> for the soup.

   several

3. We went to the new <u>market</u> on Brown Street.

   new

4. I asked for three <u>pounds</u> of chicken.

   three

5. I bought a few <u>carrots</u> too.

   few

6. Eli got two fresh <u>peppers</u>.

   two, fresh

7. We also needed some small <u>onions</u>.

   some, small

8. Everything fit into one large <u>bag</u>.

   one, large

9. At home we took out the big, heavy <u>pot</u>.

   big, heavy

10. There are many <u>ways</u> to make soup.

    many

11. We put in white <u>rice</u> and a dash of pepper.

    white

12. A dash of pepper is a tiny <u>bit</u>.

    tiny

13. Then we cooked it on a low <u>flame</u>.

    low

14. I like soup that is a golden <u>color</u>.

    golden

15. Everyone enjoyed the delicious, hot <u>soup</u>.

    delicious, hot

Copyright © Houghton Mifflin Company. All rights reserved.

An adjective can come after the word it describes. It usually follows a form of the verb *be*.

> The project is ready.
>
> I am excited.

You know that adjectives can describe nouns. They can also describe words like *I, it,* and *we,* which take the place of nouns.

GUIDED PRACTICE

Find the adjective in each sentence. What word does it describe? **Adj. is underlined once; word, twice.**

Example: The weather is beautiful.
beautiful   weather

1. The day is perfect.
2. The fair is exciting.
3. We were eager.
4. The bread is tasty.
5. It was difficult to make.
6. The rides are popular.
7. Paula is proud.
8. The chicken is fat.
9. The eggs are large.
10. Peter is afraid.
11. The sky is dark now.
12. I am tired.

Copyright © Houghton Mifflin Company. All rights reserved.

REMINDER

▶ An adjective can follow the word it describes. It usually follows a form of the verb *be*.

Science <u>is</u> **interesting**.   They <u>were</u> **easy**.
<u>Experiments are</u> **useful**.   It <u>was</u> **fun** too.

INDEPENDENT PRACTICE

Write the adjective that follows each underlined word.

Example: The <u>class</u> was busy in science.   **busy**

1. The <u>class</u> was curious about eggs.   curious

2. <u>Carmen</u> is familiar with chickens.   familiar

3. Carmen's <u>hens</u> are beautiful.   beautiful

4. The <u>eggs</u> are brown.   brown

5. <u>Carmen</u> is proud of the eggs.   proud

6. An <u>experiment</u> was possible.   possible

7. <u>Ms. Amato</u> was helpful with the experiment.   helpful

8. <u>We</u> were excited about it.   excited

9. The <u>machine</u> was large.   large

10. The <u>eggs</u> were warm in the machine.   warm

11. Soon the <u>eggs</u> were open.   open

12. The <u>chicks</u> are tiny now.   tiny

13. <u>They</u> are weak too.   weak

14. <u>Maria</u> is gentle with them.   gentle

15. <u>She</u> is careful about the food.   careful

16. <u>I</u> am happy about the experiment.   happy

Copyright © Houghton Mifflin Company. All rights reserved.

Using a, an, and the

The words *a*, *an*, and *the* are special adjectives called **articles.** Learn these rules for using articles.

With singular nouns:

Use *a* if the next word begins with a consonant.　　**a f**lower

Use *an* if the next word begins with a vowel.　　**an i**ris

Use *the* if the noun names a particular person, place, or thing.　　**the** garden

With plural nouns:

Use *the*.　　**the** flowers

　　the irises

GUIDED PRACTICE

Which article or articles could be used before each word?

Example: contest　　*a*　*the*

1. award　　an, the
2. orchid　　an, the
3. students　　the
4. prize　　a, the
5. roses　　the
6. bushes　　the
7. evergreen　　an, the
8. seeds　　the
9. area　　an, the
10. weed　　a, the

Copyright © Houghton Mifflin Company. All rights reserved.

REMINDER

▶ *A*, *an*, and *the* are special adjectives called **articles.**

▶ Use *a* before a word that begins with a consonant sound.

▶ Use *an* before a word that begins with a vowel sound.

With Singular Nouns: a coin   **an** old coin   **the** coin

With Plural Nouns: **the** coins   **the** old coins

INDEPENDENT PRACTICE

Write the correct article in ( ) to complete each sentence. The underlined letters are clues.

Example: Chang spent last summer on

_____**an**_____ island. **(a, an)**

1. One day Chang took _____a_____ long walk. **(a, an)**

2. _____The_____ sun was bright that day. **(An, The)**

3. Chang passed _____a_____ white fence. **(a, an)**

4. He walked beyond _____the_____ small cottages. **(a, the)**

5. Soon he reached _____the_____ water. **(an, the)**

6. _____The_____ high waves were splashing. **(A, The)**

7. There he saw _____a_____ sand castle. **(a, an)**

8. It was _____an_____ enormous castle. **(a, an)**

9. Did _____a_____ child build it? **(a, an)**

10. Did _____an_____ adult do this careful work? **(a, an)**

11. Chang looked at _____the_____ tall towers. **(a, the)**

12. He peeked into _____an_____ opening. **(a, an)**

13. _____An_____ old coin lay inside the castle. **(A, An)**

14. Who could have left such _____a_____ strange coin? **(a, an)**

15. Chang returned _____the_____ next day. **(an, the)**

16. _____The_____ old coin and the castle were gone. **(A, The)**

Copyright © Houghton Mifflin Company. All rights reserved.

Making Comparisons

Sometimes you may want to tell how things are alike or how they are different. You can use adjectives to compare.

You usually add *-er* to an adjective to compare two persons, places, or things, and *-est* to compare three or more.

Mindy took a **long** trip. (one trip described)
Lou's trip was **longer** than hers. (two trips compared)
I took the **longest** trip of all. (three or more compared)

Rules for Adding *-er* and *-est*

1. **If the adjective ends with e:**
   Drop the *e* before adding the ending.

   wid**e** + -er = **wider**
   wid**e** + -est = **widest**

2. **If the adjective ends with a single vowel and a consonant:**
   Double the consonant and add the ending.

   th**in** + -er = **thinner**
   th**in** + -est = **thinnest**

3. **If the adjective ends with a consonant and *y*:**
   Change the *y* to *i* before adding the ending.

   ti**ny** + -er = **tinier**
   ti**ny** + -est = **tiniest**

GUIDED PRACTICE

What adjective completes each sentence?

1. Hawaii is _newer_ than Alaska. (new)

2. However, every other state is _older_ than Alaska. (old)

3. Alaska is the _biggest_ of all the states. (big)

Copyright © Houghton Mifflin Company. All rights reserved.

REMINDER

▶ Add -er to most adjectives to compare two persons, places, or things.

▶ Add -est to most adjectives to compare three or more persons, places, or things.

Adjective	Comparing Two	Comparing Three or More
tall	tall**er**	tall**est**
gentle	gentl**er**	gentl**est**
fat	fa**tter**	fa**ttest**
easy	eas**ier**	eas**iest**

INDEPENDENT PRACTICE

Write the correct adjective in ( ) to complete each sentence.

Example: This elephant is _____taller_____ than that one. **(taller, tallest)**

1. Elephants are the _largest_____ of all land animals. **(larger, largest)**

2. Elephants are one of the _heaviest_____ of all animals at birth. **(heavier, heaviest)**

3. Do elephants have the _biggest_____ brains of any land animals? **(bigger, biggest)**

4. African elephants are _bigger_____ than Indian elephants. **(bigger, biggest)**

5. Indian elephants have _smaller_____ ears than African elephants. **(smaller, smallest)**

6. Indian elephants have _smoother_____ skin than African elephants. **(smoother, smoothest)**

7. They also have _shorter_____ tusks than African elephants do. **(shorter, shortest)**

Copyright © Houghton Mifflin Company. All rights reserved.

You know that you add *-er* or *-est* to some adjectives when you want to compare. With long adjectives, use the words *more* and *most* to compare persons, places, or things. Use the word *more* to compare two. Use *most* to compare three or more.

Tiger is a **playful** cat. (one cat described)

Ginger is a **more playful** cat than Tiger. (two cats compared)

Ike is the **most playful** cat of all. (three or more compared)

Never add *-er* and *more* or *-est* and *most* to the same adjective.

Incorrect: Tiger is <u>more</u> <u>smarter</u> than Ginger.
Tiger is the <u>most</u> <u>intelligentest</u> cat.

Correct: Tiger is **smarter** than Ginger.
Tiger is the **most intelligent** cat.

GUIDED PRACTICE

What adjective completes each sentence correctly?

Example: Cats are among the <u>**most common**</u> of all pets.   (common)

1. Only the dog is <u>more popular</u> than the cat. (popular)

2. One of the <u>most popular</u> of all breeds of cat is the Siamese.   (popular)

3. Some people think that a Persian cat is <u>more beautiful</u> than any other cat.   (beautiful)

Copyright © Houghton Mifflin Company. All rights reserved.

REMINDER

▶ Use *more* with long adjectives to compare two
persons, places, or things.

▶ Use *most* with long adjectives to compare three or
more persons, places, or things.

The buffalo is an **enormous** animal.

The elephant is **more enormous** than a buffalo.

The blue whale is the **most enormous** animal of all.

Incorrect: The giraffe is <u>more</u> <u>taller</u> than the buffalo.

  Its eyes are its <u>most</u> <u>usefulest</u> tool.

Correct: The giraffe is <u>taller</u> than the buffalo.

  Its eyes are its <u>most</u> <u>useful</u> tool.

INDEPENDENT PRACTICE

Write <u>more</u> or <u>most</u> to complete each sentence correctly.

Example: A giraffe is one of the _____**most**_____ interesting of
all animals.

1. Is the giraffe the _____**most**_____ unusual creature in the zoo?

2. It certainly has the _____**most**_____ amazing neck of all animals.

3. It is _____**more**_____ difficult for a giraffe to eat low leaves than
high ones.

4. The giraffe is one of the _____**most**_____ silent of all animals.

5. The giraffe's sense of sight is _____**more**_____ important than
its hearing.

6. Sight is the _____**most**_____ important of the giraffe's five senses.

7. Sleeping giraffes are _____**more**_____ comfortable standing up than
lying down.

8. A baby giraffe is one of the _____**most**_____ enormous of all
animal babies.

9. The mother giraffe is _____**more**_____ careful with the young
than the father.

Copyright © Houghton Mifflin Company. All rights reserved.

What Is a Pronoun?

You know that nouns name a person, a place, or a thing. You do not have to keep repeating nouns in your writing. Instead, you can use words called **pronouns**. A **pronoun** takes the place of one or more nouns. Read these two paragraphs.

Sara asked Jack and Leah to go to the seashore with Sara. Sara, Jack, and Leah spoke to Ms. Lanski. Ms. Lanski gave Sara, Jack, and Leah a special book. The book was about sea life.

Sara asked Jack and Leah to go to the seashore with **her**. **They** spoke to Ms. Lanski. **She** gave **them** a special book. **It** was about sea life.

What pronoun takes the place of the noun *Sara* in the first sentence of the second paragraph? What pronoun replaces *Sara, Jack, and Leah* in the second sentence?

Like the nouns they replace, pronouns are singular or plural. Look at the lists below. Notice that the pronoun *you* can be either singular or plural.

> **Singular Pronouns:** I, me, you, he, him, she, her, it
> **Plural Pronouns:** we, us, you, they, them

GUIDED PRACTICE

Which words in these sentences are pronouns? Is each pronoun singular or plural?

Example: Sara said, "Come with me to the seashore."
      me   singular

1. Leah carried a pail. <u>She</u> planned to collect shells. **S**____

2. Jack took a notebook. Sara wanted <u>him</u> to take notes. **S**____

3. As the children walked along, <u>they</u> looked carefully. **P**____

Copyright © Houghton Mifflin Company. All rights reserved

REMINDER

▶ A **pronoun** is a word that can take the place of one or more nouns.

Singular Pronouns: I, me, you, he, him, she, her, it
Plural Pronouns: we, us, you, they, them

Nouns

Dennis went to the park.
Dennis watched the squirrels.

Pronouns

He went to the park.
Dennis watched **them**.

INDEPENDENT PRACTICE

Underline the pronoun in each sentence. Then write *singular* or *plural* for each pronoun.

Example: Dennis had a camera. He took some pictures.   **singular**

1. He went to the park with Maya.   singular

2. She brought a camera along too.   singular

3. At the park, they started taking pictures.   plural

4. A little squirrel raced past them.   plural

5. Maya snapped a picture of it.   singular

6. The squirrel ran past her and behind a tree.   singular

7. "Don't run away from us," Maya called.   plural

8. "We have to be quick," said Dennis.   plural

9. Then he heard two soft voices.   singular

10. Two little boys walked up to him.   singular

11. "Show me how a camera works," a boy said to Dennis.   singular

12. "Please take pictures of us," said the other boy.   plural

13. "Both of you smile at the camera," said Maya.   plural

Copyright © Houghton Mifflin Company. All rights reserved.

You have learned that a pronoun can take the place of a noun. Like a noun, a pronoun can be used as the subject of a sentence. Remember that the subject tells whom or what the sentence is about.

Nouns

Juan did a project on insects.

Lola worked with Juan.

Juan and Lola gave a report.

Vin and I enjoyed the report.

Pronouns

He did a project on insects.

She worked with Juan.

They gave a report.

We enjoyed the report.

Not all pronouns can be used as subjects. Only the **subject pronouns** *I, you, he, she, it, we,* and *they* can be used as the subjects of sentences.

Subject Pronouns

Singular	Plural
I	we
you	you
he, she, it	they

GUIDED PRACTICE   Which subject pronoun could take the place of the underlined word or words in each sentence?

Example: Matt said to Barb, "Barb found a ladybug."   **You**

1. Matt and I know that ladybugs are helpful insects.   **We**

2. Matt told Barb more about ladybugs.   **He**

3. Ladybugs are not really bugs. Ladybugs are beetles.   **They**

4. This beetle eats insects that destroy plants.   **It**

5. Barb did not disturb the ladybug.   **She**

Copyright © Houghton Mifflin Company. All rights reserved.

REMINDER

▶ Use only subject pronouns as the subjects of sentences.

Singular Subject Pronouns: I, you, he, she, it
Plural Subject Pronouns: we, you, they

Nouns	Pronouns
<u>Tara</u> has an exciting new toy.	**She** has an exciting new toy.
<u>Tara and Rico</u> play with the toy.	**They** play with the toy.

INDEPENDENT PRACTICE

Write the subject pronoun in ( ) that can take the place of the underlined word or words.

Example: <u>Aunt Lori</u> bought great toys for Rico.
(She, We)

She

1. <u>Rico</u> is only four years old. **(He, You)**

He

2. <u>Aunt Lori</u> has found toys to help Rico learn. **(She, I)**

She

3. <u>This toy</u> teaches children to tell time. **(It, They)**

It

4. <u>Those toys</u> are for making music. **(We, They)**

They

5. <u>Tara</u> showed Rico a brand-new toy. **(You, She)**

She

6. "<u>Tara and I</u> will play with the toy," said Rico. **(They, We)**

We

7. "<u>Rico</u> will play with this toy all day," said Rico. **(You, I)**

I

8. <u>Tara</u> showed Aunt Lori a new puzzle. **(She, They)**

She

9. <u>This puzzle</u> was a map of the fifty states. **(It, They)**

It

10. "<u>My brother and I</u> also have paints," Tara said. **(We, He)**

We

11. <u>Uncle Joe and Aunt Lori</u> had bought these paints.

(She, They)

They

12. <u>Uncle Joe</u> told Tara about toys of long ago. **(He, We)**

He

13. <u>The toys</u> were balls made of wood. **(It, They)**

They

14. <u>Hoops</u> were also used as toys long ago. **(You, They)**

They

Copyright © Houghton Mifflin Company. All rights reserved.

You know that subject pronouns may be used as the subjects of sentences. The pronouns *me, you, him, her, it, us,* and *them* are called **object pronouns**. Object pronouns follow action verbs and words such as *to, with, for,* and *at.*

Nouns	**Pronouns**
Ms. Rossi fed **the horses**.	Ms. Rossi fed **them**.
Sal helped **Ms. Rossi**.	Sal helped **her**.
Sal showed a pony to **Ed and me**.	Sal showed a pony to **us**.
Then Sal gave **the pony** a carrot.	Then Sal gave **it** a carrot.

Object Pronouns

Singular	Plural
me	us
you	you
him, her, it	them

Never use the object pronouns *me, him, her, us,* and *them* as subjects. You can use the pronouns *you* and *it* as either subject or object pronouns.

GUIDED PRACTICE

Which object pronoun could take the place of the underlined word or words in each sentence?

Example: Sally rides <u>horses</u> every day. **them**

1. Ed said to Sally, "Please teach <u>Ed</u>." **me**

2. Sally took Ed to the stable with <u>Sally</u>. **her**

3. Sally told Ed, "I will teach <u>Ed</u> grooming first." **you**

4. She handed a brush to <u>Ed</u>. **him**

5. Then Sally and Ed brushed <u>the horse</u>. **it**

Copyright © Houghton Mifflin Company. All rights reserved.

▸ Use **object pronouns** after action verbs and words such as *to*, *with*, *for*, and *at*.

Singular Object Pronouns: me, you, him, her, it
Plural Object Pronouns: us, you, them

Nouns

Firefighters spoke to the children.

Chief Drake gave Andrea a book.

Pronouns

Firefighters spoke to **them.**

Chief Drake gave **her** a book.

INDEPENDENT PRACTICE

Write the object pronoun in ( ) that can take the place of the underlined word or words.

Example: "We can help Andrea," said the chief. **(her, she)** her

1. One day Andrea smelled smoke in the house. **(it, them)** it

2. She knew what the firefighters had taught Andrea.
    (her, she) her

3. She felt the door before she opened the door. **(them, it)** it

4. The door did not feel hot to Andrea. **(her, she)** her

5. Andrea phoned the firefighters. **(they, them)** them

6. "Give Chief Drake the address," said Chief Drake. **(me, I)** me

7. Andrea gave the address to Chief Tom Drake. **(he, him)** him

8. The fire trucks were ready for the firefighters.
    (they, them) them

9. Soon the firefighters arrived at the house. **(it, you)** it

10. Andrea's mother was outside with Andrea. **(her, she)** her

11. "Can you help Andrea and me?" asked Mrs. Katz.
    (we, us) us

12. The firefighters hooked a hose to the truck. **(it, me)** it

Copyright © Houghton Mifflin Company. All rights reserved.

Using *I* and *me*

When you talk or write about yourself, you use the pronoun *I* or *me*. Do you ever have trouble deciding whether to use *I* or *me* with another noun or pronoun? For example, should you say *Kim and me study* or *Kim and I study*? One way to check is to say the sentence to yourself with only *I* or *me*.

Kim and I study.	**I** study.
Mrs. Perez teaches **Kim and me**.	Mrs. Perez teaches **me**.
Ali studies with **Kim and me**.	Ali studies with **me**.

Remember to use *I* as the subject of a sentence. Use *me* after action verbs and after words such as *to, with, for,* and *at.*

When you talk about yourself and another person, always name yourself last.

Incorrect: I and Kim help Ali.   Ali thanks me and Kim.
Correct: **Kim and I** help Ali.   Ali thanks **Kim and me**.

GUIDED PRACTICE

Which words complete each sentence correctly?

Example: (Jen and I, I and Jen) met Maria.
Jen and I

1. Maria invited (me and Jen, Jen and me) to her house.
2. (I and Jen, Jen and I) walked home with Maria.
3. Maria talked to (Jen and me, me and Jen) about Mexico.
4. Jen and (I, me) were very interested.
5. Maria helped prepare dinner for Jen and (I, me).
6. Jen and (I, me) ate with Maria's family.
7. The food tasted wonderful to Jen and (I, me).

Copyright © Houghton Mifflin Company. All rights reserved.

REMINDER

▶ Use the pronoun *I* as the subject of a sentence.

▶ Use the pronoun *me* after action verbs and after words such as *to, with, for,* and *at.*

▶ When speaking of yourself and another person, always name yourself last.

Rami and **I** talked about fishing.   **I** talked about fishing.

Klaus listened to Rami and **me**.   Klaus listened to **me**.

INDEPENDENT PRACTICE

Write the sentence in each pair that is correct.

Example: Klaus and I like summer.   I and Klaus like summer.

Klaus and I like summer.

1. Klaus and me enjoy hot weather and sunny days.
    Klaus and I enjoy hot weather and sunny days.
    Klaus and I enjoy hot weather and sunny days.

2. I like to swim and fish on long summer afternoons.
    Me like to swim and fish on long summer afternoons.
    I like to swim and fish on long summer afternoons.

3. Klaus loves to go swimming and fishing with me.
    Klaus loves to go swimming and fishing with I.
    Klaus loves to go swimming and fishing with me.

4. Klaus and I fish for hours in the Ohio River.
    I and Klaus fish for hours in the Ohio River.
    Klaus and I fish for hours in the Ohio River.

5. My mother has told many fishing stories to Klaus and I.
    My mother has told many fishing stories to Klaus and me.
    My mother has told many fishing stories to Klaus and me.

Copyright © Houghton Mifflin Company. All rights reserved.

Possessive Pronouns

You have learned that possessive nouns show ownership. You can use pronouns in place of possessive nouns. A pronoun that shows ownership is a **possessive pronoun**.

Possessive Nouns

Pamela feeds **Pamela's** pet.

She fills **the pet's** dish.

The boys' gerbil is playful.

Possessive Pronouns

Pamela feeds **her** pet.

She fills **its** dish.

Their gerbil is playful.

Possessive Pronouns

Singular	Plural
my	our
your	your
her, his, its	their

GUIDED PRACTICE

Which possessive pronoun should you use in place of the underlined word or words?

Example: Max and I help Mr. Lee at <u>Mr. Lee's</u> shop.   **his**

1. Max likes <u>Max's</u> job at the pet store.   his

2. He gives the puppies <u>the puppies'</u> food.   their

3. Agnes is saving <u>Agnes's</u> money for a pet.   her

4. She will buy the parakeet and <u>the parakeet's</u> cage.   its

5. Agnes, you and <u>Agnes's</u> sister will like the parakeet.   your

Copyright © Houghton Mifflin Company. All rights reserved.

> ▶ A possessive pronoun may be used in place of a possessive noun.
>
> **Singular Possessive Pronouns:** my, your, her, his, its
> **Plural Possessive Pronouns:** our, your, their
>
> | **Possessive Nouns** | **Possessive Pronouns** |
> |---|---|
> | Nola is <u>Mack's</u> sister. | Nola is **his** sister. |
> | This is <u>Nola and Mack's</u> playhouse. | This is **their** playhouse. |

INDEPENDENT PRACTICE

Write each sentence. Use the possessive pronoun in ( ) that can take the place of the underlined word or words.

Example: I have seen <u>Mack and Nola's</u> new playhouse. **(his, their)**
I have seen their new playhouse.

1. Nola and Mack built <u>Nola and Mack's</u> new playhouse. **(its, their)**
Nola and Mack built their new playhouse.

2. Nola is proud of <u>Nola's</u> curtains for the playhouse. **(her, its)**
Nola is proud of her curtains for the playhouse.

3. The children visited <u>Mack's</u> friend Mr. Rey. **(their, his)**
The children visited his friend Mr. Rey.

4. Mr. Rey uses <u>Mr. Rey's</u> tools to make small furniture. **(your, his)**
Mr. Rey uses his tools to make small furniture.

5. He said, "Nola, this chair is for <u>Nola's</u> playhouse." **(my, your)**
He said, "Nola, this chair is for your playhouse."

6. Nola said, "I will keep the chair away from <u>Nola's</u> dog." **(its, my)**
Nola said, "I will keep the chair away from my dog."

7. "The dog has enough of <u>the dog's</u> own toys," said Mack. **(its, their)**
"The dog has enough of its own toys," said Mack.

Copyright © Houghton Mifflin Company. All rights reserved.

You know that homophones are words that sound alike but have different spellings and meanings. Writers often confuse some contractions and their homophones because these words sound alike. Study the chart below. Learn the spelling and the meaning of each homophone.

Homophone	Meaning	Sentence
it's	it is	**It's** a beautiful bird!
its	belonging to it	Take **its** picture.
they're	they are	**They're** odd birds.
their	belonging to them	**Their** wings are big!
there	in that place	**There** is another.
you're	you are	**You're** very lucky.
your	belonging to you	Get **your** camera.

GUIDED PRACTICE

Which word would you use to complete each sentence correctly?

Example: I hear (you're, your) entering the photo contest. *you're*

1. Which of (you're, <u>your</u>) pictures will you enter?
2. (They're, There) all so good!
3. The puppies love having (they're, <u>their</u>) picture taken.
4. The picture (their, <u>there</u>) on your desk is interesting.
5. (It's, <u>Its</u>) colors are sharp and clear.
6. (<u>It's</u>, Its) hard to choose the best one!

Copyright © Houghton Mifflin Company. All rights reserved.

> ▸ Do not confuse the contractions *it's*, *they're*, and *you're* with their homophones *its*, *their*, *there*, and *your*.

Homophones:

You're a good painter.   **Your** picture is pretty.
It's a picture of a bird.   **Its** colors are bright.
They're going to paint too.   **There** are **their** paints.

INDEPENDENT PRACTICE

Write the words in ( ) to complete the sentences in each pair. Begin each sentence with a capital letter.

Example: All the children brought ____their____ paints. **(they're, their)** ____They're____ going to paint masks.

1. "May I use __your__ yellow paint?" asked Teresa. **(your, you're)**
   "__You're__ welcome to use it," said Nikos.

2. "__It's__ going to be a large mask," said Olive. **(its, it's)**
   "I am painting __its__ eyes yellow," Teresa said.

3. "__They're__ the strangest eyes!" said Nikos. **(they're, there)**
   "Paint some black spots right __there__," he added.

4. "Now __its__ eyes look better," said Teresa. **(its, it's)**
   "__It's__ a wonderful mask!" exclaimed Olive.

5. "__Your__ mask looks like a tiger," said Nikos. **(you're, your)**
   "__You're__ right about that," replied Teresa.

6. "Only __its__ whiskers are missing," said Olive.
   (it's, its) "__It's__ time to clean up," said Teresa.

Copyright © Houghton Mifflin Company. All rights reserved.

You know that an adjective is a word that describes a noun or a pronoun. Another kind of describing word is called an adverb. An **adverb** can describe a verb.

Adverbs give us more information about an action verb or a form of the verb *be*. They tell *how, when,* or *where.* Adverbs can come before or after the verbs they describe.

How:	Maggie typed the letter carefully.
When:	Then I sealed the envelope.
Where:	All the stamps were upstairs.

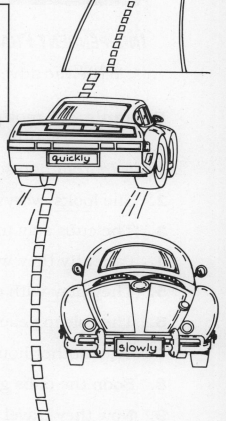

Study the lists below. They show adverbs that you use often in your writing. Most adverbs telling *how* end with *-ly*.

How	When	Where
angrily	always	downtown
carefully	finally	inside
fast	often	off
loudly	once	out
quickly	sometimes	there
sadly	then	upstairs

GUIDED PRACTICE   Find the adverb that describes each underlined verb. Does the adverb tell *how, when,* or *where?*

1. The mail carrier <u>finally</u> <u>arrived</u>.   when

2. We <u>ran</u> <u>out</u> to meet her.   where

3. Maggie <u>clapped</u> her hands <u>excitedly</u>.   how

4. I <u>quickly</u> <u>opened</u> the gold envelope.   how

Copyright © Houghton Mifflin Company. All rights reserved.

REMINDER

▶ An **adverb** is a word that describes a verb.

▶ An adverb can tell *how*, *when*, or *where*.

How: The baby lion's eyes opened **slowly**.

When: **Then** it yawned.

Where: The baby lion looked **around**.

INDEPENDENT PRACTICE

Write the adverb that describes each underlined verb.

Example: A mother lion <u>carries</u> her cubs
gently.

gently

1. A mother lion sometimes <u>leaves</u> her cubs.

   sometimes

2. She <u>looks</u> everywhere for food.

   everywhere

3. The cubs <u>stay</u> inside.

   inside

4. Patiently they <u>wait</u> for their mother.

   Patiently

5. They <u>play</u> with each other happily.

   happily

6. They <u>sleep</u> peacefully.

   peacefully

7. The mother lion finally <u>returns</u>.

   finally

8. Soon the cubs <u>grow</u> big and strong.

   Soon

9. Now they <u>travel</u> with their group.

   Now

10. Lions always <u>travel</u> as a group.

    always

11. A young lion <u>learns</u> quickly from the other lions.

    quickly

12. The older lions carefully <u>guard</u> the younger ones.

    carefully

13. The big lions <u>roar</u> loudly.

    loudly

14. Strange lions <u>stay</u> away.

    away

15. The lions <u>see</u> a zebra there.

    there

16. Then they <u>chase</u> it.

    Then

Copyright © Houghton Mifflin Company. All rights reserved.

Comparing with Adverbs

You have already learned how adjectives are used to compare people, places, and things. You can also use adverbs to make comparisons. Add *-er* to short adverbs to compare two actions. Add *-est* to compare three or more actions.

> Bill skis **fast**. (one action)
> Louise skis **faster** than Bill does. (two actions)
> Kara skis **fastest** of the three. (three or more actions)
>
> For most adverbs that end with *-ly*, use *more* to compare two actions. Use *most* to compare three or more actions.
>
> Dee swam **gracefully**. (one action)
> Did Kato swim **more gracefully** than Dee? (two actions)
> Ty swam **most gracefully** of all. (three or more actions)
>
> Do not use *-er* or *-est* to compare adverbs that end with *-ly*. Never use *-er* with *more*. Never use *-est* with *most*.
>
> **Incorrect:** Faith skates <u>smoothlier</u> than Don.
>   Don fell <u>most hardest</u> of all the skaters.
>
> **Correct:** Faith skates **more smoothly** than Don.
>   Don fell **hardest** of all the skaters.

GUIDED PRACTICE What form of the adverb in ( ) correctly completes each sentence?

1. Today we practiced <u>longer</u> than we did yesterday. (long)

2. Of all the team members, Ruth skated <u>most skillfully</u>. (skillfully)

3. Does Leslie skate <u>more quickly</u> than Shawn? (quickly)

4. Andrew jumps <u>highest</u> of us all. (high)

5. Of everyone on the team, Tara tries <u>hardest</u>. (hard)

LANGUAGE AND USAGE

Copyright © Houghton Mifflin Company. All rights reserved.

REMINDER

▶ Add *-er* or *-est* to short adverbs to compare actions.

▶ For adverbs that end with *-ly,* use *more* or *most* to compare actions.

▶ Never use *-er* with *more.* Never use *-est* with *most.*

Adverb	Comparing Two	Comparing Three or More
fast	fast**er**	fast**est**
swiftly	**more** swiftly	**most** swiftly

INDEPENDENT PRACTICE

Write each sentence. Use the correct form of the adverb in ( ).

Example: Amy arrived at the pool (later, latest) than Ruth did.
Amy arrived at the pool later than Ruth did.

1. Amy works (harder, hardest) of all the divers in her class.
Amy works hardest of all the divers in her class.

2. Amy learned the swan dive (more quickly, most quickly) than Ruth did.
Amy learned the swan dive more quickly than Ruth did.

3. The back flip took (longer, longest) of all to learn.
The back flip took longest of all to learn.

4. Ben dives (more skillfully, most skillfully) than Amy's last teacher.
Ben dives more skillfully than Amy's last teacher.

5. He works (more closely, most closely) of all with Amy.
He works most closely of all with Amy.

6. Does Ben keep his legs (straighter, straightest) than Amy does?
Does Ben keep his legs straighter than Amy does?

7. Amy tries to spring (higher, more higher) than Ben does.
Amy tries to spring higher than Ben does.

Copyright © Houghton Mifflin Company. All rights reserved.

Using good and well

Sometimes it may be hard to decide whether to use *good* or *well*. How can you make sure that you use these words correctly? Remember, *good* is an adjective that describes nouns. *Well* is an adverb that describes verbs.

Adjective	Adverb
Marcia is a <u>good</u> pilot.	She flies <u>well</u>.
This suit is <u>good</u>.	I choose my suits <u>well</u>.

GUIDED PRACTICE

Which word is correct?

Example: Kipp's trips are all (good, well).   *good*

1. He plans (good, <u>well</u>) for his adventures.

2. Kipp's guidebook is (<u>good</u>, well).

3. His road maps are (<u>good</u>, well) too.

4. He has learned to read maps (good, <u>well</u>).

5. Kipp speaks several languages (good, <u>well</u>).

6. Talking to people helps him learn (good, <u>well</u>) about another country.

7. Kipp is (<u>good</u>, well) at taking pictures.

8. Photos help him remember his trips (good, <u>well</u>).

9. Kipp describes his travels (good, <u>well</u>).

10. Everyone listens (good, <u>well</u>) to his stories.

11. The presents that he brings to his family are always (<u>good</u>, well).

12. They think that Kipp's trips are (<u>good</u>, well)!

Copyright © Houghton Mifflin Company. All rights reserved.

REMINDER

▶ Use the adjective *good* to describe nouns.

▶ Use the adverb *well* to describe verbs.

Adjective	Adverb
Audrey chooses **good** colors.	Audrey paints **well**.
This color is **good**.	Audrey chooses colors **well**.

INDEPENDENT PRACTICE

Write *good* or *well* to complete each sentence correctly. The underlined nouns and verbs are clues.

Example: Audrey had a _____**good**_____ idea.

1. Audrey wanted to give her room a **good** _____ paint job.

2. She went to a **good** _____ store for paint.

3. She knew the store owner **well** _____.

4. He showed Audrey a **good** _____ way of choosing colors.

5. His color wheel showed colors that match **well** _____.

6. Red goes **well** _____ with yellow.

7. Blue is **good** _____ for a cool look.

8. Light colors are **good** _____ for making rooms seem larger.

9. A **good** _____ shade of pink makes a room seem warmer.

10. Audrey planned her paint job **well** _____.

11. She thought gray would be **good** _____ for the windows and the door.

12. Light pink would be a **good** _____ color for the walls.

13. Audrey painted her room **well** _____.

14. Before painting, she covered the furniture **well** _____.

15. After painting, she cleaned the paintbrushes **well** _____.

Copyright © Houghton Mifflin Company. All rights reserved.

Sometimes when you write sentences, you use the word *no* or words that mean "no." A word that makes a sentence mean "no" is a **negative**. These sentences have negatives.

No one picked the beans.   I **didn't** water the garden.

The words *no, no one, nobody, none, nothing, nowhere,* and *never* are negatives. The word *not* and contractions made with *not* are also negatives. Never use two negatives together in a sentence.

Incorrect	**Correct**
There <u>weren't</u> <u>no</u> trees.	There **weren't** any trees.
	There were **no** trees.
I <u>won't</u> <u>never</u> rake leaves!	I **won't** ever rake leaves!
	I will **never** rake leaves!

Notice that there may be more than one correct way to write a sentence with a negative.

GUIDED PRACTICE

Which word in ( ) is correct?

Example: Eli doesn't want (any, no) leaves on the ground.   *any*

1. He can't go (nowhere, <u>anywhere</u>) until he has finished raking.
2. He never likes (<u>anything</u>, nothing) about yard work.
3. No one (never, <u>ever</u>) has time to help him.
4. Luckily there (<u>are</u>, aren't) no leaves left on the trees.
5. There won't be (no, <u>any</u>) more leaves to rake until next fall!

Copyright © Houghton Mifflin Company. All rights reserved.

▶ A **negative** is a word that means "no."

▶ Do not use two negative words together in a sentence.

  I had **never** heard about Helen Keller.

  No one had told me about her.

Incorrect: I **never** knew **nothing** about Helen Keller.

Correct: I **never** knew **anything** about Helen Keller.

  I knew **nothing** about Helen Keller.

INDEPENDENT PRACTICE

Write the correct word in ( ) to complete each sentence.

Example: Helen Keller's parents didn't have (any, no) help.   **any**

1. Helen Keller couldn't see or hear (nothing, anything).   anything

2. Her parents had never given her (any, no) training.   any

3. No one had (never, ever) helped their daughter.   ever

4. Helen couldn't go (nowhere, anywhere) by herself.   anywhere

5. Her parents couldn't teach her (anything, nothing).   anything

6. She hadn't (no, any) teacher until Annie Sullivan came.   any

7. Annie had never taught (anyone, no one) as bright.   anyone

8. At first Helen didn't want (none, any) of Annie's lessons.   any

9. Helen wouldn't do (nothing, anything) Annie wanted.   anything

10. Annie wouldn't (ever, never) let Helen misbehave.   ever

11. Helen hadn't met (anybody, nobody) as patient as Annie.   anybody

Copyright © Houghton Mifflin Company. All rights reserved.

CAPITALIZATION, PUNCTUATION, AND USAGE GUIDE

ABBREVIATIONS

Abbreviations are shortened forms of words. Most abbreviations begin with a capital letter and end with a period.

Titles	Mr. *(Mister)* Mr. Juan Albino	Sr. *(Senior)* John Helt, Sr.
	Mrs. *(Mistress)* Mrs. Frances Wong	Jr. *(Junior)* John Helt, Jr.
	Ms. Leslie Clark	Dr. *(Doctor)* Dr. Janice Dodds

Words used in addresses	St. *(Street)*	Blvd. *(Boulevard)*
	Rd. *(Road)*	Ave. *(Avenue)*

Days of the week	Sun. *(Sunday)*	Thurs. *(Thursday)*
	Mon. *(Monday)*	Fri. *(Friday)*
	Tues. *(Tuesday)*	Sat. *(Saturday)*
	Wed. *(Wednesday)*	

Months of the year	Jan. *(January)*	Apr. *(April)*	Oct. *(October)*
	Feb. *(February)*	Aug. *(August)*	Nov. *(November)*
	Mar. *(March)*	Sept. *(September)*	Dec. *(December)*

Note: May, June, and July are not abbreviated.

States

The United States Postal Service uses two capital letters and no period in each of its state abbreviations.

AL *(Alabama)*	HI *(Hawaii)*	MA *(Massachusetts)*
AK *(Alaska)*	ID *(Idaho)*	MI *(Michigan)*
AZ *(Arizona)*	IL *(Illinois)*	MN *(Minnesota)*
AR *(Arkansas)*	IN *(Indiana)*	MS *(Mississippi)*
CA *(California)*	IA *(Iowa)*	MO *(Missouri)*
CO *(Colorado)*	KS *(Kansas)*	MT *(Montana)*
CT *(Connecticut)*	KY *(Kentucky)*	NE *(Nebraska)*
DE *(Delaware)*	LA *(Louisiana)*	NV *(Nevada)*
FL *(Florida)*	ME *(Maine)*	NH *(New Hampshire)*
GA *(Georgia)*	MD *(Maryland)*	NJ *(New Jersey)*

Copyright © Houghton Mifflin Company. All rights reserved

CAPITALIZATION, PUNCTUATION, USAGE

States (continued)		
NM *(New Mexico)*	PA *(Pennsylvania)*	VT *(Vermont)*
NY *(New York)*	RI *(Rhode Island)*	VA *(Virginia)*
NC *(North Carolina)*	SC *(South Carolina)*	WA *(Washington)*
ND *(North Dakota)*	SD *(South Dakota)*	WV *(West Virginia)*
OH *(Ohio)*	TN *(Tennessee)*	WI *(Wisconsin)*
OK *(Oklahoma)*	TX *(Texas)*	WY *(Wyoming)*
OR *(Oregon)*	UT *(Utah)*	

TITLES

Underlining	**Titles of books, newspapers, magazines, and TV series are underlined. The important words and the first and last words are capitalized.**
	Life on the Mississippi Newsweek Nova
Quotation Marks	**Put *quotation marks (" ")* around the titles of short stories, articles, songs, poems, and book chapters.**
	"The Necklace" *(short story)* "Home on the Range" *(song)*

QUOTATIONS

Quotation Marks	**A *direct quotation* tells a speaker's exact words. Use *quotation marks (" ")* to set off a direct quotation from the rest of the sentence.**
	"Please put away your books now," said Mr. Emory.
	Begin a quotation with a capital letter. When a quotation comes at the end of a sentence, use a comma to separate the quotation from the words that tell who is speaking. Put end marks inside the last quotation mark.
	The driver announced, "This is the Summer Street bus."
Writing a conversation	**Begin a new paragraph each time a new person begins speaking.**
	"Are your seats behind home plate or along the first-base line?" asked the voice on the phone.
	"I haven't bought any tickets yet," said Mr. Williams. "I was hoping that you would reserve three seats for me now."

Copyright © Houghton Mifflin Company. All rights reserved.

CAPITALIZATION

Rules for capitalization	**Capitalize the first word of every sentence.** What an unusual color the roses are!

Capitalize the pronoun *I*.
What should I do next?

Capitalize every important word in the names of particular people, pets, places, and things (proper nouns).
Rover   District of Columbia   Elm Street   Lincoln Memorial

Capitalize titles and initials that are parts of names.
Governor Bradford   Emily G. Hesse   Senator Smith

Capitalize family titles when they are used as names or as parts of names.
We visited Uncle Harry.   May we play now, Grandma?

Capitalize the names of months and days.
My birthday is on the last Monday in March.

Capitalize the names of groups.
Sutton Bicycle Club   National League

Capitalize the names of holidays.
Memorial Day   Fourth of July   Veterans Day

Capitalize the first and last words and all important words in the titles of books and newspapers.
From Earth to the Moon   The New York Times

Capitalize the first word in the greeting and the closing of a letter.
Dear Marcia,   Yours truly,

In an outline, each Roman numeral and capital letter is followed by a period. Capitalize the first word of each main topic and subtopic.
I. Types of libraries
   A. Large public library
   B. Bookmobile

CAPITALIZATION, PUNCTUATION, USAGE

Copyright © Houghton Mifflin Company. All rights reserved.

End marks	**There are three end marks. A *period (.)* ends a statement or a command. A *question mark (?)* follows a question. An *exclamation point (!)* follows an exclamation.** The scissors are on my desk. *(statement)* Look up the spelling of that word. *(command)* How is the word spelled? *(question)* This is your best poem so far! *(exclamation)*
Apostrophe	**To form the possessive of a singular noun, add an apostrophe and *s ('s).*** baby's Russ's grandmother's family's
	For a plural noun ending in *s*, add only an apostrophe ('). sisters' families' Smiths' hound dogs'
	For a plural noun that does not end in *s*, add an apostrophe and *s ('s).* women's mice's children's
	Use an apostrophe in contractions in place of dropped letters. isn't *(is not)* wasn't *(was not)* I'm *(I am)* can't *(cannot)* we're *(we are)* they've *(they have)* won't *(will not)* it's *(it is)* they'll *(they will)*
Comma	**A *comma (,)* tells the reader to pause between the words that it separates.**
	Use commas to separate items in a series. Put a comma after each item in the series except the last one. Clyde asked if we had any apples, peaches, or grapes.
	You can combine two short, related sentences to make one compound sentence. Use a comma and the connecting word *and, but,* or *or.* Some students were at lunch, but others were studying.
	Use commas to set off the words *yes, no,* and *well* when they are at the beginning of a sentence. Well, it's just too cold out. No, it isn't six yet.

Copyright © Houghton Mifflin Company. All rights reserved.

Comma (continued)	**Use a comma or commas to set off the names of people who are spoken to directly.**
	Jean, help me fix this tire. How was your trip, Grandpa?
	Use a comma to separate the month and the day from the year.
	Our nation was born on July 4, 1776.
	Use a comma between the names of a city and a state.
	Chicago, Illinois Miami, Florida
	Use a comma after the greeting in a friendly letter.
	Dear Deena, Dear Uncle Rudolph,
	Use a comma after the closing in a letter.
	Your nephew, Sincerely yours,

PROBLEM WORDS

Words	Rules	Examples
a, an, the	These words are special adjectives called articles.	
a, an	Use *a* and *an* before singular nouns. Use *a* if a word begins with a consonant sound. Use *an* if a word begins with a vowel sound.	a banana an apple
the	Use *the* with both singular and plural nouns.	the apple the apples
	Use *the* to point out particular persons, places, or things.	The books that I like are long.
are	*Are* is a verb.	Are these gloves yours?
our	*Our* is a possessive pronoun.	This is our car.

Copyright © Houghton Mifflin Company. All rights reserved.

CAPITALIZATION, PUNCTUATION, USAGE

CAPITALIZATION, PUNCTUATION, USAGE

Words	Rules	Examples
doesn't	Use *doesn't* with singular nouns, *he, she,* and *it.*	Dad <u>doesn't</u> swim.
don't	Use *don't* with plural nouns, *I, you, we,* and *they.*	We <u>don't</u> swim.
good	Use the adjective *good* to describe nouns.	The weather looks <u>good</u>.
well	Use the adverb *well* to describe verbs.	She sings <u>well</u>.
its	*Its* is a possessive pronoun.	The dog wagged <u>its</u> tail.
it's	*It's* is a contraction of *it is.*	<u>It's</u> cold today.
let	*Let* means "to allow."	Please <u>let</u> me go swimming.
leave	*Leave* means "to go away from" or "to let stay."	I will <u>leave</u> soon. <u>Leave</u> it on my desk.
set	*Set* means "to put."	<u>Set</u> the vase on the table.
sit	*Sit* means "to rest or stay in one place."	Please <u>sit</u> in this chair.
their	*Their* is a possessive pronoun.	<u>Their</u> coats are on the bed.
there	*There* is an adverb. *There* means "in that place."	Is Carlos <u>there</u>? <u>There</u> is my book.
they're	*They're* is a contraction of *they are.*	<u>They're</u> going to the store.
two	*Two* is a number.	I bought <u>two</u> shirts.
to	*To* means "toward."	A squirrel ran <u>to</u> the tree.
too	*Too* means "more than enough" and "also."	I ate <u>too</u> many cherries. Can we go <u>too</u>?
your	*Your* is a possessive pronoun.	Are these <u>your</u> glasses?
you're	*You're* is a contraction of *you are.*	<u>You're</u> late again!

Copyright © Houghton Mifflin Company. All rights reserved.

Use adjectives to describe nouns. Use adverbs to describe verbs.

This plant is <u>tall</u>. *(adj.)* It grew <u>fast</u>. *(adv.)*

Comparing

To compare two people, places, or things, add *-er* to many adjectives and adverbs.

This plant is <u>taller</u> than the other one. It grew <u>faster</u>.

To compare three or more people, places, or things, add *-est* to many adjectives or adverbs.

This plant is the <u>tallest</u> of the three. It grew <u>fastest</u>.

Double comparisons

Never combine *-er* with the word *more*. Do not combine *-est* with the word *most*.

She is a <u>better</u> (*not* more better) skier than he.
The third <u>book</u> is the <u>longest</u> (*not* most longest).

good, bad

When you use the adjectives *good* and *bad* to compare, you must change their form. Use *better* or *worse* to compare two. Use *best* or *worst* to compare three.

The weather today is <u>worse</u> than it was yesterday.
The forecast for tomorrow is the <u>best</u> one of the week.

more, most

With most long adjectives and with adverbs that end in *-ly*, use *more* to compare two people, places, things, or actions. Use *most* to compare three or more.

This song is <u>more beautiful</u> than the first one.
Of the five songs, this one was sung the <u>most powerfully</u>.

NEGATIVES

A negative word or negative contraction says "no" or "not." Do not use two negatives to express one negative idea.

INCORRECT: He can't see nothing.
CORRECT: He can't see <u>anything</u>.
CORRECT: He <u>can</u> see <u>nothing</u>.

Copyright © Houghton Mifflin Company. All rights reserved.

CAPITALIZATION, PUNCTUATION, USAGE

PRONOUN USAGE

I and me	**Use the pronoun *I* as the subject of a sentence. Use the pronoun *me* after action verbs and after words such as *to, with, for,* and *at.* When using *I* or *me* with other nouns or pronouns, name yourself last.** Jan and I are going to the movies. She will telephone me. Beth and I will leave. Give the papers to Ron and me.
Subject and object pronouns	**A pronoun used as a subject (*I, you, he, she, it, we,* or *they*) is called a subject pronoun.** She did not disturb the grasshopper.
	A pronoun used as an object (***me, you, him, her, it, us,*** or ***them***) **is called an object pronoun. Use object pronouns after action verbs and after words such as *to, with, for,* and *at.*** The puppy likes us. Let's play with him.

VERB USAGE

Tenses	**Avoid unnecessary shifts from one tense to another.** The trains stopped, and everyone was (*not* is) surprised.
Irregular verbs	**Irregular verbs do not add *-ed* or *-d* to show past action. Because irregular verbs do not follow a regular pattern, you must remember their spellings.**

Present	Past	Past with helping verb	Present	Past	Past with helping verb
be	was	been	have	had	had
begin	began	begun	know	knew	known
break	broke	broken	make	made	made
bring	brought	brought	say	said	said
come	came	come	sing	sang	sung
drive	drove	driven	take	took	taken
eat	ate	eaten	tell	told	told
give	gave	given	throw	threw	thrown
grow	grew	grown	wear	wore	worn

Copyright © Houghton Mifflin Company. All rights reserved.

Language and Usage Lessons

Overview

Language and Usage Lessons have been provided in the *Student Resource Book* as an optional resource for teachers who wish to integrate these skills into their reading/language arts curriculum. A Capitalization, Punctuation, and Usage Guide has also been provided as a useful handbook for students' own reference.

The Language and Usage Lessons provide opportunities for direct instruction in key language areas. Instruction, modeling, guided practice, and independent practice are provided for each skill. Students using *Houghton Mifflin Reading: The Literature Experience* will have a rich variety of reading, writing, listening, and speaking projects and activities; this section provides a useful support for those language arts areas.

The Language and Usage Lessons are organized into the following six major sections: The Sentence, Nouns, Verbs, Adjectives, Pronouns, and Adverbs.

Format of the Lessons

Each lesson is two pages in length. The first page provides instruction and guided practice. The second page provides a skill reminder and independent practice. Instruction, written to the student, can be used as a basis for a teacher-led discussion. Suggestions for modeling each lesson can be found on pages 158 – 162 of the *Student Resource Book Teacher's Annotated Edition.* Guided practice begins with an example and gives students an opportunity to practice the skill with the guidance and support of the teacher. Directions for the independent practice are clearly written and easy to follow. An example is provided to reinforce both the directions and the skill. Throughout, vocabulary has been kept at a level that allows students to focus on the skill.

How to Use the Lessons

The teacher's goals, style of teaching, and classroom organization will guide the use of this section. Because the lessons are grouped into skill categories and in many cases build sequentially, it is best to use them in the order presented. Some ideas for incorporating the lessons into your teaching plan follow.

1. You might decide to teach one of the language and usage skill categories with each of the seven themes in the student Anthology. For example, you might introduce the Capitalization, Punctuation, and Usage Guide during Theme 1 and encourage students to familiarize themselves with its contents so they can use it independently. You might then teach the six categories of Language and Usage Lessons sequentially, with the six remaining themes.

2. You might choose to use this section as a resource to supplement your own or a published instructional program in language, mechanics, and usage.

3. Annotations in the *Dinosauring* Journal Teacher's Edition provide suggestions for coordinating the activities in the student Journal with lessons in this section. You might find it helpful to familiarize yourself with this section and, knowing the contents, to use those suggestions to help students who indicate in their speech or writing a need for work in a particular area.

The flexibility of this section permits it to be used in a variety of ways. You, as a teacher, will know best how to use it.

Capitalization, Punctuation, and Usage Guide

This guide is a helpful handbook for student reference throughout the year. It can also be used for instruction. It includes the following sections, with rules and examples provided for each section: Abbreviations, Titles, Quotations, Capitalization, Punctuation, Problem Words, Adjective and Adverb Usage, Negatives, Pronoun Usage, and Verb Usage.

This guide will be a valuable resource to students in their writing. Annotations in the *Dinosauring* Journal Teacher's Edition note times when, as students are completing the activities in their Journals, it would be helpful to suggest that they refer to this guide.

Throughout the year you might want to remind students of the existence of this resource and to refer them to it whenever they indicate in their speech or writing a need for this support.

Copyright © Houghton Mifflin Company. All rights reserved.

Modeling the Lessons

Page 85

Statements and Questions

Hold up a paper bag with a small object inside, such as a pencil. Tell students they can ask five questions to find out what it is. Write their questions on the board. (For example: What is it made of? It is made of wood and rubber.) Call attention to the sentences on the board. Ask students what is different about the end punctuation of the sentences. Help them see that some sentences end with periods and others end with question marks.

Page 87

Commands and Exclamations

Surprise students by dramatically slamming a book on a desk. Have them suggest sentences that describe their reactions. (For example: It scared me! I jumped in my seat!) Write these on the board. Explain that the exclamation point represents strong feelings in a sentence. Next, have students name things you often ask them to do. List these commands on the board. (For example: Pay attention. Open your books.) Point out that a sentence that tells someone to do something ends with a period.

Page 89

Complete Subjects and Complete Predicates

Draw two columns on the board, labeling one *Who or What* and the other *What Is or What Happens*. Remind students that a complete sentence has information for each column. Then have students suggest sentences, telling which part of the sentence belongs in which column. Write the suggestions in the appropriate columns. Tell students that in this lesson, they will learn more about these two sentence parts.

Page 91

Simple Subjects

Write this sentence on the board: *The ballplayer ran.* Have students name the complete subject (the ballplayer) and then expand the subject by adding words that describe the ballplayer more exactly. (For example: The tall, black-haired ballplayer ran.) Write students' sentences on the board, underlining the word *ballplayer* in each. Explain that no matter how long the complete subject is, there is always one main word that tells *who or what*.

Page 93

Simple Predicates

Write this sentence on the board: *The campers slept.* Remind students that a predicate includes all the words that tell what the subject of a sentence is or does. Ask students to identify the predicate (slept) and expand it by adding words that tell more about how or where the campers slept. (For example: The campers slept in their bunks in the cabin.) Write students' sentences on the board, underlining the word *slept*. Explain that a simple predicate is the main word that tells what the subject is or does.

Page 95

Combining Sentences: Subjects and Predicates

Point out to students that a compound sentence combines two simple sentences. Have students use a compound to name two things on their desk. (For example: A book is on my desk, and a pencil is on my desk.) Then ask them to think of another way to present the same information, using fewer words. Write this pattern on the board:

A _____ and a _____ are on my desk.

Have students use the pattern to change compound sentences into simple sentences with compound subjects.

Using the same method, direct students in writing sentences with compound predicates. Put this pattern on the board:

The skater _____ and _____ .

Ask students to supply the missing words.

Point out that a sentence can have both a compound subject and a compound predicate. You may also wish to explain that a compound subject or predicate can be connected with *or* instead of *and*.

Page 97

Correcting Run-on Sentences

Write the following on the board:

Li's family visited the Smithsonian Institution this museum has over 75 million items only a small number are displayed at one time.

Copyright © Houghton Mifflin Company. All rights reserved.

Read the passage aloud without pausing after each complete thought. Help students see that ideas are confusing when they are run together in this way. Ask students to read the passage aloud, telling where they think one complete idea ends and another begins.

Page 99

Common and Proper Nouns

Write these words in a column on the board: *boy, girl, teacher, principal, school, town, park, river, store.* Point out that these words are nouns. Then ask volunteers to supply actual names of people and places that correspond to each noun on the board, and write these nouns in a second column. Point out that the nouns in the first column give the general name of a person, place, or thing while those in the second column name a particular place or thing.

Page 101

Singular and Plural Nouns

Write these word pairs on the board:

dollar   dollars
friend   friends

Ask a volunteer to tell which word in each pair he or she would rather have. Have the volunteer explain why dollars are preferable to a dollar and why friends are preferable to a friend. (The nouns *dollar* and *friend* stand for one and are called singular nouns. *Dollars* and *friends* stand for more than one and are called plural nouns.)

Tell students to use context clues to tell if a noun should be singular or plural. Words such as *many* and *all* precede plural nouns, while the word *a* means the noun following it is singular.

Page 103

Nouns Ending with *y*

Hold up a penny in one hand and a key in the other, and ask students to identify them. Write *penny* and *key* on the board. Next, hold up two pennies and two keys. Ask for the names and spellings of the plural nouns *pennies* and *keys,* and write them on the board. Have students look at the two plural forms and note that they are formed differently. Have volunteers suggest reasons for this. Explain that this lesson gives rules for forming plurals of nouns ending with *y.*

Page 105

More Plural Nouns

Ask students to listen to this poem, which makes fun of certain English plural nouns.

The plural of *man* is always *men.*
Is the plural of *pan* ever *pen?*
One is a *mouse;* two are *mice.*
One is a *house.* Are two ever *hice?*
I have a *foot;* I have two *feet.*
I have a *boot.* Have I two *beet?*
A *goose* and a *goose* equal *geese,*
But a *moose* and a *moose* are never —
    meese!

Have students name the made-up plural forms in the poem.

Page 107

Action Verbs

Write various action verbs —*jump, shave, cook, read*—on slips of paper. Then ask volunteers to pick a slip randomly and pantomime the action for the class. Have the class watch to determine the action being pantomimed. As students guess each action, write the verb on the board. Explain that these words are called action verbs. Then have students suggest other action verbs. Write these on the board.

Page 109

Main Verbs and Helping Verbs

Draw two columns on the board. In the first column, list the helping verbs *am, is, are, was,* and *were.* In the second, list the verbs *reading* and *playing.* Call on volunteers to combine a word in column 1 with a word in column 2. Ask them to use these two-word verbs in sentences. Repeat the process with *have, has,* and *had* in one column and *read* and *played* in another. Explain that the words in the first column are helping verbs because they help describe an action.

Page 111

Present, Past, and Future

Write the words *learn, learned,* and *will learn* on the board. Ask students for sentences with the word *learn* that tell what they are doing now. Guide them to give sentences with the present tense form. (For example: We learn about verbs.) Ask for sentences that use the word *learned* and that tell what students have learned in the

Copyright © Houghton Mifflin Company. All rights reserved.

past. Follow a similar procedure with the words *will learn* and future activities. Sum up by telling students that different forms of verbs tell when actions take place.

Explain that the word *tense* as used in the lesson simply means "time."

Page 113

Making Subjects and Verbs Agree

Ask two students to hop up and down as you write on the board:

The student___ hop___ .

Ask what letter needs to be added to the sentence to describe the action. (an *s* to make the subject plural)

Next, ask one of the students to sit down. Remove the *s* from *students*. As the remaining student hops, ask the class what the sentence needs now. Elicit that an *s* must be added to *hop*. Add it, saying that the *s* ending makes the present tense verb singular to agree with the singular subject.

Page 115

Irregular Verbs

Explain that some verbs do not end in *ed* in the past tense. Then write these sentences on the board:

I sing today.

I _____ yesterday.

I have _____ for years.

Have students complete the sentences with the correct past tense forms for *sing*. (sang, sung) Point out that *sing* changes its spelling rather than adding *ed*. Have volunteers write three similar sentences for the irregular verbs *drive* and *tell*.

Page 117

The Special Verb *be*

Write the following on the board:

Mr. Wong teaches history.
Mr. Wong is a teacher.

Have students identify the verb in each sentence and tell which verb shows action. (teaches) Tell them that the other verb, *is*, does not show action, but, instead, tells what someone or something is like. Write *am*, *are*, *is*, *was*, and *were* on the board. Explain that these are all forms of the verb

be. Have students make up sentences with these verbs as the simple predicate.

Page 119

What Is an Adjective?

Ask a volunteer to choose an object in the room. Without revealing its identity, the volunteer should give three words that describe the object. Write the words on the board. Have students use these describing words to guess the object. Once the object has been revealed, have students suggest other words to describe it. Write these additional words on the board. Tell students that describing words are called adjectives.

Tell students that the words *a*, *an*, and *the* are special kinds of adjectives that they will study soon.

Page 121

Adjectives After *be*

Write the following incomplete sentences on the board:

1. I am _____ .

2. The _____ is _____ .

For Sentence 1, ask volunteers to supply an adjective that they would use to describe themselves. For Sentence 2, ask volunteers to supply the name of an object for the first blank and an adjective that describes the object for the second blank. Indicate with an arrow that the adjective in each sentence comes after the noun or pronoun it describes.

Page 123

Using *a*, *an*, and *the*

Read these sentences aloud:

1. Do you want a banana?
2. Do you want the banana?

Ask students to tell how the meanings of the two sentences differ. (The word *the* refers to a particular banana while *a* means any banana at all.) Write this sentence on the board:

I want an apple and a banana.

Ask students why one fruit is preceded by *an* and one by *a*. (The word *an* is used before words beginning with vowel sounds. The word *a* is used before words beginning with consonant sounds.)

Copyright © Houghton Mifflin Company. All rights reserved.

Page 125

Making Comparisons

Display three books that students use. Ask volunteers to provide three sentences that compare the books. Write the sentences on the board. (For example: The math book is thick. The reader is thicker. The social studies book is thickest of all.) Then ask students to compare the same books with other adjectives, such as *easy, hard,* or *heavy.* Point out the *-er* and *-est* endings. Help students conclude that the *-er* ending is used to compare two books while the *-est* ending is used to compare three or more.

Page 127

Comparing with *more* and *most*

Write these sentences on the board and ask volunteers to read each pair aloud:

May was enjoyabler than June.
May was more enjoyable than June.

My cat is the curiousest of all.
My cat is the most curious of all.

Ask students to identify the adjectives and tell which sounds better — *curiousest* or *most curious, enjoyabler* or *more enjoyable.* Tell students that since long adjectives sound awkward with *-er* and *-est* endings, we use the words *more* and *most* with such adjectives to make comparisons.

Tell students that some two-syllable adjectives compare with *-er* and *-est* endings, such as *quieter/quietest,* while others use *more* and *most,* as in *more helpful/most helpful.* Tell students to check their dictionaries if they are not sure about the correct form. Point out that adjectives with three or more syllables almost always compare with *more* and *most.*

Page 129

What Is a Pronoun?

Remind students that nouns name people, places, and things. Ask students to give examples of singular nouns and plural nouns. Write the examples on the board. Choose one of the examples and have students give three or four sentences about this noun. Write the sentences on the board as a paragraph without pronouns; that is, repeat the noun in every sentence. Call attention to the awkwardness of repeating the noun every time. Tell students that in

this lesson they will be learning about words that replace nouns.

Page 131

Subject Pronouns

Write the following sentences on the board and ask volunteers to name the subject of each:

Sir Edmund Hillary climbed Mount Everest.
That mountain is the earth's highest mountain.

Then write the words *He* and *It* on the board. Have volunteers choose the pronoun that can replace the subject in each sentence and read the sentence with the pronoun. Have students supply two more sentences for which the words *He* and *It* can be used as the subjects.

Page 133

Object Pronouns

Help students name the subject pronouns they have studied. *(I, you, we, he, she, they, it)* Then help them list the remaining pronouns that are not subject pronouns. *(me, him, her, us, them)* Have them use these pronouns in sentences. Write sentences with object pronouns on the board. Ask students to comment on the position of these pronouns in the sentences. Explain that they do not serve as the subject of a sentence.

Page 135

Using *I* and *me*

Ask students to supply sentences about the activities they enjoy with friends. Write the sentences that contain *I* and *me* on the board. Remind students that *I* is a subject pronoun and *me* is an object pronoun. Point to any sentences in which *I* or *me* is used with another noun or pronoun. Help students to conclude that when *I* or *me* is used with another noun or pronoun, it is written or spoken last.

Stress that *me* should be used after words like *to, with, for,* and *at.* Explain that people sometimes mistakenly use *I* after these words because they think it sounds correct.

Page 137

Possessive Pronouns

Write the names of a few students on the

Copyright © Houghton Mifflin Company. All rights reserved.

board. Ask each of these students to name a favorite possession. Write the item after each name to show the possessive, such as *Hilary's bicycle*. Remind students that possessive nouns show ownership.

Point out that certain pronouns can take the place of possessive nouns. Write *my, your, hers, his, its, our,* and *their* on the board. Have students rewrite the phrases, using possessive pronouns in place of the students' names, as in *her bicycle*.

Point out that *'s* is not added to possessive pronouns as it is to possessive nouns.

Page 139

Pronouns and Homophones

Write these sentences on the board:

It's my dog, and its name is Jo.
You're looking for your dogs.
They're there with their friends.

Ask students to identify the words in each sentence that sound alike. Then ask them to identify which words are contractions *(it's, you're, they're)* and which are possessive pronouns *(its, your, their)*. Point out that *there* is an adverb that means "in that place." Ask volunteers to use these pronouns and contractions in sentences.

Stress that a contraction uses an apostrophe while a possessive pronoun does not.

If students have trouble deciding when to use the contractions *it's, you're,* and *they're,* suggest they insert *it is, you are,* or *they are* in the sentence instead to see whether it makes sense.

Page 141

What Is an Adverb?

Write this sentence on the board:

Joe was singing.

Ask volunteers to suggest words that tell how Joe might have sung. (loudly, happily) Next, ask for single words that tell where he sang (upstairs, here) and when he sang (today, earlier). Proceed similarly with these sentences:

Jill was dancing.
Harry was eating.

Explain that words telling how, when, and where an action takes place are called adverbs.

Page 143

Comparing with Adverbs

Have students turn back to page 141, and have three students each read one paragraph from the page. After they have finished, write *loudly, fast,* and *clearly* on the board. Have students use these three adverbs to discuss and compare how the students read. (For example: Don read faster than Sue. Sue read the most clearly.) Write on the board the sentences that students suggest. Point out that adverbs can be used to compare two or more actions.

Stress that any adverb ending in *-ly,* even a short two-syllable adverb like *slowly,* should be used with *more* or *most* when making comparisons.

Page 145

Using *good* and *well*

On the board, write:

What a good drummer Dan is!
He also plays the piano well.

Ask students to name the word that *good* describes in the first sentence. (drummer) Then ask them to name the word in the second sentence that *well* describes. (plays) Help students see that *good* is an adjective because it describes a noun and that *well* is an adverb because it describes a verb. Ask students to use *good* and *well* in sentences that tell about their own skills and talents.

Page 147

Negatives

Shake your head to show "no," and ask students to tell what the gesture means. Write their suggestions on the board. (For example: No! Never! I can't. Don't do it! It's not right.) Then have students think of situations in which they have shaken their heads. Ask them to tell what they meant to say by doing this. Write their responses, underlining the negative word in each. Point out that the underlined words all mean "no." Explain that words that mean "no" are called negatives.

Remind students that a contraction is a shortened form of two words. Many contractions are formed from a helping verb and *not.* (For example: does + not = doesn't)

Copyright © Houghton Mifflin Company. All rights reserved.

UNIVERSITY OF RHODE ISLAND

3 1222 00991 287 7

NO LONGER THE PROPERTY
OF THE
UNIVERSITY OF R. I. LIBRARY